HISTORY OF GUJARAT

HISTORY OF GUJARAT

(MUSALMAN PERIOD, A.D. 1297-1760)

by

MAJOR J. W. WATSON,
ACTING POLITICAL AGENT, REWA' KA'NTA'

GYAN

Published by

GYAN

Gyan Publishing House
5, Ansari Road
Daryaganj, New Delhi-110002
Phone: 011-47034999, 9811692060
E-mail: books@gyanbooks.com

Distribution Network
gyanbooks.com
India, USA, Canada, UK, Australia, France

ISBN : 978-81-212-6020-6 (PB)
First Published, 1876

2nd Impression 2021

Printed at: Gyan Press, Delhi.

History of Gujarat
Author: Major J. W. Watson

HISTORY

OF

GUJARAT.

(MUSALMAN PERIOD, A.D. 1297-1760.)

BY

MAJOR J. W. WATSON,
ACTING POLITICAL AGENT, REWA' KA'NTA'.

Written for the Bombay Gazetteer.

Bombay:
PRINTED AT THE GOVERNMENT CENTRAL PRESS.
1876

PREFACE.

This historical sketch is mainly based on two Persian works, the Mirat-i-Sikandri for the earlier portion up to Akbar's conquest (A.D. 1573), and the Mirat-i-A'hmadi for the subsequent part (A.D. 1573-1760). These are the two most authentic of the Persian histories of Gujarát, and were compiled by men who, themselves and their fathers before them, held high positions and were actors in the scenes described.

I have also borrowed both from local tradition and from numerous other works, prominent among which are :—

1. Grant Duff's History of the Maráthás.
2. Elphinstone's History of India.
3. Elliot's History of India.
4. Forbes' Rás Málá.
5. The Gáekwár and his relations with the British Government.
6. Briggs' Cities of Gujaráshtrá.
7. Briggs' Ferishta.
8. Dow's Hindustán.
9. Bird's Gujarát.
10. The Government Selections relating to Gujarát.
11. The Tabakát-i-Akbari, by Nizám-ud-din A'hmad Bakshi.

JOHN W. WATSON.

Baroda, September 1876.

ERRATA.

	For	Read
Page 1, line 14 from top ...	"two centuries"	"one century."
,, 4 ,, 17 ,,		
,, 5 ,, 5 ,, ...	"*sirkárs*"	"*sarkárs.*"
,, 18, foot-note 1, line 4		
,, 17, line 2 from bottom ...	"*matsudi*"	"*mutsadi.*"
,, 22, foot-note 1	"Ome's"	"Orme's."
,, 22 ,, 2, line 2 ...	"eighteenth century"	"sixteenth and seventeenth centuries."
,, 37, line 2 from top		
,, 44, lines 4, 13, 17 and 19 from top. ...	"ráwál	"ráwal."
,, 62, line 7 from top ...	"Khán Khán"	"Khán Khánán."
,, 77 ,, 20 ,, bottom ...	"renewed"	"removed."
,, 78 ,, 20 ,, top ...	"Mándwár"	"Mándwá."
,, 91 ,, 8 ,, bottom ...	"of minis Surat"	"of Surat."
,, 91 ,, 10 ,, ...	"ter"	"minister."
,, 131 ,, 2 ,, ...	"Moráwar"	"Zoráwar."
,, 133 ,, 2 ,, ...	"Wanthalis"	"Wanthali."

Note.—Since these chapters have been printed, it has been found that the word written Sonnáth in Bird's History of Gujarát (p. 136), should be Sunth (in Rewá Kántá).

At note 2, page 2, and page 14, line 14 from top, omit Somnáth, and at page 17, line 7 from bottom, *for* Somnáth in Káthiáwár, *read* Sunth in Rewá Kántá.

HISTORY OF GUJARAT.

INTRODUCTION.

Muhammadan rule in Gujarát lasted from their conquest of the province, shortly before the close of the thirteenth century A.D., to their final defeat by the Maráthás and loss of the city of A'hmadábád in A. D. 175. Musalmán ascendancy in Gujarát, 1297-1760.

This whole term of Musalmán ascendancy, stretching over slightly more than four-and-a-half centuries, may conveniently be divided into three parts. The first—the rule of the early sovereigns of Delhi—lasting throughout almost the whole of the fourteenth century, or, more strictly, from A.D. 1297 to A.D. 1403; the second—the rule of the A'hmadábád kings—a term of nearly Two Centuries and three-quarters, from A.D. 1403 to A.D. 1573; the third—the rule of the Moghal emperors—when for little less than two hundred years, A.D. 1573-1760, Gujarát was administered by viceroys of the court of Delhi. Period how divided.

In the course of these 450 years, the limits of Gujarát varied greatly at different times. In the fourteenth century A.D., the territory nominally under the control of the Musalmán governors of Pátan (Anhilpur) extended southwards from Jhálor, now in Rájputáná, to the neighbourhood of Bombay,[1] and in breadth from the line of the Málwá and Limits of Gujarát.

1 The first notice of the exercise of sovereignty on the part of the Musalmán rulers of Gujarát in lands further south than the neighbourhood of Surat is in A.D. 1428, when King A'hmad I. (A.D. 1412-1443) contested with the Deccani sovereign the possession of Máhim (N. Lat. 19° 40', E. Long. 72° 47'). The ruler of Máhim was then a Hindu tributary to Gujarát; and as no record of the conquest of this territory by the Musalmáns remains, it

Introduction.

Khándesh Hills to the western shores of peninsular Gujarát. The earlier kings of A'hmadábád (A.D. 1403-1450), content with establishing their power on a firm footing, did not much extend the limits of their kingdom. Afterwards, during the latter part of the fifteenth and the beginning of the sixteenth centuries (A.D. 1450-1530), the dominions of the A'hmadábád kings became gradually wider, including to the east and north-east large tracts of territory formerly in the possession of the rulers of Khándesh and Málwá. Again, during the time of misrule, that lasted from about A.D. 1530 to A.D. 1573, the western parts of Khándesh and the north of the Konkan ceased to form part of the kingdom of Gujarát. Finally, under the arrangements introduced by the emperor Akbar in A.D. 1583, more lands were restored to Málwá and Khándesh, and with the exception of the districts of Jhálor and Sirohi in the north, since handed over to Rájputáná and A'jmir, the limits of Gujarát still remain almost as they were then laid down.

Limits of Sorath.

Though, under the Musalmáns, peninsular Gujarát did not bear the name of Káthiáwár, it was then, as at present, considered to form a part of the province of Gujarát. During the early times of Musalmán rule, the peninsula, together with a small portion of the adjoining mainland, was known as Sorath, a shortened form of Saurásthrá, the name originally applied by the Hindus to a long stretch of sea-coast between the banks of the Indus and Daman.[1] Towards the close of the sixteenth century the official use of the word Sorath was confined to a portion, though by much the largest part, of the peninsula.[2] But, at the same time,

---

seems probable that Bombay and the Northern Konkan fell into the possession of the Musalmáns in A.D. 1297 as part of the recognized territories of the lords of Anhilpur (Pátan).—Rás Málá, I., 350.

[1] At one time the whole country from the Indus to Daman was called Su-ráshtrá, and its inhabitants Suráshtrian, from which Ptolemy (A.D. 150) has made Syrastrene, now called Sorath and Surat. Afterwards, as in the Puráns, the country known as Saurásthrá, or Surasht, extended only as far as Jambusar, and from thence to the Tápti was Gujarát.—Wilford in As. Res. VIII. 336, and IX. 231.

[2] From the details given of the settlement of the country by the emperor Akbar in A.D. 1583, it would seem that, besides Sorath, divisions (Independent) and Nawánagar (Islámnagar)[1] were recognized division of the peninsula. Sorath, however, included by much the largest part of the peninsula with sixty-three sub-divisions, as compared with seventeen under Nawánagar. In the Ain-i-Akbari (A.D. 1590) Sorath with its nine divisions includes the whole area of the peninsula except Jháláwár in the north, then part of A'hmadábád.—Gladwin, II. 64 and 66-71.

Introduction.

in common use, this name would seem then, and for long after, to have been applied to the whole peninsula. For the author of the Mirat-i-A'hmadi, writing as late as the middle of the eighteenth century (A.D. 1748-1762), speaks of the whole country (Sorath) as then divided into five districts, or *zillah*,—Hállar, Káthiáwár, Gohelwár, Bábariáwár, and Jetwár,—and notices that though Nawánagar (Islámnagar) was considered a separate district, its tribute was included in the revenue derived from Sorath.[1] But during the past hundred years the area of the country known by this name has been greatly narrowed, so that at present Sorath stretches no further than the limits of the States of Junágarh on Bántwá, and other holdings.

Limits of Káthiáwár.

The use of the name Káthiáwár, on the other hand, is of recent origin. It was not until after the establishment of Musalmán power in Gujarát that any portion of the peninsula came to be called after the tribe of Káthis, and, as noticed above, even as late as the middle of the eighteenth century, the name Káthiáwár was applied only to one of the five sub-divisions of the peninsula. In the disorders that prevailed during the latter part of last century the Káthis made themselves conspicuous; and as it was from the hardy horsemen of this tribe that the Maráthás met with the greatest resistance in the collection of their tribute, they came to speak of the whole peninsula as the land of the Káthis. This use, adopted in their writings by the early British officers, has since then been continued.

Administra- of Gujarát, 1403-1573.

With regard to the form of government under the A'hmadábád kings, Gujarát, as is still the case under British rule, was divided, politically, into two main parts. Of these, one was administered directly by the central authority; and the other, on payment of a certain tribute, in service or in money, was allowed to remain under the control of its former rulers. The amount of tribute paid by the different chiefs depended, not on the value of their territory, but on the terms granted to them when they agreed to become feudatories of the kings of A'hmadábád. Nor was this tribute paid with regularity or willingly, but was extorted by the pressure of an armed force. This expedition, generally headed by the

---

1 Bird's History of Gujarát, 418.

Introduction.

king in person, was afterwards known by the name of *mulk-giri*, or the country-seizing circuit.

Feudatory States.

As far as the feudatory chiefs were concerned, the internal management of their States was unaffected by the fact of their paying tribute. Justice was administered and the revenue collected in the same way as under the Anhilpur kings. The revenue consisted, as before, of a share of the crops received in kind, supplemented by the levy of special cesses, trade, and transit dues. The chief's share of the crops differed according to the locality, but rarely exceeded one-third of the produce, or was less than one-sixth. From some parts of his territory this share was realized directly from the cultivators by agents called *mantri,* while in other parts the collection was made through the medium of landowners of the superior class.[1]

Directly governed districts.

The portion of their territory under the direct authority of the A'hmadábád kings was divided into districts, or *sirkárs.* These districts were administered in one of two ways: they were either assigned to nobles in support of a certain contingent of troops; or they were set apart as crown domains, and managed by paid officers. The officers placed in charge of districts set apart as crown domains were called *maktáa.*[2] Their chief duties were to preserve the peace and to collect the revenue. For the maintenance of order, a body of soldiers from the head-quarters of the army at A'hmadábád was detached for service in each of these divisions, and placed under the command of the district governor. At the same time, in addition to the presence of this detachment of regular troops, there were in every district certain fortified outposts called *thána,* varying in number according to the character of the country and the temper of the people. These posts, in charge of officers called *thánádár,* subordinate to the district governor, were garrisoned by bodies of local soldiery, for whose maintenance, in addition to money payments, a small assignment of land was set apart in the neighbourhood of the post. Except on the occasion of the yearly tribute-collecting circuit—when the governors

Management of crown lands.

Military arrangements.

---

1 Rás Málá, I., 241.

2 This word and *iktáa*—the term used for the district administered by a *maktáa*—both come from the Arabic root, *kataa*, to cut off, in allusion to the public revenue diverted for the pay of those officers and their establishments.

of the districts through which it passed were expected to join the main body of the army with their local contingents —the district governors had ordinarily no control over the feudatory chiefs in the neighbourhood of their charge. **Introduction.**

For fiscal purposes these districts, or *sirkárs,* were again distributed among a certain number of sub-divisions styled *parganáh,* each placed under the charge of a paid official called *tehsildár.* These sub-divisional officers realized the state demand, nominally a one-half share of the produce, by the help of the head-men of the villages under their charge. The village head-men, styled *patels,* or, according to the Musalmán writers, *mukadams,* in the sharehold villages of Northern Gujarát, and in the simple villages of the South known as *desáis,* arranged for the final distribution of the total payment among the shareholders in joint villages and, in simple villages, from the individual cultivators.[1] A statement of the accounts of the villages in his sub-division was then presented by the sub-divisional officer to the district officer, whose record of the revenue of his whole district was in turn forwarded to the head revenue officer at court. As a check on the internal management of his charge, and especially to help him in the work of collecting the revenue, with each district governor was associated an accountant. And that each of these officers might be the greater check on the other, king A'hmad I. (A.D. 1412-1443) made it a rule that when the governor was chosen from among the royal slaves the accountant should be a free man, and similarly that, if the accountant was a slave, the district governor should be chosen from some other class. This practice was maintained till the end of the reign of Muzafar Sháh (A.D. 1511-1526). But at last, according to the authority of the Mirat-i-A'hmadi, during the reign of Bahádur Sháh (A.D. 1526-1536) the army became much increased, and the ministers, condensing the details of revenue, farmed it on contract, so that many parts formerly yielding one rupee now produced ten, and many others seven, eight, or nine, and in no place was there a less increase than from ten to twenty (per cent). Many other changes occurred at the same time, and, the overseer of the regulations having been dismissed from his office, mutiny and confusion were spread over Gujarát.[2]

Fiscal arrangements.

Management of crown lands, 1403-1573.

---

1 Some further particulars as to the position of these village head-men will be found below (p. 20).

2 Bird's History of Gujarát, 192.

Introduction.

Management of assigned lands, 1403-1573.

With regard to the second class of directly governed districts,—the lands assigned to nobles for the maintenance of their contingent of troops,—it would seem that, as in other parts of India, these assignments were at first for specific sums equal to the pay of the contingent. But when such assignments were of long standing, and were large enough to swallow up the whole revenue of a district, it was natural to simplify the arrangement by transferring the collection of the revenue and the whole management of the district to the chief of the military body. As long as the central power was strong, precautions were, no doubt, taken to prevent the holder of the grant from unduly rack-renting his district and appropriating to himself more than the pay of the troops, or exercising any powers not vested in the local governors of the districts included within the crown domains. As in other parts of India, those stipulations were probably enforced by the appointment of certain civil officers directly from the Government to inspect the whole of the noble's proceedings, as well in the managing his troops as in the administration of his lands.[1] But with the decline of the king's power the nobles became freed from all check or control in the management of their lands; and when, in A.D. 1536, the practice of farming was introduced in the crown domains, it would seem to have been adopted by the military leaders in their lands, and to have been continued from that time till the annexation of Gujarát by the emperor Akbar in A.D. 1573.

Administration of the province, 1573-1760.

It was not the policy of Akbar to introduce a new form of government, but rather to perfect the existing system. After, as has been noticed above, to some extent contracting the limits of Gujarát, he constituted it a province, or *subáh*, of the empire, appointing to its government an officer of the highest rank, with the title of *subahdár*, or viceroy.

Management of crown lands, 1573-1760.

As was the case under the A'hmadábád kings, the province was still divided, politically, into territories continued under the management of feudatory chiefs, and districts administered by officers appointed by the court of Delhi, or by the viceroy. The head-quarters of the army still remained at A'hmadábád, and detachments were told off and placed under the orders of the officers in charge of the directly administered divisions. These district governors, as before, belonged to two classes—paid officers responsible for the management of

---

1 Elphinstone's History, 76.

Introduction.

Management of crown lands, 1573-1760.

the crown domains, and military leaders in possession of lands assigned to them in pay of their contingent of troops. The governors of the crown domains, who were now known as *foujdár*, or commanders, had, in addition to the command of the regular troops, the control of the out-posts maintained within the limits of their charge, and, like their predecessors, accompanied the viceroy in his yearly circuit for the collection of tribute.

As a check on the military governors, and to help them in the collection of the revenue, the distinct class of account officers, formerly established by king A'hmad I. (A.D. 1420), was again introduced. The head of this branch of the administration was an officer, second in rank only to the viceroy, appointed direct from the Court of Delhi with the title of *diwán*. Besides acting as collector-general of the revenues of the province, this officer was also the head of its civil administration. His title *diwán* is generally translated by minister; and though this word does not express the functions of the office, it represents with sufficient accuracy the relation in which the holder of the office of *diwán* generally stood to the viceroy. For the revenue administration of the province in each district, an officer styled *mutsadi*, or revenue clerk, was placed immediately under the orders of the collector-general. The duties of this officer were to collect and submit to his superior the statements of revenue received from the officers in charge of the different fiscal sub-divisions which his district included. These sub-divisional officers realized the revenues by the help of the hereditary men of local position, the *desáis* and *mukadams*.

The arrangements introduced by Akbar in the end of the sixteenth century remained in force till the death of Aurangzeb (A.D. 1707). Then trouble and perplexity, daily increasing, began to spread, till, in A.D. 1724-25, Hámid Khán usurped the Government lands, and, seeking to get rid of the servants and assignments, gradually obtained possession of the volumes of the record of the Registry office. The keepers of the records were scattered, and yearly revenue statements ceased to be received from the districts.[1]

---

1 Bird's History of Gujarát, 93. Though under the Moghal Viceroys the State demand was at first realized in grain, at the last the custom was to assess each sub-division, and probably each village, at a fixed sum or *jamá*.

Introduction.

Management of assigned lands, 1573-1760.

The system of assigning lands to military leaders in payment of their contingent of troops was also continued by Akbar. Immediately after the annexation in A.D. 1573, the whole country was, according to the author of the Mirat-i-A'hmadi, divided among the great nobles;[1] and though two years afterwards mention[2] is made of the revenues of several districts being set aside for the imperial exchequer, the greater part of the directly governed portions of the province would seem to have been in the hands of military leaders, who employed their own agents for the collection of the revenue. During the seventeenth century the submission of the yearly record of the revenues of their districts, and the power of the viceroy to bring them to account for misgovernment, exercised a check on the management of these officers, and during this time a yearly surplus revenue of 600,000*l.* (Rs. 6,000,000) from the assigned and crown lands was on an average forwarded from Gujarát to Delhi. In the eighteenth century the decay of the viceroy's authority was accompanied by a gradual increase in the power of the military leaders in possession of assigned districts, till finally, as in the case of the Nawábs of Broach and of Surat, they openly claimed the position of independent rulers.

Minor branches of administration.

Of the other officials who took a part in the general management of the province, those most commonly referred to in the following history are the Musalmán judge, *kázi;* the city police-magistrate, *kotwál;* the superintendent of customs, *ámin,* under whose orders military guards were posted in the neighbourhood of the chief cities; the pay-master, *bakshi;* and the officers in charge of military posts, *thánádár.* There was nothing, however, either in the position or in the nature of the duties of these officers in Gujarát that calls for special notice.

Land tenures.

Besides the class of vernacular terms that belong to the administration of the province, certain technical words connected with the tenure of land are of frequent occurrence

---

The total amount for the sub-division was collected by an officer called *majmudár,* the village head-men, *patels* or *mukadams* being responsible each for his own village.—W.

1 Bird's History of Gujarát, 325.

2 Bird's History of Gujarát, 341.

Introduction.

Land Tenures, 1573-1760.

in the history of this period. For each of these the English equivalent has, as far as possible, been given in the text; but, in addition to this, some further explanation seems to be necessary. During the period to which this history refers, the superior holders of the land of the province belonged to two main classes,—those whose claims dated from a time prior to the Musalmán conquest, and those whose interest in the land was based on some grant in their favour by the Musalmán authorities. By the Musalmán historians, landholders of the first class, who were all Hindus, are called *zamindárs*, while landholders of the second class—Musalmáns as a general rule—are spoken of under the title of *jágirdárs*. Though the term *zamindár* was used to include the whole body of superior Hindu landholders, yet, in practice, a marked difference was always maintained between the almost independent chief, who still enjoyed his Hindu title of *rájá*, *ráwal*, *ráv*, or *jám*, and the petty claimants to shares in Government villages, who in a Hindu State would have been known as *garásiás*.[1]

Hereditary Hindu landholders.

The larger landholders, who had succeeded in avoiding complete subjection, were, as noticed above, liable only for the payment of a certain fixed sum, the collection of which by the central power always required the presence of a military force. But with regard to the settlement of the claims of the smaller landholders of the superior class, whose estates fell within the limits of the directly administered districts, no steps would seem to have been taken till the reign of A'hmad Sháh I. (A.D. 1412-1443). About the year A.D. 1420, the peace of his kingdom was so broken by agrarian disturbances, that A'hmad Sháh agreed, on condition of their paying tribute and performing certain military service, to re-grant, as hereditary possessions for the landholders of the *zamindár* class, a one-fourth share of their former village lands. From this time the portion so set apart was called *wántá*, or share, and the remainder,

---

1 The title *rájá* is applicable to the head of a family only. The payment of tribute to the Moghals or Maráthás does not affect the right to use this title. *Ráná* and *ráv* seem to be of the same dignity as *rájá*. *Ráwál* is of lower rank. The sons of *rájás*, *ránás*, *rávs*, and *ráwals* are called *kuwar*, or prince, and their sons *thákors*. The younger sons of *thákors* become *bhumiás*, land-owners, or *garásiás*, owners of *garás*, literally a mouthful. *Jám* is the title of the chiefs of the *Jhádejá* tribe—of the head of the elder branch in Cutch as well as of the younger branch in Nawánagar, or little Cutch, in Káthiáwár.—Rás Málá, II., 277.

Introduction.

Hereditary Hindu landholders.

retained as State land, was called *talpat*. This agreement continued to be observed till, in the year A.D. 1545, during the reign of Muhammad Sháh III. (A.D. 1536-1553), an attempt was made to annex these private shares to the crown. But this measure, which caused much discontent and disorder, was reversed by the emperor Akbar (A.D. 1556-1605), who, as part of the settlement of the province in A.D. 1583, restored the landholders to their one-fourth share, and, except that the Maráthás afterwards levied an additional quit-rent from these lands, the arrangements then introduced have since continued in force.[1]

Garásiá exactions.

During the decay of Musalmán rule in Gujarát in the first half of the eighteenth century A.D., shareholders of the *garásiá* class in Government villages, who were always ready to increase their power by force, levied many irregular exactions from their more peaceful neighbours, the cultivators or inferior landholders. These levies, known as *grás* (a mouthful), *vol* (a forced contribution), or *pál* (protection), have this peculiar characteristic, that they were paid by the cultivators of crown lands to petty marauders to purchase immunity from their attacks, and in no case partook of the nature of dues imposed by a settled government on its own subjects.

Holders of service lands.

The second class of superior landholders were those whose title was based on a grant by the Musalmán authorities. Such grants were either assignments of large tracts of land to the viceroy, district-governors, and nobles, to support the dignity of their position and maintain a certain contingent of troops, or allotments on a smaller scale as a reward for some special service. Land granted with these

1 With the introduction of Maráthá rule the title *zamindár* was bestowed on the farmers of the land revenue, and it is to men of the revenue farmer class that this word is, by the early English writers in Gujarát, generally applied. In consequence of this change in the application of the word *zamindár*, small landholders of the superior class, in directly administered districts, came again to be called by their original Hindu name of *garásiá*. Mr. Elphinstone (History 79 and note 13) includes under the term *zamindár* :—(1) half-subdued chieftains, (2) independent governors of districts, and (3) farmers of revenue. He also notices that until Aurangzeb's time only such chiefs as enjoyed some degree of independence were called *zamindár*. But in Colonel Walker's time, A.D. 1805, at least in Gujarát (Bombay Government Selection XXXIX., 25), the term *zamindár* included *desáis*, *majmudárs* (district accountants), *patels*, and *talátis* (village clerks).

Introduction.

Holders of service lands.

objects was called *jágir*, and the holder of the land *jágirdár*. Such possessions, on the death of the original grantee, were, in theory, strictly resumable, but, in practice, they tended to become hereditary. Though no regular payments were required from proprietors of this class, yet under the name of *peshkash* certain contributions were occasionally demanded from them. These contributions, however, consisting generally of presents,—such as a horse, an elephant, or some other article of value,—had more of the nature of a free-will offering than of an enforced tribute. During the time of Musalmán rule payments of this kind only were exacted from proprietors of the *jágirdár* class. But the Maráthás, in addition to levies of this nature, imposed on members of the *jágirdár* class a regular tribute, similar to that paid by the representatives of the original class of superior Hindu landholders.

Great part of Gujarát, under its Musalmán rulers, was always in the hands of landholders of the *jágirdár* class, and so powerful were they at times allowed to become, that on two occasions under the A'hmadábád kings, in A.D. 1554 and A.D. 1572, the leading nobles distributed among themselves the entire area of the kingdom.[1] Again, during the eighteenth century, when the rule of the Moghal emperors was on the decline, landholders of this class by degrees, as has been noticed above, won for themselves positions of almost complete independence.[2]

---

[1] From details of the year A.D. 1571 given in the Mirat-i-A'hmadi, the chief nobles, who were bound to furnish cavalry contingents, varying in strength from 25,000 to 4,000 horse, held lands estimated to yield yearly revenues of from 1,620,000*l*. to 160,000*l*.—Bird, 109-127.

[2] According to the European travellers in India during the seventeenth century, provincial governors, and probably to some extent all large holders of service lands, employed various methods for adding to the profits which the assigned lands were meant to yield them. The chief of these would seem to have been two—the practice of supporting a body of horse smaller than the number agreed for, and the practice of purveyance, or levying their supplies without payment. Sir Thomas Roe, from A.D. 1615 to 1618 English ambassador at the court of the emperor Jahángir, gives in his journal some idea of the extent to which, at that time, these irregular practices were carried :—" The (Pátna) viceroy's government was estimated at 5,000 horse, the pay of each trooper being 20*l*. (Rs. 200) yearly ; of which he kept only 1,500 on foot, being allowed the surplus as dead pay. On one occasion this governor wished to present me with 100 loaves of the finest sugar, as white as snow, each loaf weighing fifty pounds ; and on my declining, said—'You refuse these from me, thinking I am poor ; but being made in my government it costs me nothing, as it comes to me gratis.' " —Sir Thomas Roe in Kerr's Voyages, IX, 282-284.

The same writer, the best qualified of the English travellers of that time

Introduction.

Condition of Gujarát.

The changes noticed in the extent of territory and in the form of administration throw some light on the character of the government and on the condition of the people during the different periods of Musalmán rule. At the same time, before proceeding to the detailed narrative of the history, it seems advisable shortly to summarize the leading characteristics of each of the main divisions of the four-and-a-half centuries of Musalmán ascendancy.

Under the early Governors, 1297-1403.

On conquering Gujárát in A.D. 1297, the Musalmáns found the country in a state of disorder. The last kings of Anhilpur (Pátan), suffering, perhaps, under the defects of an incomplete title, held even their crown lands with no firmness of grasp, and allowed the outlying territory to escape almost entirely from their control. Several of the larger and more distant rulers had resumed their independence; the aboriginal tribes—the Bhils and Kolis—were in revolt; and stranger chiefs, driven southwards by the Musalmán conquests in Upper India, had robbed the central power of considerable portions of its territory.[1] The records of the rule of the early Musalmán governors of the province (A.D. 1297-1391) show suspicion on the side of the Delhi court, and disloyalty on the part of more than one of the viceroys; much confusion throughout the province, and but little in the way of government beyond the exercise of military force. At the same time, in spite of wars and rebellions, the country would seem, in parts at least, to have been well cultivated, and trade and manufactures to have been flourishing.[2]

---

to form a correct opinion, thus describes the administration of the Musalmán governors of the seventeenth century :—" They practice every kind of tyranny against the natives under their jurisdiction, oppressing them with continual exactions, and are exceedingly averse from any way being opened by which the king may be informed of their infamous proceedings. They grind the people under their government to extract money from them, often hanging men up by the heels to make them confess that they are rich, or to ransom themselves from faults merely imputed with a view to fleece them."—Sir Thomas Roe in Kerr's Voyages, IX., 338.

1 Of these settlements the principal was that of the Ráthor chief, who founded Idar, now one of the States of the Máhi Kántá Division. About the same time also, 13th century A.D., the Gohils from the north, and the Shodá Parmárs, and the Káthis from Sindh, entered Gujarát.—Rás Málá II., 269.

2 The following is a description of Gujarát about the year A.D. 1300 :—" The air of Gujarát is healthy, and the earth picturesque ; the vineyards bring forth blue grapes twice a year, and the strength of the soil is

Introduction.

Under the A'hmadábad Kings, 1403-1573.

The period of the rule of the A'hmadábád kings (A.D. 1403-1573) contains two sub-divisions,—one lasting from A.D. 1403 to A.D. 1530, on the whole a time of strong government and growing power and prosperity; the other consisting of forty-three years, from A. D. 1530 to the transfer of the province to the emperor Akbar in A.D. 1573, a time of disorder and misrule. When Gujarát separated from Delhi (A. D. 1403) the new king had but a narrow territory on the plain. On the north-west were the independent rájás of Jhálor and Sirohi, from whom he occasionally levied contributions. On the east the rájá of Idar, another Rájput prince, was in possession of the nearer part of the hills and forests, and the rest of that tract was held by the mountain tribes of Bhils and Kolis. On the west the peninsula was in the hands of nine or ten Hindu tribes, probably tributary, but by no means obedient.[1] In the midst of so unsettled and warlike a population, all the efforts of Muzafar, the founder of the dynasty, were spent in establishing his power. It was not until the reign of his successor A'hmad I. (A.D. 1412-1443) that steps were taken to settle the different classes of the people in positions of permanent order. About the year A.D. 1420 two important measures were introduced,—one assigning lands for the support of the troops, the other recognizing the rights of the superior class of Hindu landholders to a portion of the village lands they had formerly held. The effect of these changes was to establish order throughout the districts directly under the authority of the crown. And though, in the territories subject to feudatory chiefs, the presence of an armed force was still required to give effect to the king's claims of tribute, his increasing power and wealth made efforts at independence more hopeless, and gradually ended in the subjection of the greater number of

such that the cotton plants spread their branches like willows and plane trees, and yield produce for several years successively; and besides Cambay, the most celebrated of the cities of Hind in population and wealth, there are 70,000 towns and villages, all populous, and the people abounding in wealth and luxuries."—Elliot's Hist. of India, III., 31, 32, and 43. Marco Polo, about A. D. 1292, says:— "In Gujarát there grows much pepper, and ginger, and indigo. They have also a great deal of cotton. Their cotton-trees are of very great size, growing full six paces high, and attaining to an age of 20 years."—Yule's Ed., II., 328. (The cotton referred to was probably the variety known as *devkapás* (*Gossypium religosum* or *peruvianum*), which grows from 10 to 15 feet high, and bears for several years.—Royle, 149-150).

1 Elphinstone's History, 762.

Introduction.

Under the A'hmadábád Kings, 1403-1573.

his vassals. During the latter part of the fifteenth and the first quarter of the sixteenth century the power of the A'hmadábád kings was at its height. At that time their dominions included twenty-five divisions or *sirkárs*. There were, besides, the nine districts—Pátan, A'hmadábád, Godhrá, Chámpáner, Baroda, Broach, Nádod (Rajpiplá), and Surat—among which the central plain of Gujarát was distributed ; in the north four divisions,—Jodhpur, Jhálor, Nágor, and Sirohi, now in Rájputáná ; in the north-east two—Dungarpur and Bánswádá, now in Málwá ; in the east and south-east three—Nandurbár, now in Khándesh, Mulher (Báglán), now in Násik, and Rám Nagar (Dharampur), now in Surat ; in the south four—Dandá Rájápur (Jinjirá), Bombay, Bassein, and Daman, now in the Konkan ; in the west three—Somnáth, Sorath, Nawánagar, now in Káthiáwár ; and Cutch in the north-west. Besides the revenues of these districts, there was a tribute from the rulers of Ahmadnagar, Bijápur, Berár, Golkondá, and Barhánpur, and custom-dues from twenty-five ports on the western coast of India, and twenty-six foreign marts, some of them in India, and others in the Persian Gulf and along the Arabian coast.[1] The total revenue realized from these three sources of income is said, in prosperous times, to have amounted to a yearly sum of 11,460,000*l.* (Rs. 11,46,00,000). Of this total sum the territorial revenue from the 25 districts yielded 5,840,000*l.* (Rs. 5,84,00,000), or slightly more than one-half of the whole amount. Of the remaining 56,20,000*l.* (Rs. 5,62,00,000), about one-fifth part was derived from the Deccan tribute, and the rest from custom dues.[2]

---

1 Bird's History of Gujarát 110, 129, and 130.

2 The passage from the Mirat-i-A'hmadi, Bird 109, is: "A sum of 25 láks of *huns* and one kro orf *ibráhims*, that were two parts greater, being altogether nearly equal to 5 krors and 62 láks of rupees, was collected from the Deccan tribute and the customs of the European and Arab ports." The word *hun*, from an old Carnátic word for gold, is the Musalmán name for the coin known among Hindus as *varáha*, or the wild-boar coin, and among the Portuguese as the pagoda, or temple coin.—Prinsep Ind-Anti, Thomas, Ed., II. U. T. 18. The old specimens of this coin weigh either 60 grains the *máda*, or half pagoda, or 120 grains the *hun*, or full pagoda—Thomas, Chron. Pat. Ks. II., 224, note. The star pagoda, in which English accounts at Madras were formerly kept, weighs 52·56 grains, and was commonly valued at 8*s.*, or Rs. 4 (Prinsep as above). At this rate in the present sum the 25 láks of *huns* would equal one kror (100 láks) of rupees. The *ibráhim*, "two parts greater than the *hun*," would seem to be a gold coin, perhaps a variety of the Persian *ashrafi* (worth about 9*s.* English—Marsden N. O. 455). Taking the two parts of a *hun* as *fánams*, or sixteenths, this would give the *ibráhim* a

Introduction.

Under the A'hmadábád Kings, 1403-1573.

The buildings at A'hmadábád, and the ruins of Chámpáner and Mehmadábád,[1] prove how much wealth was at the command of the sovereign, while the accounts of the travellers who visited Gujarát at this time, seem to show that the expenditure of the court was not greater than the kingdom was well able to bear. The Portuguese traveller Duarte Barbosa, who was in Gujarát between A.D. 1511 and A.D. 1514, gives a detailed account of the province:— "Inland" he found "the capital Chámpáner, a great city, a very fertile country of abundant provisions, and many cows, sheep, goats, and plenty of fruit, so that it was full of all things;" and A'hmadábád "still larger, very rich and well supplied, embellished with good streets and squares, with houses of stone and cement." It was not, however, from the interior districts of the province that the A'hmadábád kings derived the chief part of their wealth, but from those lying along the coast, enriched by manufactures and sea-trade.[2] So it was that along the shores of the Gulf of Cambay, and southward as far as Bombay, the limit of the Gujarát kingdom, besides many small seaports,

---

value of Rs. 4 as. 8, and make a total custom revenue of 450 láks of rupees. This statement of the revenues of the kingdom is, according to the author of the Mirat-i-A'hmadi, taken from such times as the power of the Gujarát kings continued to increase. The total revenue of the 25 districts (5,840,000*l.*) is the amount recovered in the year A.D. 1571. But the receipts under the head of Tribute must have been compiled from accounts of earlier years. For, as will be seen lower down, the neighbouring kings ceased to pay tribute after the end of the reign of Bahádur (A.D. 1536), while the custom revenues entered as received from Daman, and other places must have been taken from the accounts of some years previous to A.D. 1560.

1 The remains at Chámpáner in the British district of the Panch Mahâls are well known. Of Mehmadábád, the town of that name in the district of Kairá, 18 miles from A'hmadábád, a few ruins only are now left. But in A.D. 1590, this city is said to have contained many "grand edifices, surrounded with a wall 11 miles (7 *kos*) square, and at every ¾ mile (½ *kos*) of which is erected a pleasure house, with an enclosure, in which are deer and other game."—(Ain Akbari, Gladwin II. 64.) With regard to the share of the total revenue of the province received by the sovereign, nothing is specially mentioned in the Mirat-i-A'hmadi. But the greater part of the 5,620,000*l.* derived from tribute and customs would probably go to the king, besides the lands specially set apart as crown-domains, which in A.D. 1571 were returned as yielding a yearly revenue of 900,000*l* (900,000,000 *tankás*). This would bring the total income of the crown to a little more than 6½*l.* millions sterling.

2 So Sikandar bin Bahlul, emperor of Delhi, A.D. 1488-1517, is reported to have said—"The magnificence of the kings of Delhi consists of wheat and barley, whilst that of the king of Gujarát, who has eighty-four ports under him, has its foundation on coral and pearls."—Bird, 132.

Introduction.

Under the A'hmadábád Kings, 1403-1573.

Barbosa chooses out for special mention twelve "towns of commerce, very rich and of great trade." Among these was Diu, off the south coast of Káthiáwár, yielding so large a revenue to the king as to be "a marvel and amazement;" and chief of all Cambay, in a goodly, fertile, and pretty country full of abundant provisions; with rich merchants and men of great prosperity; with craftsmen and mechanics of subtle workmanship in cotton, silk, ivory, silver, and precious stones; the people well dressed, leading luxurious lives, much given to pleasure and amusement.[1] From the defeat of king Bahádur (A.D. 1526-1536) by the emperor Humayan in A.D. 1535 to the annexation of Gujarát by Akbar in A.D. 1573 was a time of confusion and misgovernment. During those years, abroad, the superiority of Gujarát over the neighbouring powers was lost, and the limits of the kingdom were curtailed, while at home, after the attempted confiscation (A.D. 1545) of the shares in village-lands held by superior land-owners, disaffection became general, and the court, beyond the narrow limits of the crown domains, ceased to

---

1 The twelve Gujarát ports mentioned by Barbosa are:—On the south coast of the peninsula, two Patenixi (Patán-Somnáth, now Veráwal), very rich and of great trade—Surati-Mangalor, a town of commerce, and Diu. On the shores of the Gulf of Cambay four—Gogári (Gogo), a large town; Barbesy (Broach); Guandari or Gandar (Gandhár), a very good town; and Cambay. On the western coast five—Ravel (Ránder), a rich place; Surat, a city of very great trade; Denvy (Gandevi), a place of great trade; Baxay (Balsár), a good seaport in which much goods are exchanged; and Tanamayambu (Tháná—Mahim), a town of great Moorish mosques, but of little trade.—(Stanley's Barbosa, 59—68.) The only one of these ports whose identification seems doubtful is Ravel, described by Barbosa (p. 67) as a pretty town of the Moors on a good river 20 leagues south of Gandhár. This agrees with the position of Ránder on the Tápti, nearly opposite Surát, mentioned under the name Ránir, both in the Ain Akbari (A. D. 1590) and in the Mirat-i-A'hmadi for the year A.D. 1571, as a place of trade, "in ancient times a great city." In his description of the wealth of Cambay, Barbosa is supported by the other European travellers of the 15th and beginning of the 16th centuries. According to Nicolo de Conti (A.D. 1420-1444), the town, including its suburbs, was twelve miles in circuit, abounding in spikenard, lac, indigo, myrobalans, and silk. Athanasius Nikotin (A.D. 1468-1474) found it a manufacturing place for every sort of goods—as long gowns, damasks, and blankets; and Varthema (A.D. 1503-1508) says of it, "abounding in grain and very good fruits, supplying Africa, Arabia, and India with silk and cotton stuffs, it is impossible to describe its excellence." Barbosa's account of A'hmadábád is also borne out by the statement of the author of the Mirat-i-A'hmadi, that it once contained 380 quarters (*purás*), each quarter of considerable size, containing good buildings and markets filled with everything valuable and rare, so that each is almost a city. (Bird, 311.) (In the Ain Akbari, Gladwin II., 63, the whole number of the quarters of the city is given at 360.)

Introduction.

Under the A'hmadábád Kings, 1403-1573.

exercise any substantial control, either over its chief nobles or the more turbulent classes of the population. Still, in spite of these forty years of disorder, the province retained so much of its former prosperity, that the boast of the local historian—that Gujarát was still (A.D. 1783) in every respect allowed to be the finest country in Hindustán—is to some extent supported by the details shortly afterwards (A.D. 1590) given by the author of the Ain-i-Akbari. This writer describes the high road from Pátan (Anhilpur) to Baroda as being throughout all its length of 150 miles (100 *kos*) lined on both sides with mango-trees; the fields bound with hedges; and so great an abundance of mango and other fruit-trees that the whole country seemed a perfect garden. The people, too, were well housed in dwellings with walls of brick and mortar and with tiled roofs; many of them rode in carriages drawn by oxen; and the province was famous for its painters, carvers, in-layers and other craftsmen.[1]

Under the Moghal Viceroys, 1573-1760.

The period of Moghal rule, like the period of the rule of the A'hmadábád Kings, contains two divisions—a term on the whole, of good government, lasting from A.D. 1573 to A.D. 1700, and a time of disorder, from A.D. 1700 to A.D. 1760. Under the arrangements introduced by the emperor Akbar in A.D. 1583, the area of the province was considerably reduced. Of its twenty-five districts nine were restored to the States from which they had been conquered, by the vigour of the A hmadábád kings. Of these two—Jodhpur and Jálor—were transferred to Rajputáná; one—Nágor—to Ajmir; two—Mulher and Nandurbár—to Khándesh; three—Bombay, Bassein, and Daman—were allowed to remain under the Portuguese; and one—Dandá Rájápur (Jinjirá), was made over to the nizám Sháhi (A.D. 1490-1595), rulers of Ahmadnagar in the Deccan. Of the remaining 16, six—Dungarpur and Bánswádá, now in Málwá; Sirohi, now in Rajputáná; Cutch; Sûnth is Rewa Ka, and Rám Nagar (Dharampur) in Surat—were, on the payment of tribute, allowed to continue in the hands of their Hindu rulers. The ten remaining districts were administered directly by imperial officers. But as the revenues of the district of Surat had been separately assigned to its manager (*mátsadi*, literally revenue-clerk), only nine districts with 184 sub-divisions, or *parganahs*, were

---

1 Gladwin's Ain Akbari II., 62-63.

Introduction.

Under the Moghal Viceroys, 1573-1760.

entered in the collections from the viceroy of Gujarát. These nine districts were in continental Gujarát,—Pátan with 17 subdivisions; A'hmadábád with 33; Godhrá with 11; Chámpáner with 13; Baroda with 4; Broach with 14; and Rájpiplá (Nádod) with 12. In the peninsula were Sorath with 63, and Nawánagar with 17 sub-divisions. This lessening of the size of the province would seem to have been accompanied by even more than a corresponding reduction in the amount of the State demand. Instead of 5,840,050*l*. (Rs. 5,84,00,500), the revenue recovered in A.D. 1571, two years before the province was annexed, under the arrangement introduced by the emperor Akbar; the total amount, including the receipts from Surat and the tribute of the six feudatory districts, is returned at 1,999,113*l*. (Rs. 1,99,91,130), or but little more than one-third part of what was formerly collected.

According to the author of the Mirat-i-A'hmadi this revenue of 1,999,113*l*. continued to be realized as late as the reign of Muhammad Sháh (A.D. 1719-1748). But before the time in which he was writing (A.D. 1748-1762) the whole revenue had fallen to 1,235,000*l*. Of 1,999,113*l*. (Rs. 1,99,91,130), the total amount levied by Akbar on the annexation of the province, 520,501*l*. (Rs. 52,05,010), or a little more than a quarter, were set apart for the imperial use and royal expenses; 55,000*l*. (Rs. 5,50,000) were assigned for the support of the viceroy and the personal estates of the nobles; and the remainder was settled for the pay of other officers of rank and court officials. Nearly 30,000*l*. (Rs. 3,00,000) were given away as rewards and pensions to religious orders and establishments.[1]

---

[1] Bird's History of Gujarát. Another detailed statement of the revenue of Gujarát given in the Mirat-i-A'hmadi, apparently for the time when the author wrote (A.D. 1750) gives: Revenue from crown lands 2,107,518*l*.; tribute-paying divisions or *sirkárs*, 12,700*l*.; Mahi Kánta tribute, 178,741*l*.; Wátrak Kántá tribute, 159,768*l*.; and Sámbar Kántá tribute, 121,151*l*,—in all 2,579,878*l*.; adding to this 20,000*l*. for Káchh, 40,000*l*. for Dungarpur, and 5,000*l*. for Sirohi, or a total of 65,000*l*., gives a grand total of 2,644,878*l*. According to a statement given by Bird in a note at page 108 of his History, the revenue of Gujarát under Jahángir (A.D. 1605-1617) averaged 1,250,000*l*.; under Aurangzib (A.D. 1658-1707) 1,519,622*l*.; and under Muhammad Sháh (A.D. 1719-1748) 1,218,360*l*. In this passage the revenue under the emperor Akbar (A.D. 1556-1605) is given at 668,454*l*., but this total is taken from Gladwin's Ain Akbari; and at vol. II., p. 73 of that work there would seem to be some miscalculation, for while the total number of *dams* ($\frac{1}{40}$ of a rupee) is 43,68,02,301, the conversion into rupees is

Introduction.

Under the Moghal Viceroys, 1573-1760.

Besides lightening the pressure of the State demand, three measures were introduced by the emperor Akbar to improve the condition of the province. These were—(1) the survey of the land; (2) the payment of the chief men, *mukadam*, of government villages; and (3) the restoration to the small landholders of the superior class of the share they formerly enjoyed in the lands of Government villages. The survey, which was entrusted to rájá Todar Mal, the revenue minister of the empire, was completed in A.D. 1575. The operations were, however, confined to only a small portion of the whole area of the province. Besides the six tributary districts which were unaffected by the measure, Godhra in the east, the western peninsula, and a large portion of the central strip of directly governed lands were excluded, so that of the 184 sub-divisions only 64 were surveyed. Of 7,261,849 acres (12,360,594 bighás), the whole area measured, 4,920,818 acres (8,374,498 bighás), or about two-thirds, were in A.D. 1575 found to be fit for cultivation, and the remainder was waste. In those parts of the directly governed districts, where the land was not measured, the old method of determining the government share of the produce, by selecting a portion of the field while the crop was still standing, or dividing the grain heap at harvest time, was continued. In surveyed districts the amount paid was determined by the area and character of the land under cultivation. Payment was made either in grain or in money, according to the instructions issued to the revenue-collectors, "that when it would not prove oppressive the value of the grain should be taken in ready money at the market price."[1] But the chief

---

Rs. 10,96,123 instead of Rs. 10,920,057½. The corresponding returns given by Mr. Thomas (Rev. of the Mog. Emp., p. 52) are in Akbar, A.D. 1594, 1,092,412*l.*; under Sháh Jahán, A.D. 1648, 13,25,000*l.*; under Aurangzeb, A.D. 1654, 2,173,220*l.*; A.D. 1663-66, 1,339,500*l.*; A.D. 1697, 2,330,500*l*; A.D. 1707, 1,519,623*l.* The varieties in the currency employed in different parts of the accounts cause some confusion in calculating the Gujarát revenue. Under the A'hmadábád kings the accounts were kept in *tankhás*, or $\frac{1}{100}$ of rupees, while under the Moghals *dams*, $\frac{1}{40}$th of a rupee, took the place of *tankhás*. The revenues from Surat, Baroda, Broach, and other districts south of the Mahi, were returned in *changizis*, a coin varying in value from something over ⅔rds of a rupee to slightly less than ½; the revenues from Rádhanpur and Morvi were entered in *mahmudis*, a coin nearly identical in value with the *changizi*; while, as noticed above, the tribute and custom dues are returned in a gold currency, the tribute in *huns* of about 8*s.* (Rs. 4), the customs in *ibráhims* of 9*s.* (Rs. 4-8.)

1 Ain Akbari (Gladwin) I., 305. Four ways of calculating the amount of the State share in an unsurveyed field are given in the Ain Akbari:—(1)

Introduction.

Under the Moghal Viceroys, 1573-1760.

change in the revenue management was that, instead of each year calculating the Government share from the character of the crop, a uniform demand was fixed to run for a term of ten years.

Another important effect of this survey was, to extend to cultivators in simple villages the proprietary interest in the soil formerly enjoyed only by the shareholders of joint villages. By this change the power of the military nobles to make undue exactions from the cultivators in their assigned lands was to some extent checked. It was, perhaps, also an indirect effect of this more definite settlement of the State demand that the revenue agents of Government and of the holders of assigned lands, finding that the revenues could be realised without their help, refused to allow to the heads of villages certain revenue dues which, in return for their services, they had hitherto enjoyed. Accordingly, in A.D. 1589-90, these heads of villages appealed to Government, and Akbar decided that from the collections of Government lands—in assigned districts as well as in the crown domains—two-and-a-half per cent should be set apart as a perquisite for men of this class.[1]

---

to measure the land with the crops standing and make an estimate; (2) to reap the crops, collect the grain in barns, and divide it according to agreement; (3) to divide the field as soon as the seed is sown; and (4) to gather the grain into heaps on the field and divide it there.

1 The men to whom this 2½ per cent was granted are referred in the Mirat-i-A'hmadi as *desdis* and *mukadams.* Whatever doubt there may be as to the precise meaning of these terms, this much seems clear, that it was as head-men of the villages that they petitioned for and received this grant. These were the heads of the villages with whom, as noticed above, the Government agent for collecting the revenue dealt, and who, agreeing for the whole amount that was to be recovered from the village, themselves carried out the actual details of collection from the individual cultivators. In the sharehold villages north of the Narbadá, the head-man, who would be entitled to this 2½ per cent, would be the representative of the body of village shareholders. South of the Narbadá, in the villages "originally colonised by officers of the State, who, placed in charge of a district or part of a district, collected cultivators, assigned them sites, gave them advances of food, money, and materials, and thus founded villages of which they had the entire management" (*see* "Indian Enconomist" for 1869, page 83)—it would be by the representatives of these officers that the 2½ per cent grant would be enjoyed. Persons holding the position of heads of villages in Southern Gujarát were called *desáis,* and acted as district hereditary revenue officers; but it was not as district hereditary revenue officers, but as heads of villages, that they received from Akbar this 2½ per cent assignment. In Northern Gujarát there were *desáis* who were only district revenue officers. These men would seem to have received no part of

When the heads of villages laid their own private grievance before Government, they also brought to its notice that the Koli and Rájput land-owners, whose shares in Government villages had been resumed by the crown in A.D. 1545, had since that time continued in a state of discontent and revolt, "and were then causing the ruin of the subjects and a deficiency of the Government collections." An inquiry was instituted, and, to satisfy the claims of land-owners of this class, it was agreed that, on furnishing good security for their conduct and receiving the Government mark on their contingent of cavalry, they should again be put in possession of a one-fourth share of the lands of Government villages. While the province was managed agreeably to these regulations, says the author of the Mirat-i-A'hmadi, it continued to increase in prosperity.[1]

Still, though these measures did much to put a stop to internal disorder, Gujarát, for several years after it came under imperial control, continued to be much disturbed by insurrections among the nobles, and so imperfectly protected was it from the attacks of foreign enemies that between the years A.D. 1573 and 1609 each of its three richest cities—A'hmadábád, Cambay, and Surat—were in succession taken and plundered.[2] During the rest of the seventeenth century, though the country was from time to time disturbed by Koli and Rájput risings, and towards the end of the century suffered

---

Akbar's grant in 1589-90, for as late as A.D. 1766 the emperor Aurangzeb, having occasion to make inquiries into the position of *desáis*, found that hitherto they had been supported by cesses and illegal exactions, and ordered that a stop should be put to all such exactions, and a fixed assignment of 2½ per cent on the revenues of the villages under their charge be allowed to them. It does not appear whether the Surat *desáis* succeeded in obtaining this grant of 2½ per cent as district revenue officers in addition to the Akbar (A.D. 1589) assignment of 2½ per cent as heads of villages.

1 Bird, 409.

2 A'hmadábád (A.D. 1583) by Muzafar Sháh, the former king of Gujarát; Cambay (A.D. 1573) by Muhammed Husain Mirzá; and Surat (A.D. 1609) by Malik Amber, a general of the Deccani king. As regards the general order maintained in the country, it seems that in the beginning of the 17th century native merchants trading between A'hmadábád and Cambay travelled in large weekly caravans, resting at nights in a space barricaded by a circle of carts (Kerr IX., 127 and 201). The English merchants, on their way from one factory to another, were accompanied by an escort, and, in spite of their guard, were on more than one occasion attacked by large bands of Rajputs (Kerr IX., 187,203). As regards the state of the different parts of the province, Nicholas Ufflet, who went from Agra to Surat about 1610, describes the north, from Jhálor to A'hmadábád, as throughout the whole way a

Introduction.

Under the Moghal Viceroys, 1573-1760.

much from the attacks of the Maráthás, the viceroys were, on the whole, able to maintain their authority, repressing the outbreaks of the disorderly classes, and enforcing the imperial claims for tribute on the more independent feudatory chiefs. Throughout the greater part of the century the general state of the province would seem to have been prosperous. Its cities were the wonder of European travellers. Surat, which only since the transfer of Gujarát to the Moghal Empire had risen to hold a place among its chief centres of trade, was, in A.D. 1664, when taken by Siváji, rich enough to supply him with plunder, in treasure and precious stones, worth a million sterling;[1] and at that time Cambay is said to have been beyond comparison greater than Surat, and A'hmadábád much richer and more populous.[2]

From the beginning of the eighteenth century disorders increased in Gujarát. Unable to rely for support on the imperial court, the viceroys failed to maintain order among the leading nobles, or to enforce their tribute from the more powerful of the feudatory chiefs. And while the small Koli and Rájput landholders, freed from the control of a strong central power, were destroying the military posts, taking possession of the State share of the village lands, and levying dues from their more peaceful neighbours, the tribute claims of the Maráthás were from year to year becoming a heavier burden on the province. During the last ten years of Musalmán rule,

---

sandy and woody country, full of thievish, beastly men, and savage beasts such as lions and tigers; from A'hmadábád to Cambay the road was through sands and woods, much infested by thieves; from Cambay to Broach it was a woody and dangerous journey; but from Broach to Surat the country was goodly, fertile, and full of villages abounding in wild date-trees (Kerr VIII, 303). Passing through from the mouth of the Tapti to Surat Mr. Copland (24th December 1613) was quite delighted to see at the same time the goodliest spring and harvest combined I had ever seen anywhere. "Often of two adjoining fields, one was as green as a fine meadow, and the other waving yellow like gold and ready to be cut down, and all along the roads were many goodly villages." (Kerr IX., 119.)

1 Ome's Historical Fragments, 12.

2 The following are some of the notices of A'hmadábád and Cambay by the European travellers of the eighteenth century:—Cambay, 1598, trade so great that if he had not seen it he would not have believed it possible (Cæsar Frederick); 1638, beyond comparison larger than Surat (Mandelslo, 101-108); 1663-1671, twice as big as Surat (Baldæus, Churchill, III., 506). A'hmadábád, 1598, a very great city and very populous (Cæsar Frederick); 1638, great manufactures, satin and velvet, silk and cotton (Mandelslo, 80); 1695, the greatest city in India, nothing inferior to Venice for rich silks and gold stuffs. (Gemelli Careri—Churchill, IV. 188.)

so entirely did the viceroy's authority forsake him, that, according to the author of the Mirat-i-A'hmadi, when the great landholders refused to pay their tribute, what power had the viceroy to enforce it? And so faithless had they become that he could not pass the city gate without an escort from them.[3]

Introduction. Under the Moghal Viceroys, 1573-1760.

---

[3] Bird, 441.

CHAPTER I.

EARLY MUSALMA'N GOVERNORS, A.D. 1297-1403.

With the exception of the great expedition of Muhammad Ghaznavi against Somnáth,[1] A.D. 1024-1026; the defeat of Muhammad Ghori by Bhim Dev II. of A'nhalwáḍá[2] about A.D. 1178; and the subsequent sack of A'nhalwáḍá and defeat of Bhim by Kutb-ud-din Eibak A.D. 1194, Gujarát was, until the reign of Alá-ud-din Ḵhiljy, A.D. 1295-1315, free from all interference from the Muhammadans. But in A.D. 1297, A'laf Khán, general of Alá-ud-din, was, together with Nasrat Khán Vazir, sent against A'nhalwáḍá,[2] which they conquered, expelling Karan Wághela, usually called Ghelo or "The Mad," who took refuge at Devgarh[3] with Rámdeva, the sovereign of that principality. They then conquered Khambhát (the modern Cambay), and, appointing a local governor, returned to Delhi. From this time Gujarát fell under the Muhammadan power, and A'laf Khán, a man of great energy, by repeated expeditions, consolidated the conquest and established the Muhammadan rule. The Kánaddeva Rásá says that he plundered Somnáth, and there is no doubt but that he conquered Jhálor[4] (the ancient Jhálindar) from the Songarh Chohâns. A'laf Khán held the government of Gujarát for about 20 years, when, at the instigation

Ala'-ud-din Ḵhiljy, Emperor, 1295-1315.

Musalmán conquest of Gujarát, 1297.

ALAF KHA'N, Governor, 1297-1317.

---

1 Somnáth (N. Lat. 20° 55', E. Long. 70° 23'), the temple of Mahádev, "Lord of the Moon," near the southern extremity of the peninsula of Káthiáwár.

2 A'nhalwáḍá (N. Lat. 23° 48', E. Long. 72° 2'), Nehrwalá, or Pátan, on the south bank of the Saraswati River, 65 miles N.E. of A'hmadábád, from A.D. 746 to A.D. 1194 the capital of the Rájput dynasties of Gujarát.

3 Deogarh; this is supposed to have been Daulatábád in the Deccan, situated about 10 miles N.W. of Aurangábád (N. Lat. 19° 57', E. Long. 75° 18').

4 Jhálor (N. Lat. 25° 23', E. Long. 72° 40'), in the Rájput State of Jodhpur, 71 miles S.W. by S. from the town of that name.

Chapter I.

Early Musalma'n Governors.

of Malik Káfur, he was recalled and put to death by the emperor Alá-ud-din.

AIN-UL-MULK, Governor, 1318.

After his departure Muhammadan power in Gujarát was much shaken, and Malik Kámil-ud-din, sent by Mubárak Khiljy to quell the disturbances, was slain in battle, and the sedition spread. It was now that Ain-ul-Mulk Multáni arrived with a powerful army, and through his exertions the rebels were beaten and order re-established. He was succeeded by Zufar Khán, who completed the subjection of the country. But this able governor was also recalled, and his place supplied by Hisám-ud-din Parmár. This officer, showing treasonable intentions, was imprisoned and succeeded by Malik Waji-ud-din Kuraishi, who was afterwards ennobled by the title of Táj-ul-Mulk. Khusrav Khán Parmár was then appointed governor, but it is not clear whether he ever joined his appointment; and the next governor of whom we have any account was Táj-ul-Mulk, who about A.D. 1320 was, for the second time, chosen as governor by sultán Gheiás-ud-din Toghlak. He was succeeded by Malik Mukbil, who held the titles of Khán Jahán and Náib-i-Mukhtár, and who was appointed by sultán Muhammad Toghlak A.D. 1325-1351. Subsequently the same emperor granted the government of Gujarát to A'hmad Eiáz, Malik Mukbil continuing to act as his deputy. Afterwards when A'hmad Eiáz, who received the title of Khwájá Jahán, proceeded as governor to Gujarát, Malik Mukbil acted as his minister. And about A.D. 1338, when Khwájá Jahán was sent against the emperor's nephew Kursháp, and the rájá of Kampila[1] who had sheltered him, Malik Mukbil succeeded to the post of governor. Finally, Malik Mukbil was, about A.D. 1347, sent to Daulatábád, and his place supplied by Moiz-ud-din.

Order established, 1318.

TAJ-UL-MULK, Governor, 1320.

Muhammad Toghlak, Emperor, 1325 1351.

The emperor quells an insurrection, 1347.

About A.D. 1346 certain Muhammadan nobles of Gujarát, leaguing with the Hindu chieftains, rebelled and defeated one Aziz, who was appointed by the emperor to march against them. On this occasion Muhammad Toghlak, in the year A.D. 1347, advancing in person against the rebels, totally defeated them, and, at the same time, sacked the towns of Cambay and Surat. It was also during this campaign that he drove the Gohel chief Mokheráji out of his stronghold at Piram

---

[1] In the Carnatic, probably on the Tungabhadrá River near Vijayanagar. —Briggs' Muhammadan Power in India, 418 and 428.

Chapter I.

Early Musalma'n Governors.

Island, near Gogo, on the Gulf of Cambay, and then, landing his forces, after a stubborn conflict, defeated the Gohels, killing Mokheráji and capturing Gogo. Muhammad Toghlak then departed for Daulatábád in the Deccan, and in his absence the chiefs and nobles under one Malik Togh4n again rebelled, and, obtaining possession of Pátan, imprisoned Moiz-ud-din the viceroy. The insurgents then plundered Cambay, and afterwards laid siege to Broach. Muhammad Toghlak at once marched for Gujarát and relieved Broach, Malik Toghán retreating to Cambay, whither he was followed by Malik Yusuf, whom the emperor sent in pursuit of him. In the battle that ensued near Cambay, Malik Yusuf was defeated and slain, and all the prisoners, both of this engagement and those who had been previously captured, were put to death by Malik Toghán. Among the prisoners was Moiz-ud-din, the governor of Gujarát. Muhammad Toghlak now marched to Cambay in person, whence Malik Toghán retreated to Pátan, pursued by the emperor, who was forced by stress of weather to halt at Asáwal.[1] Eventually the emperor came up with Malik Toghán near Kadi and gained a complete victory, Malik Toghán fleeing to Thattá in Sindh. Muhammad Toghlak now turned his attention to the establishment of good order in Gujarát, and marched against the hill fortress of Girnár,[2] from the chief of which he extorted tribute. He then went to Cutch, and after subduing that country returned to Sorath. Here, at Gondal, he contracted a fever, and before he was entirely recovered, with the view of subduing the Sumrá chief of Thattá, who had sheltered Malik Toghán, he advanced through Cutch into Sindh. Ere reaching Thattá, however, he succumbed to the fever, and died in the spring of the year A.D. 1351. Shortly before his death he appointed Nizám-ul-Mulk to the government of Gujarát.

Subdues the Chiefs of Girnár and Cutch, 1350.

Advancing into Sindh dies, 1351.

Muhammad Toghlak was, in A.D. 1351, succeeded on the throne of Delhi by Firoz Toghlak. Shortly after his accession the emperor marched to Sindh and sent a force against Malik Toghán. Some years later, about A.D. 1360, he again advanced to Sindh against Jám Bábuniá. From Sindh he

Firoz Toghlak, Emperor, 1351-1388.

---

[1] Asáwal (N. Lat. 23° 0', E. Long. 72° 36'), a town of some size, afterwards, A.D. 1413, made the capital of the Musalmán kings of Gujarát, and called A'hmadábád.

[2] Girnár (N. Lat. 21° 30', E. Long. 70° 42'), in the Sorath sub-division of the peninsula of Káthiáwár.

Chapter I.

Early Musalmán Governors.

ZUFAR KHÁN Governor, 1371.

FARHAT-UL-MULK, Governor, 1376-1391.

proceeded to Gujarát, where he stayed during some months. In the following year, on leaving for Sindh for the third time, he bestowed the government of Gujarát on Zufar Khán in place of Nizám-ul-Mulk. Zufar Khán dying in about A.D. 1373, according to Ferishta, and A.D. 1371 according to the Mirat-i-Áhmadi, was succeeded by his son Darya Khán as viceroy. Darya Khán, however, appears to have governed by a deputy named Shams-ud-din Anwar Khán. In A.D. 1376 the revenue from Gujarát being less than in former years, one Shams-ud-din Damgháni offered a considerable advance on the usual collections. As Darya Khán would not agree to pay this sum he was displaced and Shams-ud-din Damgháni was appointed governor. Finding himself unable to pay the stipulated amount this officer rebelled and withheld the revenue entirely. Firoz Toghlak sent an army against him, and by the aid of the chieftains and people, whom he had greatly oppressed, Shams-ud-din was slain. The government of the province was then entrusted to Farhat-ul-Mulk Rásti Khán. In about A.D. 1388, a noble, named Sikandar Khán, was sent to supersede Farhat-ul-Mulk, but was defeated and slain by him. No notice was, however, taken of this conduct by the Imperial Government, and in this same year Firoz Toghlak died and was succeeded by Gheiás-ud-din Toghlak, in whose short reign no change was made in the government of Gujarát. During the brief rule of Ábu Bakar, Farhat-ul-Mulk continued undisturbed. But about A.D. 1390, on the accession of Násir-ud-din Muhammad Toghlak II., Farhat-ul-Mulk again rebelled and endeavoured to become independent.

Rebels and is succeeded by

ZUFAR KHÁN, Governor, 1391-1403.

In A.D. 1391, a noble of the name of Zufar Khán was, accordingly, appointed governor of Gujarát, and despatched with an army to recall and, if necessary, expel Farhat-ul-Mulk.

Zufar Khán a converted Rájput.

This Zufar Khán was the son of Waji-ul-Mulk, who belonged by birth to the Tánk tribe, a class of Rájputs claiming to be of the Suryavansi race, who together with the Gujars appear from very early times to have inhabited the plains of the Panjáb. Driven from the Panjáb by the pressure of the Muhammadan conquests in Northern India, these tribes, especially the Gujars, would seem, about the end of the 13th century A.D., to have been found by the Musalmán conquerors in considerable numbers near Mount Abu and in the neighbourhood of Pátan. As this city was made the seat of

Chapter I.

Early Musalma'n Governors.

His rise to power.

Musalmán government, the name of the chief inhabitants of the neighbouring country would seem to have been applied by the Musalmáns to the whole province of which Pátan became the capital.[1] The following story is told of Waji-ul-Mulk's rise to power at the Delhi Court. Before he sat on the throne of Delhi, Firoz Toghlak, when hunting in Gujarát, is said, one day, to have lost his way, and to have come to the village of Thásrá,[2] then held by chieftains of the Tánk tribe. Here he was hospitably entertained by two brothers of the chief's family, named Saháran and Sádhu, and became enamoured of their beautiful sister. When his hosts learned who the stranger was, they gave him their sister in marriage and followed his fortunes. Afterwards, Firoz Toghlak, persuading them to embrace Islám, conferred on Saháran the title of Waji-ul-Mulk, and on Sádhu the title of Shamsher Khán. Finally, in A.D. 1351, when Firoz Toghlak ascended the throne, he made Shamsher Khán and Zufar Khán, the son of Waji-ul-Mulk, his cup-bearers and raised them to the rank of nobles.

Battle of Jitpur; Farhat-ul-Mulk slain, 1391.

In A.D. 1391, on being appointed viceroy, Zufar Khán marched without delay for Gujarát. In passing Nágor[3] he was met by a deputation of the inhabitants of Cambay, complaining of the tyranny of Rásti Khán. Consoling them, he proceeded to Pátan, the seat of government, and thence marched against Rásti Khán. The armies met near the village of Kambhu,[4] a dependency of Pátan, and Farhat-ul-Mulk Rásti Khán was slain and his army defeated. Zufar Khán, to commemorate the victory, founded a village on the battle-field, which he named Jitpur (the city of victory), and then, starting for Cambay, redressed the grievances of the people.

Zufar Khán attacks the Chief of Idar, 1393.

Zufar Khán's first warlike expedition was against the ráv of Idar,[5] who, in A.D. 1393, had refused to pay the customary tribute, and this chief he humbled. From the contemporary histories, it would seem that the previous governors had estab-

---

1 See Cunningham's Ancient Geography, I., 322.

2 Thásrá, the head-quarters of the sub-division of that name in the British district of Kaira (*Kheda*).

3 Nágor (N. Lat. 27° 10', E. Long. 73° 50'), in the Rájput State of Jodhpur, 84 miles N.W. of Nasirábád.

4 The Tabakát Akbari has Khánpur or Kánpur.

5 Idar, the principal Rájput State of the Mahi Kántá. The chief town N. Lat. 23° 50', E. Long. 73° 3'.

Chapter I.

Early Musalma'n Governors.

lished tribute on all or most of the chiefs of Gujarát except the ráv of Junágarh[1] and the rájá of Rájpiplá,[2] who hitherto had retained their independence. Zufar Khán now planned an expedition against the celebrated Hindu shrine of Somnáth, but, hearing that A'dil Khán of A'sir Burhánpur had invaded Sultánpur and Nandurbár,[3] he moved his troops in that direction, and A'dil Khán retired to A'sir.[4] In A.D. 1394, he marched against the ráv of Junágarh and exacted tribute. Afterwards, proceeding to Somnáth, he destroyed the temple and introduced Islám into the city of Pátan Somnáth or Deva Pátan. He now heard that the Hindus of Mándu[5] were oppressing the Maslims, and, accordingly, marching thither, he beleaguered that fortress for a year, but failing to take it contented himself with accepting the excuses of the rájá. From Mándu he performed a pilgrimage to A'jmir.[6] Here he proceeded against the chiefs of Sámbhar and Dandwána, and then attacking the Rájputs of Delwárá and Jháláwár,[7] he defeated them, and returned to Pátan in A.D. 1396. About this time his son Tátár Khán, leaving his baggage in the fort of Pánipat,[8] made an attempt against Delhi. But Ikbál Khán took the fort of Pánipat, captured Tátár Khán's baggage, and forced him to withdraw to Gujarát. In A.D. 1397, Zufar Khán determined to reduce Idar, and, accordingly, besieged the fort, laying waste the neighbouring country. But before he had taken the fort news arrived of Timur's conquests, and concluding a peace with the Idar rájá, Zufar Khán returned to Pátan. In A.D. 1398, hearing that the Somnáth chief affected independence, Zufar Khán led an army against him, and subduing him established Islám on a firm footing.

Zufar Khán exacts tribute from Junágarh, 1394.

Lays siege to Idar Fort, 1397.

Establishes Islám at Somnáth, 1398.

1 Junágarh in the Sorath sub-division of the Káthiáwár peninsula. This is Briggs' Rai of Jehrend. Junágarh was formerly called Jirangarh, both names meaning ancient fortress.

2 Rájpiplá in the Rewá Kántá division of Gujarát.

3 Sultánpur and Nandurbár now form parts of the British district of Khándesh.

4 Asir, now Asirgarh (N. Lat. 21° 26′, E. Long. 76° 26′), beyond the north-eastern frontier of Khándesh.

5 Mándu (N. Lat. 22° 20′, E. Long. 75° 27′), the capital of the Pathán dynasty of Málwá A.D. 1404-1561, has long been in ruins.

6 A'jmir (N. Lat. 26° 29′, E. Long. 74° 43′), the chief town of the district of the same name to which Sámbhar and Dandwána also belong.

7 Delwárá is probably A'bu and Jháláwár, the modern Jháláwár in Gujarát, which in those days included Mándal, Viramgám and part of the Chunwál.

8 Pánipat (N. Lat. 29° 23′, E. Long. 77° 2′), 78 miles north of Delhi.

CHAPTER II.

THE A'HMADA'BA'D KINGS—A.D. 1403-1573.

Chapter II.

A'hmada'ba'd Kings.

Though Zufar Khán had, from the time of his first appointment as governor of Gujarát, A.D. 1391, acted as an independent ruler, he did not till, A.D. 1403, openly throw off all forms of allegiance to the emperor of Delhi. In that year he formally invested his son Tátár Khán with the sovereignty of Gujarát, under the title of Násir-ud-din Muhammad Sháh.

The period of the rule of the dynasty thus established in Gujarát, extending over 170 years and including the names of fifteen sovereigns, may conveniently be divided into two parts. The first, lasting for a little more than a century and a quarter, when Gujarát, under strong rulers, rose to a position of consequence among the kingdoms of Western India; the second, from A.D. 1536 to A.D. 1573, a time of confusion, during almost the whole of which the nominal sovereigns were minors, and the wealth and supremacy of Gujarát were sacrificed to the struggles for power among the chief nobles.

Muhammad I., 1403-1404.

On ascending the throne in A.D. 1403, Muhammad Sháh made Asáwal his capital, and, after humbling the chief of Nándod,[1] marched against Delhi by way of Pátan. On hearing of his intentions, Ikbál Khán, who at this time was master of Delhi, was greatly alarmed. The Gujarát king was, however, taken ill at Pátan and died there, and was there buried, and the expedition, in consequence, came to nothing.[2]

---

1 One of the capitals of the State of Rájpiplá, then independent. The word is always written Nádot by the Muhammadan historians.

2 Another account, perhaps more probable, is that Tátár Khán deposed and imprisoned his father and himself ascended the throne, and that when he reached Pátan on this expedition persons friendly to his father poisoned him.

Chapter II.

A'hmad-a'ba'd Kings.

Zufar Khán reigns as Muzafar, 1407-1410.

After the death of Muhammad Sháh, Zufar Khán asked his own younger brother Shams Khán to carry on the government, but he refused, and Zufar Khán, accordingly, sent him to Nágor in place of Jalál Khán Ghoghar, and in A.D. 1407-8, at the request of the nobles and chief men of the country, himself formally mounted the throne and assumed the title of Muzafar Sháh. At this time A'lp Khán, son of Diláwar Khán of Málwá, was rumoured to have poisoned his father and ascended the throne with the title of sultán Hushang Ghori. On hearing this, Muzafar Sháh marched against him and besieged him in Dhár.[1] This town he finally reduced, handing over A'lp Khán to the charge of his brother Shams Khán, on whom had been conferred the title of Nusrat Khán. A'lp Khán remained a year in confinement, and Musá Khán usurped his authority. On hearing this, A'lp Khán begged to be released, and Muzafar Sháh not only agreed to his prayer, but sent his grandson, A'hmad Khán, with an army to reinstate him. This expedition was successful; the town of Mándu was taken and the usurper Musá Khán put to flight. A'hmad Khán then returned to Gujarát in A.D. 1409-10. In this year the king marched against the chief of Kanbah Kot,[2] and in A.D. 1410-11 died, poisoned as is generally believed by his grandson A'hmad Khán, who now succeeded him with the title of Násir-ud-dunya Wa-ud-din Abul fateh A'hmad Sháh.

Dies, 1410.

A'hmad I., 1411-1443.

Shortly after A'hmad Sháh's accession, his cousin Moid-ud-din Firoz Khán, governor of Baroda, allying himself with Nizám-ul-Mulk Bhandári and certain other of the nobles, collected an army at Nadiád in Kaira, and, laying claim to the crown, defeated the king's followers. Jivandás, one of the insurgents, then proposed to march upon Pátan, but the others refused; and a dispute arose in which Jivandás was slain, and the rest sought and obtained A'hmad Sháh's forgiveness. Moid-ud-din Firoz Khán, however, went to Cambay, and was there joined by Masti Khán, son of Muzafar Sháh, who was governor of Surat: on the king's advance they fled from Cambay to Broach, to which fort A'hmad Sháh laid siege. As soon as the king arrived Moid-ud-din's army went over to his side, and Masti Khán also submitted. After a few days A'hmad Sháh sent for

---

[1] Dhár (N. Lat. 22° 35', E. Long. 75° 20'), the chief place of a small State of the same name in Málwá.

[2] Kanbah Kot. The Tabakát Akbari has Kanthkot, a dependency of Kutch, which is probably correct.

Chapter II.

Ahmad-a'ba'd Kings.

and forgave Moid-ud-din, and returned to Asáwal victorious and triumphant.

A'hmad I. builds A'hmadábád, 1413.

Shortly afterwards, in A.D. 1413-1414, A'hmad Sháh attacked and defeated A'sa Bhil, chief of Asáwal, and, finding the site of that town suitable for his capital, he changed its name to A'hmadábád, and busied himself in enlarging and fortifying the city. During this year Moid-ud-din Firoz Khán and Masti Khán again revolted, and, joining the Idar rájá, took shelter in that fortress. A force under Fateh Khán was despatched against the rebels, and finally Firoz Khán and the Idar rájá were forced to flee. The rájá at length, seeing that all hope of success was gone, made his peace with the king by surrendering to him the elephants, horses, and other baggage of Moid-ud-din Firoz Khán and Masti Khán, who now fled to Nágor,[1] where they were sheltered by Shams Khán Dandáni. A'hmad Sháh after levying the stipulated tribute departed. Moid-ud-din Firoz Khán was afterwards slain in the war between Shams Khán and rána Mokal of Chitor. In A.D. 1414-15 Othmán A'hmad and Shekh Malik, son of Sher Malik, and Sulimán Afghán called A'zam Khán, and Isá Sálár, rebelled and wrote secretly to sultán Hushang of Málwá, inviting him to invade Gujarát, and promising to seat him on the throne and expel A'hmad Sháh. They were joined in their rebellion by Jhálá Satarsálji[2] of Pátri and other chiefs of Gujarát. A'hmad Sháh despatched Latif Khán and Nizám-ul-Mulk against Shekh Malik and his associates, while he sent Imád-ul-Mulk against sultán Hushang, who retired, and Imád-ul-Mulk, after plundering Málwá, returned to Gujarát. Latif Khán was equally successful, and the king returned with joyful heart to A'hmadábád.

Defeats the Idar Chief, 1414.

Suppresses a revolt, 1414.

Spread of Islám in Káthiáwar, 1414.

Though the Muhammadans had with their first possession of the country, A.D. 1297-1318, introduced their faith throughout the length and breadth of Gujarát, from Pátan to Broach, the rest of the province for long remained unconverted. But by degrees, through the efforts of the A'hmadábád kings, the power of their rule became more directly felt in all parts of the province. Many districts, till then all but independent, accepted the Musalmán faith at the hands of A'hmad Sháh, and agreed to the payment of a regular tribute. In A.D.

---

1 Nágor in the Rájput State of Jodhpur (see above p. 29).

2 Called in the Tabakát Akbari the rájá of Mándal.

Chapter II. A'hmad-a'ba'd Kings.

1414 he sent an army against the rájá of Girnár and defeated him in the field, on which the rájá retired to the fortress of Girnár. A'hmad Sháh, though unable to capture the citadel, gained the lower fort of Junágarh. Finding further resistance vain, the chief offered his submission, and Junágarh was admitted among the tributary states. This example was followed by the greater number of the Sorath chiefs, who, for the time, resigned their independence. Leaving Syad A'bdúl Khair and Syad Kásim to collect the tribute, A'hmad Sháh returned to A'hmadábád. Next year he marched against Sidhpur,[1] and from that on to Dhár in Málwá. At this time the more powerful feudatories of the kingdom were the ráv of Junágarh, the ráwal of Chámpáner,[2] the rájá of Nándod, the ráv of Idar, the rájá of Jháláwár, and others. The chiefs of Chámpáner, Idar, Nándod, and Jháláwár, alarmed at the activity of A'hmad Sháh and his zeal for Islám, instigated sultán Hushang of Málwá to invade Gujarát; but A'hmad Sháh, by promptly marching to Morásá,[3] forced sultán Hushang of Málwá to retire, and afterwards he broke up the conspiracy, reproving but pardoning the chiefs concerned. The Sorath chiefs, too, about this time, withheld their tribute, but the patience and unwearied activity of the king overcame all opposition, and none of these risings became formidable.

A'hmad I. quells a second revolt, 1416.

After quelling these rebellions A'hmad Sháh marched to Málwá against sultán Hushang, whom he defeated, and, after capturing the treasure and elephants of the Málwá prince, returned to his own dominions. It was always A'hmad Sháh's policy to separately engage his enemies, and thus endeavour to destroy them in detail. In accordance with these tactics, he, in A.D. 1418, marched to chastise Tribhovandás of Chámpáner, and though unable to take that fortress he laid waste the surrounding country. In A.D. 1419 he ravaged the lands round Songarh,[4] and built a

Expedition against Málwá, 1417.

Attacks Chámpáner, 1418.

---

[1] Sidhpur (N. Lat. 23° 50′, E. Long. 72° 20′), on the Saraswati, 58 miles north of A'hmadábád.

[2] Chámpáner (N. Lat. 22° 30′, E. Long. 73° 30′), in the British district of the Panch Máháls, from A.D. 1483 to A.D. 1560 the chief city of Gujarát, now in ruins.

[3] Morásá (N. Lat. 23° 27′, E. Long. 73° 21′), 40 miles N.E. of the town of Kairá.

[4] Songarh, a few miles to the south of the Tápti in the Nausári district of His Highness the Gáekwár's territory. It is near to the Khándesh frontier.

fort there and a mosque within the fort; he also built a wall round the town of Mangni,[1] and then marched upon Mándu. Sultán Hushang, however, sending ambassadors, made peace, on which A'hmad Sháh, returning towards Chámpáner, again laid waste the surrounding country. During the following year he remained in A'hmadábád, devoting his time to bringing his own dominions into thorough subjection by establishing fortified posts in different places, and by humbling the chiefs and destroying their strongholds. Amongst other works he built at this time the fort of Dohad[2] on the Málwá frontier. He next attacked Málwá and took the fort of Mesar, and after a short siege of Mándu, in which he was unsuccessful, he went to Ujain,[3] and thence again besieged Mándu; but unable to capture this fortress, he marched to Sárangpur and besieged that town. Sultán Hushang now, sending ambassadors concluded a peace; but while A'hmad Sháh was returning to Gujarát, sultán Hushang made a night attack on his army and committed much havoc. A'hmad Sháh, however, collecting what men he could, waited till dawn and then fell on and defeated the Málwá troops, who were busy plundering. After this sultán Hushang took shelter in the fort of Sárangpur, to which A'hmad Sháh laid siege; but after a time relinquishing the siege he retreated towards Gujarát, and was closely followed by sultán Hushang, who was eager to wipe out his former defeat. On his approach A'hmad Sháh, halting his troops, joined battle and repulsed sultán Hushang. He then returned to A'hmadábád in A.D. 1422.

War with Málwá, 1422.

In A.D. 1425 he led an army against Idar, defeating the force brought to meet him and driving their leader to the hills. Idar was always a troublesome neighbour to the A'hmadábád kings and one difficult to subdue, for when his country was threatened, the chief could retire to his hills, where he could not easily be followed. As a permanent check on his movements, A'hmad Sháh, in A.D. 1427, built the fort of Ahmadnagar,[4] on the banks of the Háthmati,

Defeats the Idar Chief, 1425.

---

[1] Mangni:—The Tabakát Akbari has Mánki; its position has not been determined.

[2] Dohad (N. Lat. 22° 50′, E. Long. 74° 15′), 77 miles N.E. of Baroda, now the chief town of the sub-division of that name in the British district of the Panch Máháls.

[3] Ujain (N. Lat. 23° 10′, E. Long. 75° 47′), at different times the capital of Málwá.

[4] Ahmadnagar (N. Lat. 23° 34′, E. Long. 73° 1′) in the Native State of Idar.

Chapter II. — A'hmad-a'ba'd Kings.

and in the following year the Idar chieftain, ráv Punjá, was killed during a foray on the frontier.

For the next two years A'hmad Sháh abstained from foreign conquests, devoting himself to the improvement of his dominions and to the working out of a system of paying his troops. The method he finally adopted was half-payment in money and half by grant of land, so as to attach the men to the country, and, while keeping them dependent on the state, free them from debt. After ráv Punjá's death A'hmad Sháh marched upon Idar, and only returned on ráv Punjá's son agreeing to pay an annual tribute of 300*l*. (Rs. 3,000).

A'hmad I. defeats the king of the Deccan at Máhim, 1429,

In A.D. 1429, on the death of Kutb Khán, governor of Máhim in the North Konkan,[1] sultán A'hmad Báhmani, (A.D. 1422-1435) seized the fort. On hearing this, A'hmad Sháh sent his youngest son Zufar Khán, with an army under Malik Iftikhár Khán, to retake it. Ships were collected from Diu, Gogo, and Cambay, and proceeding to Thání[2] attacked that city by sea and land, captured it, and regained possession of Máhim. In A.D. 1431 A'hmad Sháh advanced upon Chámpáner, and A'hmad Sháh Báhmani, anxious to retrieve his defeat at Máhim, marched an army into the Báglán[3] district and laid it waste. Hearing this A'hmad Sháh returned to Nandurbár, destroying Nándod as he passed. A'hmad Sháh Báhmani was now occupied in the siege of Tambol, a fort in Báglán. But the Gujarát king, marching for Tambol with all speed, defeated the besiegers and relieved the fort. In A.D. 1432, after contracting his son Fateh Khán in marriage with the daughter of the rái of Máhim,

and in Báglán, 1431.

---

[1] Máhim.—There are two towns of this name on the coast of the Northern Konkan—one about 22 miles north of Bassein (N. Lat. 19° 40′, E. Long. 72° 47′), and the other in the northern extremity of the island of Bombay (N. Lat. 19° 2′, E. Long. 72° 54′). The latter, Máhim, would seem to be the town referred to in the text. This part of the Konkan coast remained under the A'hmadábád kings till A. D. 1529-30, when it was conquered by the Portuguese.

[2] Thání (N. Lat. 19° 11′, E. Long. 73° 6′), the head-quarters of the British district of that name, about 24 miles north-by-east of Bombay, was from the 10th to the 16th century A.D. the chief city in Northern Konkan.

[3] Báglán, now called Satáná, the northern sub-division of the British district of Násik. The chief, a Ráthod, was converted to Islám by Aurangzeb (A.D. 1656-1707). In A.D. 1590 the chief commanded 8,000 cavalry and 5,000 infantry. The country was famous for fruit.—Ain Akbari (Gladwin) II. 73.

A'hmad Sháh marched towards Nágor, and exacted tribute and presents from the ráwál of Dungarpur.[1] From Nágor he went on to Mewár, enforcing his claims on Bundi and Kotá, two Hárá Rájput states in Central India. After this he returned to Gujarát, and during the next few years was warring principally in Málwá. He died in A.D. 1441.

Muhammad II. King, 1441-1451.

A'hmad Sháh was succeeded by his son Muhammad Sháh Gheiás-ud-dunya Wa-ud-din, also styled Zerbaksh or "Gold Bestower." In A.D. 1445 Muhammad marched against Bir rái of Idar, but on that chief agreeing to give him his daughter in marriage, he confirmed him in the possession of his state. He afterwards, in A.D. 1450, marched upon Chámpaner and took the lower fortress. The Chámpáner chief had, however, a strong ally in sultán Mahmud Khiljy, the ruler of Málwá, and on his approach Muhammad Sháh retired to Godhrá,[2] and Mahmud Khiljy continued his march upon Gujarát at the head of 80,000 horse. Muhammad Sháh was preparing to fly to Diu, when the nobles, who were disgusted at his cowardice, caused him to be poisoned, and in A.D. 1451 placed his son Jalál Khán on the throne with the title of Kutb-ud-din Sháh.

Is poisoned, 1451.

Kutb-ud-din, 1451-1459.

Sultán Mahmud of Málwá in the meantime advancing laid siege to Sultánpur,[3] a city defended on the part of Kutb-ud-din Sháh by Malik Alá-ud-din bin Sohráb. This commander was, however, prevailed on to surrender the fort, and was sent with much honour to Málwá and appointed governor of Mándu. Sultán Mahmud, now marching to Sársá-Pálri, summoned Broach, then commanded by Sidi Marján on behalf of Gujarát. The Sidi refused, and fearing to be delayed too long by Broach, the Málwá sultán proceeded by Nadiád to Baroda, which city he plundered. Kutb-ud-din Sháh now advancing met sultán Mahmud at Kapadwanj,[4] where, after a doubtful fight of some hours, he de-

War with Málwá, 1451.

Battle of Kapadwanj, 1454.

---

[1] Dungarpur (N. Lat. 23° 50', E. Long. 73° 50'), in Rájputáná, 150 miles N.W. of Mhow.

[2] Godhrá (N. Lat. 22° 45', E. Long. 73° 36'), the chief town of the sub-division of that name in the British district of the Panch Máháls.

[3] Sultánpur (N. Lat. 21° 43', E. Long. 74° 40'), in the north of the Shádá sub-division of the British district of Khándesh, till A.D. 1804 a place of consequence and the head-quarters of a large district.

[4] Kapadwanj (N. Lat. 23° 2', E. Long. 73° 9'), the chief town of the sub-division of that name in the British district of Kaira.

Chapter II.

A'hmad-a'ba'd Kings.

feated sultán Mahmud, though that prince was during the battle able to penetrate to Kutb-ud-din's camp and carry off his crown and jewelled girdle. This victory is ascribed by the Mirat-i-Sikandri in a great measure to the gallantry of certain inhabitants of Dholká[1] called Darwáziyehs. Muzafar Khán, who it is said incited the Málwá sultán to invade Gujarát, was captured and beheaded, and his head was affixed to the gate of Kapaḍwanj.

War with Nágor, 1455-1459.

In this same year sultán Mahmud Khiljy attempted to conquer Nágor. This city was then held by a certain Firoz Khán, to whose assistance Kutb-ud-din Sháh despatched an army under the command of Syad Atá-ullah. When the Gujarát force had nearly reached Sámbhar,[2] the Málwá sultán retired, and shortly after this Firoz Khán died. The ráná of Chitor[3] now began interfering in the Nágor succession on behalf of Shams Khán, who had been dispossessed by his brother Mujáhid Khán, and expelled the latter; as, however, Shams Khán refused to dismantle the fortifications of Nágor, the Chitor chief collected an army to capture Nágor, while Shams Khán repaired to Kutb-ud-din Sháh for aid and gave that sovereign his daughter in marriage. Kutb-ud-din upon this sent some of his nobles with an army to Nágor to repulse the ráná of Chitor. But in a battle near Nágor the Gujarát troops were defeated, and the ráná laying, waste the neighbourhood of that city, returned to Chitor. To revenge this raid, Kutb-ud-din Sháh, in A.D. 1455-56, marched against Chitor. On his way the Devrá rájá of Sirohi[4] attended Kutb-ud-din Sháh's camp, praying him to restore the fortress of Abu,[5] part of the ancestral domain of Sirohi which had been wrested from his house by the ráná of Chitor. Agreeing to help him, the king ordered one of his generals, Malik Shábán, to take possession of this fortress and restore it to the Devrá chieftain, while he himself continued to advance against Kumbhá-

Kutb-ud-din at war with Chitor, 1455-1459.

---

1 Dholká (N. Lat. 22° 42′, E. Long. 72° 25′), the chief town of the sub-division of that name in the British district of A'hmadábád.

2 Sámbhar (N. Lat. 26° 53′, E. Long. 75° 13′), a town in the province of A'jmir, about 51 miles N.N.E. from the city of A'jmir.

3 Chitor (N. Lat. 24° 52′, E. Long. 74° 4′), for several centuries before A.D. 1567 the capital of the principality of Udepur.

4 Sirohi (N. Lat. 24° 59′, E. Long. 72° 56′), the capital of the principality of the same name in the province of A'jmir.

5 Abu (N. Lat. 24° 45′, E. Long. 72° 49′), in the province of Sirohi.

mer. Malik Shábán was, however, entangled in the defiles near Abu, and defeated with great slaughter, and shortly after Kutb-ud-din Sháh, making a truce with Chitor, retired to his own country. On his return the Málwá sovereign proposed that they should unite against Chitor, conquer the ráná's territories, and divide them equally between them. Kutb-ud-din agreed, and in A.D. 1456-57 marched against the ráná by way of Abu, which fortress he captured and handed over to the Devrá rájá.[1] Next, advancing upon Kumbhámer, he plundered the country round, and then turned towards Chitor. On his way to Chitor he was met by the ráná, and a battle was fought, after which, though neither side had gained any marked advantage, the ráná fell back on his capital, and was there besieged by the Gujarát army. The siege was not however pressed, for, on the ráná agreeing to pay tribute and not to harass Nágor, Kutb-ud-din withdrew to Gujarát. The ráná in the meantime, by the cession of Mandisor[2] to Málwá, came to terms with the Khiljy sultán of Mándu. No sooner had Kutb-ud-din returned than he gave himself up to licentious excess, and ráná Kumbhá again attacked Nágor. Kutb-ud-din Sháh was with difficulty induced to muster his troops and sound a march. As soon as the ráná heard that the Gujarát army was actually in motion he retired, and the king returned to A'hmadábád. In A.D. 1458 he again led an army by way of Sirohi against Chitor, and laid waste the country, but soon after his return died in the month of May A.D. 1459.

Chapter II.

Ahmada'ba'd Kings.

Kutb-ud-din at war with Chitor, 1455-1459.

Dies, 1459.

Mahmud I. (Begara'), 1459-1511.

On the death of Kutb-ud-din Sháh, the nobles raised to the throne his uncle Dáud, son of A'hmad Sháh; but on his appointing low-born men to high offices and committing other foolish acts, he was deposed, and his half-brother, Fateh Khán, the son of Muhammad Sháh, son of A'hmad Sháh by Bibi Moghlái, a daughter of one of the jáms of Sindh, was, in A.D. 1459, at the age of only fourteen years, seated on the throne. Fateh Khán, who assumed the title of Mahmud Sháh, was by the death of his uncle, the late sultán Dáud, who had become a religious beggar, relieved of one source of danger. But not long after some of the nobles conspired against the minister Imád-ul-Mulk,

---

1 The rájá is called Kishan or Krishna Devra. Abu is still held by the Devrás.

2 Mandisor (N. Lat. 24° 4', E. Long. 75° 9'), the chief town of a large district of the same name in the province of Málwá.

Chapter II.

Ahmadába'd Kings.

Defeats a conspiracy of the nobles, 1459.

and on their plot being discovered marched against the palace. By the intrepidity of the young king, their designs were, however, entirely defeated. From his religious ardour, his love of justice, his bravery and his wise measures, Mahmud is, by the local historians, considered the best of the Gujarát kings. Amongst the measures which the Mirat-i-Sikandri specially notices is his sanction to grants of land being continued to the son of the holder, and in cases where there was no male issue to half the grant being continued to the daughter. His rule, too, about soldiers being forbidden to borrow money at interest is favourably noticed. He would seem to have appointed a special officer to make advances to such soldiers as could prove that they were really in need, the advances being recovered from their pay in such instalments as might be agreed upon.[1] He also devoted much attention to the culture of fruit-trees.[2] In A.D. 1461, or A.D. 1462 according to Ferishta, Nizám Sháh Báhmani A.D. 1461-1463, king of the Deccan, whose country had been invaded by sultán Mahmud Khiljy of Málwá, applied for help to the Gujarát king. Mahmud Sháh at once started to his aid, and on his way receiving another equally pressing letter from the Deccan sovereign, he

Mahmud improves the state of the soldiery, 1459-1461.

Helps the king of the Deccan, 1461.

---

1 The Gujarát cavalry of this time are thus described by the Portuguese traveller Barbosa (A.D. 1511-1514.) :—The Moors and Gentiles of this kingdom are bold riders, mounted on horses bred in the country, for it has a wonderful quantity. They ride on small saddles and use whips. Their arms are very thick round shields, edged with silk; each man has two swords, a dagger, and a Turkish bow with very good arrows. (Gujarát canes made famous arrows.—Bird, 104.) Some of them carry maces, and many of them coats-of-mail, and others tunics quilted with cotton. The horses have housings and steel head-pieces, and so they fight very well and are light in their movements. The Moorish horsemen are white and of many countries, Turks and Mamelukes ('renegade Christians,' military slaves imported from Georgia, Circassia, and Mingrelia.—Badger's Varthema 13), Arabs, Persians, Khorasanays, Turkomans, and from the great kingdom of Delhi, and others born in the country itself. Their pay is good, and they receive it regularly. They are well dressed with very rich stuffs of gold, silk, cotton, and goats' wool, and all wear caps on their heads and their clothes long, such as morisco shirts and drawers, and leggings to the knee of good thick leather, worked with gold knots and embroidery, and their swords, richly ornamented with gold and silver, are borne in their girdles, or in the hands of their pages. Their women are very white and pretty; also very richly decked out. They live well and spend much money. (Stanley's Barbosa, 55-56).

2 The chief varieties of trees which Mahmud is said to have planted are the mango, *ámbo*, Mangifera indica ; the *raen*, Mimusops hexandra ; the *jámbu*, Eugenia jambolana ; the *gular*, Ficus glomerata ; the tamarind, *ámli*, Tamarindus indica, and the shrubby Phyllanthus, *aonla*, Emblica officinalis.

Chapter II.

Ahmad-a'ba'd Kings.

pushed on with all speed by way of Burhánpur.[1] When sultán Mahmud Khiljy heard of his approach, he retired to his own country by way of Gondwáná,[2] on which occasion, from thirst and from the treacherous attacks of the Gonds, he is said to have lost from 5,000 to 6,000 men. The king of Gujarát, after receiving the thanks of the Deccan sovereign, returned to his own dominions. Afterwards, in A.D. 1462, sultán Mahmud Khiljy made another incursion into the Deccan, with the view of plundering Daulatábád. But again the Deccan sovereign applied for help to Mahmud Sháh, and on hearing of his advance the Málwá sultán a second time retired to his own dominions. Mahmud Sháh now wrote to the Málwá sultán to desist from harassing the Deccan, threatening, in case of refusal, to march at once upon Mándu.

Expedition against Junágarh, 1467.

Mahmud Sháh next turned his thoughts to the conquest of the celebrated citadel of Girnár,[3] and in A.D. 1467 made an attack on the fort of Junágarh, and receiving the submission of ráv Mandlik, the ruler of that district, returned to his capital. In the following year, it appeared that the Junágarh chief continued to visit his idol temple in state with a golden umbrella and other ensigns of royalty. Upon this an army was despatched to Junágarh, and the chief sent the obnoxious umbrella to the king, accompanied by fitting presents. Afterwards, in A.D. 1469, Mahmud again sent an army to ravage Sorath, and at length determined to attack and finally conquer both Junágarh and Girnár. While on his march, the ráv Mandlik suddenly joined him, and asking why he was so bent on his destruction when he had committed no fault, agreed to do whatsoever Mahmud might command. The king replied that there was no fault like infidelity, and ordered the ráv to embrace Islám. The chief, now thoroughly alarmed, fled by night and entered his fortress; but after a long siege he, in A.D. 1472-73, quitted the fort and handed over the keys to the king, repeating after him the Muhammadan profession of faith, on which condition his life was spared. From this date Sorath became a crown possession, and was

Capture of the Fortress, 1472.

---

1 Burhánpur (N. Lat. 21° 18′, E. Long. 76° 20′), under the Musalmáns the capital of Khándesh, now within the limits of the Berárs.

2 Gondwáná, a large hilly tract lying between N. Lat. 19° 50′ and 24° 30′, and E. Long. 77° 38′ and 87° 20′.

3 Girnár, a well-known mountain in Káthiáwár (see above p. 27).

Chapter II.

Ahmadabad Kings.

governed by officers appointed by the kings and stationed at Junágarh. At the close of the war Mahmud Sháh, charmed with the beauty of the place, sent for syads and learned men, and caused them to settle at Junágarh and other towns in Sorath. He induced the nobles also to build houses there, and himself raised a palace and made the new city his capital under the name of Mustafábád. He also repaired the fort Jahánpanah, and enforced his claim as suzerain upon all the neighbouring chiefs. These chieftains, including even the Junágarh ráv himself, had, it is true, paid tribute in the time of A'hmad Sháh; but on this occasion the rule of the A'hmadábád king was more firmly established, and the duty of collecting the tribute entrusted to an officer permanently settled in the country. The author of the Mirat-i-Sikandri specially dilates on the dense wood round Junágarh, in which were to be found mango, *khirni*, *jámbu*, *gular*, *ámli*, and *áonla*[1] trees, and says that this forest tract was inhabited by a wild race of men called Khánts.[2]

Disturbances in Chámpáner 1472.

During Mahmud Sháh's prolonged absence from his capital, Malik Jamál-ud-din was appointed governor of Ahmadábád, with the title of Muháfiz Khán. At this time Jesingh, son of Gangádás the chief of Chámpáner, appears to have meditated rebellion and to have been harassing the adjacent country. The king, therefore, appointed Bháo-ul-Mulk, who had the title of Imád-ul-Mulk, to the command of Songarh; Malik Sárang Kiwám-ul-Mulk to the command of Godhrá; and Táj Khán bin Sálár to the command of Norkha and Dakhna; and in consequence of these precautions, Jesingh abstained from rebellion. At this time the ráv Mandlik received the title of Khán Jahán, and lands were bestowed on him, while the golden idols which had been taken from the Junágarh temples were broken up and distributed among the soldiers.

Conquest of Cutch.

The next of Mahmud Sháh's expeditions was against the rulers of Cutch, who are said to have been Rájputs of the Sumrá and Sodhá tribes.[3] The Sumrás and Sodhás appear to have readily submitted to the king, and to have voluntarily

---

1 Mangifera indica, Mimusops hexandra, Eugenia jambolana, Ficus glomerata, Tamarindus indica, Emblica officinalis.

2 This tribe is still to be found in the province of Káthiáwár.

3 The Tabakát Akbari says they were Jats.

Chapter II.

Ahmad-a'ba'd Kings.

sent men of their tribe to Junágarh to be instructed in the faith of Islám. Shortly afterwards, however, they again became troublesome, and the king advancing into Cutch completely defeated them. About this time a religious man, Mullá Mahmud Samarkandi, complained to the king that he had been robbed by the pirates of Jagat (Dwárká).[1] On hearing of this outrage Mahmud Sháh marched to Jagat, took the fort and destroyed the idol temples. The pirates, in the first instance, retired to the island of Shankhodwára (Bet), but from this, too, they were driven with great slaughter. The king, after building a mosque at Jagat, entrusted the government of the place to Farhat-ul-Mulk, and himself returned to Junágarh. This was the first time that Dwárká had ever been conquered. The rájá of Dwárká, by name Bhim, was sent to Muháfiz Khán, the governor of A'hmadábád, with orders that he was to be hewn in pieces and a piece affixed to every gate of the city. After settling the affairs of Sorath, the king turned his face towards A'hmadábád, but on the way hearing that the people of the Malabár coast were, with a number of ships, annoying the vessels which visited the Gujarát ports, he marched to Gogo, and there equipped a fleet to oppose the pirates. This done he went to Cambay, and from there returned to A'hmadábád.

The pirate chief of Jagat defeated.

Expedition against Malabár pirates.

Afterwards, in A.D. 1480, when Mahmud Sháh was at Junágarh, his eldest son A'hmad was, by Khudáwand Khán and some of the soldiers, who were discontented with the king's habit of constant warfare, incited to assume the royal power. But Imád-ul-Mulk, by refusing to join, upset their plans, and on the king's return the conspiracy was stamped out. In the previous year (A.D. 1479) Mahmud Sháh sent an army to ravage the Chámpáner country, which he was now desirous of conquering; and about this time he founded the city of Mehmudábád on the banks of the Wátrak, about eighteen miles from A'hmadábád. In A.D. 1482 there was a partial famine in Gujarát, and the Chámpáner country being exempt from scarcity the commandant of Morámli or Rasulábád, a post on the Chámpáner frontier, made several forays into the dominions of that chief. He in return attacked the commandant and defeated him, killing most of his men and capturing two elephants and several horses.

Unsuccessful conspiracy against the king, 1480.

War against Chámpáner, 1482-1484.

---

[1] Dwárká (N. Lat. 22° 15, E. Long. 69'), on the north-western shore of Káthiáwár, famous for its temple of Krishná.

Chapter II.

Ahmadábád Kings.

On hearing this, Mahmud Sháh determined to finally conquer the Chámpáner country, and accordingly set out for Baroda with a powerful army. On reaching Baroda the ráwál of Chámpáner, becoming alarmed, sent ambassadors and sued for forgiveness; but the king rejected his overtures, saying "except the sword and the dagger no other message shall pass between me and you." The ráwál then made preparations for a determined resistance, and sent messengers to summon Gheiás-ud-din Khiljy of Málwá to his aid. Mahmud Sháh hearing of this, entrusted the conduct of the siege to his nobles and marched to Dohad, on which Sultán Gheiás-ud-din returned to Mándu. The ráwál, after a prolonged defence, burnt the women and all articles of value in the fort on a large pile, and rushing forth at the head of his troops made a fierce but unavailing charge.

Capture of Chámpáner, 1484.

The garrison were put to the sword and Chámpáner taken, but the ráwál and his minister Dungarshi fell wounded into the conqueror's hands, and, on refusing to embrace Islám, were by him put to death. The ráwál's son, who was entrusted to Saif-ul-Mulk and instructed by him in the Muhammadan religion, afterwards in the reign of Muzafar Sháh (A.D. 1513-1526) was ennobled by the title of Nizám-ul-Mulk. On the capture of this fortress in A.D. 1484, Mahmud Sháh built a wall round the town of Chámpáner and made it his capital under the name of Muhammadábád.

Case of compensation, 1484.

In this reign an instance is mentioned, of the form of the compensation for robbery known as *waltar*. The case was one of some merchants bringing horses and other goods for sale from Irák and Khurásán, who were plundered in Sirohi limits. The king caused them to give in writing the price of their horses and stuffs, and paying them from his own treasury recovered the amount from the rájá of Sirohi. Shortly after this, Mahmud went against Bahádur Khán Giláni, a vassal of the Bahmani king of the Deccan, who from Dábhol[1] had been harassing the Gujarát harbours. The Báhmani sultán, fearing the consequences to himself, marched against Bahádur Khán, and, capturing him alive,

1 Dábhol (N. Lat. 17° 34', E. Long. 73° 16'), on the north bank of the river Wáshishti (called Halewacko and Kalewacko by the early navigators) in the British district of Ratnágiri. About this time, according to Athanasius Nikitin (A.D. 1468-1474), Dábhol was the great meeting place for all nations living along the coast of India and Ethiopia. In A.D. 1501 it was taken by the Portuguese. Between A.D. 1626-1630 an English factory was established here, but by the end of the 17th century trade had left Dábhol and has never again returned.

Mahmud determines the Khándesh succession, 1508.

struck off his head and sent it to the Gujarát monarch, who returned to his own country. Shortly afterwards, in A.D. 1508, Mahmud interfered in the Khándesh succession, and succeeded in placing his nephew, Mirán Muhammad Adil Khán Fárukhi, on the throne of A'sir-Burhánpur. In A.D. 1506, when marching to Bassein to settle disturbances raised by the Portuguese, at that time becoming powerful along the western coast of India, he heard of the victory of Chaul[1] gained over the Portuguese by the Gujarát squadron under Malik Eiáz (Sultáni) in concert with the Turkish fleet. After rewarding Malik Eiáz he returned to his capital. His last regal progress was to Pátan in A.D. 1504, and in A.D. 1513 he died and was succeeded by his son Khalil Khán, whom he had appointed his heir.[2]

---

1 Chaul, now Rewádandá (N. Lat. 18° 33', E. Long. 72° 59), from about A.D. 1500 to 1650, first under the Ahmadnagar dynasty, and then under the Portuguese, a place of much trade.

2 Mahmud Begará seems greatly to have impressed travellers who visited Gujarát during his reign, and from the strangeness of the tales told of him this king became well known in Europe. Varthema (1503-1508) thus describes his manner of living :—"The king has constantly 20,000 horsemen. In the morning when he rises there come to his palace 50 elephants, on each of which a man sits astride, and the said elephants do reverence to the king, and, except this, they have nothing else to do. When the king eats, 50 or 60 kinds of instruments, drums, trumpets, flageolets, and fifes play, and the elephants again do him reverence. As for the king himself, his mustachios under his nose are so long that he ties them over his head as a woman would tie her tresses, and he has a white beard that reaches to his girdle. As to his food, every day he eats poison (Hudibras' Prince whose 'daily food was asp, and basilisk and toad '), not that he fills his stomach with it; but he eats a certain quantity, so that when he wishes to destroy any great person he makes him come before him stripped and naked, and then eats certain fruits which are called *chofole* (jeiphal, nutmeg), like a muscatel nut. He also eats certain leaves called *tamboli* (*pan* or betelnut) like the leaves of a sour orange, and with these he eats lime of oyster shells. When he has chewed this well he spurts it out on the person he wishes to kill, and so in the space of half an hour he falls to the ground dead. The sultán has also three or four thousand women, and every night that he sleeps with one she is found dead in the morning." Barbosa goes further than this (Stanley's trans. 57), saying that so soaked was the king with poison, that if a fly settled on his hand it swelled and immediately fell dead. This was the result of his early training. For, on Varthema's companion asking how it was that the king could eat poison in this manner, certain merchants, who were older than the sultán, answered that his father had fed him upon poison from his childhood. (Badger's Varthema, 110.) Of the origin of Mahmud's surname of Begará two explanations are given : (1) "from his mustachios being large and twisted like a cow's horn, and such a cow being called Bigarrah ; (2) that the word comes from the Gujaráti, *be*, two, and *gad*, a fort, the people giving him this title in honour of the capture of Junágarh (A.D. 1472) and Chámpáner (A.D. 1484)."—(Bird's History of Gujarát, 202).

Chapter II.

A'hmad-a'ba'd Kings.

Muzafar II. 1513-1526.

Expedition against Idar, 1514.

Khalil Khán was the son of ráni Hirábái, the daughter of a Rájput chieftain named ráná Nákah, who resided on the bank of the Mahi. On ascending the throne, this prince adopted the title of Muzafar Sháh. In A.D. 1514 ráv Bhim, the son of ráv Bhán of Idar, defeated Ain-ul-Mulk, governor of Pátan, who was coming to Ahmadábád to pay his respects to the king. This officer had turned aside to punish the ráv for some disturbance he had created, but failing in his purpose, was himself defeated. On the approach of Muzafar Sháh, Idar was abandoned by the ráv, and he only made his peace with difficulty and by agreeing to pay a heavy tribute. The king in the meantime marched to Godhrá, and so on to Málwá by way of Dohad, which fort he caused to be repaired, and soon after went on to Dhár. After a short stay in Málwá, Muzafar returned to Muhammadábád (Chámpáner). At this time Ráimal, nephew of ráv Bhim of Idar (deceased), expelling the ráv's son Bhármal by the aid of ráná Sángá of Chitor, succeeded to the chieftainship of Idar. The king was displeased at the interference of the ráná, and directed the governor of Ahmadnagar to expel Ráimal and reinstate Bhármal. In A.D. 1517, the nobles of Málwá besought Muzafar's interference, alleging that the Hindu minister, Medani Rái, was very oppressive, and that he would probably depose the Málwá sultán, Mahmud Khiljy, and usurp the throne. Muzafar Sháh promised to come to their help, and shortly after sultán Mahmud Khiljy, escaping from the surveillance of Medani Rái to Gujarát, himself sought the aid of the Gujarát monarch. Muzafar Sháh then marched by Godhrá into Málwá, and on his arrival at Dhár, that town was evacuated by Medani Rái. The Gujarát king next besieged Mándu. The garrison summoned the Chitor ráná to their aid, and he marched as far as Sárangpur. Muzafar Sháh, however, detaching a force against the ráná, caused him to retire while his soldiers exerted themselves so strenuously that they captured Mándu. This was in A.D. 1518. After this conquest Málwá was virtually in Muzafar's power, but he honourably restored the kingdom to sultán Mahmud Khiljy, and, withdrawing to Gujarát, proceeded to Muhammadábád. In A.D. 1519 news was received of the defeat and capture of sultán Mahmud Khiljy by the ráná of Chitor. Muzafar Sháh sent a force to protect Mándu. But the ráná, who distinguished himself by the honourable treatment of his prisoner the sultán of Málwá, had a continued run of good fortune. He attacked and

Disturbances in Málwá, 1517.

They march against the rebels, and capture of Mándu, 1518.

War with the ráná of Chitor, 1519.

Chapter II.

Ahmadaba'd Kings.

plundered Ahmadnagar, defeating the Gujarát forces, and then marched on Wadnagar which he spared, but plundering Visálnagar, returned to Chitor. Malik Eiáz Sultáni, the governor of Sorath, was in A.D. 1521 sent with a large force to revenge this inroad. But owing to dissensions between Malik Eiáz and the Gujarát nobles, this expedition did not effect much, and Muzafar Sháh, greatly displeased with the result, determined himself to march against Chitor. He was, however, dissuaded by a submissive embassy from that chief, who sent his son to A'hmadábád with valuable presents for the king. Muzafar Sháh shortly afterwards, on the death of Malik Eiáz, confirmed his elder son Malik Ishák in his father's rank and possessions, and he now remained in his own territory strengthening his frontier posts, especially the fort of Morásá. In about A.D. 1524 prince Bahádur Khán, dissatisfied with the smallness of his estates, left Gujarát and withdrew to Hindustán. King Muzafar, after formally appointing his son Sikandar Khán his heir, died at A'hmadábád in A.D. 1526. During this reign cultivation increased so much in Jháláwár that it became necessary to forcibly keep certain pieces of land waste for pasturing cattle.

The ráná of Chitor submits, 1521.

Death of Muzafar, 1526.

Sikandar Sháh reigned but a few months when he was murdered by Imád-ul-Mulk Khush Kadam, who seated a younger brother of Sikandar's, named Násir Khán, on the throne with the title of Mahmud II., and governed on his behalf. The nobles, however, deserted his cause, and prince Bahádur Khán, returning to Gujarát from Hindustán, was joined by a large following, prominent among whom was Táj Khán, proprietor of Dhandhuká; and marching at once on Chámpáner, he captured and executed Imád-ul-Mulk, and poisoning Násir Khán, ascended the throne in A.D. 1526 by the title of Bahádur Sháh. His brother Latif Khán, aided by rájá Bhim of Pál,[1] now asserted his claim to the throne. He was, however, defeated, and fell wounded into the hands of the Gujarát army and died of his wounds. Rájá Bhim was slain. Ráisingh, who succeeded Bhim, plundered Dohad; a large force was therefore sent against him, commanded by Táj Khán, who laid waste Raisingh's country and dismantled his forts. In the end of A.D. 1526, Bahádur Sháh visited Cambay, and ascertained that Malik Ishák, the son of Malik Eiáz, had been intriguing with the Portuguese

Sikandar, King, 1526.

Mahmud II. 1526.

Bahadur, 1526-1536.

Portuguese intrigues, 1526.

1 Pál is probably Rájpiplá, see below note 1, p. 54.

Chapter II.

A'hmad-a'ba'd Kings.

to surrender Diu. Expelling him, he entrusted Diu to Kiwám-ul-Mulk, and Junágarh to Mujáhid Khán Bhikam, and returned to A'hmadábád. During one of his numerous expeditions he went to Nándod for hunting and received the homage of the rájá. As the Portuguese were endeavouring to establish themselves on the coast of Sorath, and, if possible, to obtain Diu, the king was constantly at Cambay, Diu, and Gogo to frustrate their attempts, and he now directed the construction of the fortress of Broach. At this time Muhammad Khán bin Adil Khán, ruler of A'sir and Burhánpur, requested his aid on behalf of Imád-ul-Mulk, ruler of Berár. Bahádur Sháh marched at once to their aid, and was joined at the Narbadá River by Muhammad Khán A'siri, and

Khándesh affairs, 1528.

thence proceeded to Burhánpur, where Imád Sháh joined him from Gávalgarh. After some successes he made peace between Burhán Nizam Sháh and Imád Sháh Gávali, and returned to Gujarát. In A.D. 1529, however, at the request of Jáfar Khán, son of Imád Sháh Gávali, he again marched to the Deccan and occupied Ahmadnagar. A battle was subsequently fought near Burhánpur, in which it seems probable that Bahádur Sháh was worsted, though the Gujarát historian says that "the scales of battle were equal." Anyhow Bahádur Sháh withdrew to Gujarát and did not for some time interfere in the affairs of the Deccan.

Settlement of Turks at Diu, 1526-1530.

About this time (A.D. 1526-1530) some Turks under one Mustafa came to Gujarát, part of a Turkish fleet expected to act against the Portuguese. They were assigned Diu as a place of residence, and the command of the island was granted to Malik Toghán, son of Malik Eiáz, the former governor. In this year the king marched to Wágar, and Prathiráj, rájá of Dungarpur, obtained an audience as did the ambassadors of ráná Ratansi of Chitor. Misunderstandings here arising

War with Málwá; capture of Mándu, 1530.

between him and the sultán of Málwá, Bahádur Sháh marched upon Mándu, and taking the fortress captured sultán Mahmud Khiljy and his seven sons. In this year, hearing that Mánsingji, rájá of Halwad[1], had killed the commandant of Dasádá, Bahádur despatched Khán Khánán against him. On this occasion the districts of Viramgám and Mándal were reft from the Jhálá chieftains, and ever after formed a part of the crown dominions. The king spent the rainy season at Mándu, and in A.D. 1531 again marched to

1 Halwad is a former capital of the chief of Dhrángadhrá in Káthiáwár.

the Deccan. When sultán Mahmud Khiljy and his sons were being conveyed to the fortress of Chámpáner for confinement there, Ráisingh, rájá of Pál, endeavoured to rescue them on the way. But failing in his attempt, the prisoners were put to death by their guards. Bahádur Sháh now proceeded to Asir-Burhánpur, and bestowed on Nizám-ul-Mulk the title of Sháh, and invested him with the regal umbrella: and from this date the occupants of the Ahmadnagar (Deccan) throne were called Nizám Sháhi. At this time he also bestowed on Muhammad Khán A'siri the title of Muhammad Sháh. In A.D. 1531, hearing that the Rájput chief of Ráisin in Málwá kept Muhammadan women, he marched against him and forced him to surrender and embrace Islám. The chief, however, having secretly sent to the rání of Chitor for aid, delayed handing over the fort. On hearing of this, the king despatched a force to keep the rání in check and pressed the siege. The Rájput chief was then sent, at his own request, to endeavour to pursuade the garrison to surrender, but their reproaches so much affected him, that, joining with them, and after burning their females, he and they sallied sword in hand and were all slain. Ráisin then fell into Bahádur's hands, and this district together with those of Bhilsá and Chanderi were entrusted to the government of sultán A'lam Lodhi. The king now went to Gondwáná to hunt elephants, and, after capturing many, employed his army in reducing several minor fortresses, such as Gágrawn and others. He next, in A.D. 1532, advanced against Chitor and devoted his attention to the capture of that fort. Subsequently, however, on the receipt of an enormous ransom, the siege was raised. His troops shortly afterwards took the strong fortress of Ranthambar.

Chapter II.

A'hmad-a'ba'd Kings

A'hmadnagar affairs, 1531.

Siege of Chitor, 1532.

About this time disagreement sprung up between Bahádur Sháh and Humaiyun, emperor of Delhi. The original ground of quarrel was the shelter afforded by Bahádur Sháh to sultán Muhammad Zamán Mirza, and Humaiyun's anger was further increased by an insolent answer received from the Gujaráti king. Bahádur Sháh, however, without considering that he had provoked a powerful enemy, again laid siege to Chitor; and though he heard that Humaiyun had arrived at Gwálior, would not desist from the siege. In March 1535 Chitor fell into the hands of the Gujarát king, but his army was shortly afterwards

Disagreement with the emperor of Delhi, 1532.

Fall of Chitor, 1535.

Chapter II.

A'hmada'ba'd Kings.

First conquest of Gujarát by the Moghals, 1535.

routed by that of Humaiyun. The Gujarát historians endeavour to throw the blame of Bahádur Sháh's defeat on Rumi Khán a foreigner, and a Turk, who was the head of the artillery, and who, they say, was a traitor; but there seems every reason to consider this an excuse, and that the Gujarát army was in both valour, discipline, and tactics, inferior to the Moghals who defeated them. Bahádur Sháh, unaccustomed to defeat, lost heart and fled to Mándu, which fortress was speedily taken by Humaiyun. From this the king fled to Chámpáner, and finally took refuge in Diu. Chámpáner fell shortly to Humaiyun's efforts, and the whole of Gujarát, except Sorath, came under his rule. At this time Sher Sháh Sur revolted in Bihár and Junpur, and Humaiyun accordingly returned to A'gra to oppose him, leaving his brother Hindal Mirza in A'hmadábád, Kásam Beg in Broach, and Yádgár Násir Mirza in Pátan. As soon, however, as Humaiyun had departed, the country rose against the Moghals, and his old nobles requested the king to join them; he did so, and, defeating the Moghals near Mahmudábád, expelled them from Gujarát. During his residence at Diu, Bahádur Sháh had been compelled to court the Portuguese, who were masters of the seas, and had conceded them permission to erect a factory there, which they converted into a fort. Bahádur, now that he had recovered his kingdom, repented of what he had done, and, resolving to expel the Portuguese by stratagem, repaired to Diu and endeavoured to get the viceroy into his power. That officer, however, excused himself, but in return invited the king to visit his ship. Bahádur agreed, and returning in a barge was attacked and slain. The author of the Mirát-i-Sikandri states that the reason of Bahádur's assassination was that a paper from him to the kings of the Deccan, inviting them to join him in an alliance against the Portuguese, had fallen into the hands of the Portuguese viceroy.[1] During the thirty-seven years from the death of king Bahádur to the second and final conquest of Gujarát by the Moghals, the representatives of the A'hmadábád dynasty, being for the most part minors, were rulers only in name. This period is throughout a struggle for power among the

Bahádur recovers Gujarát, 1536.

Difficulties with the Portuguese at Diu, 1536.

Death of king Bahádur, 1536.

[1] The Musalmán and Portuguese accounts of the death of king Bahádur differ in some particulars. But the result would seem to show that while both sides had treacherous designs, neither party was able to carry out his original plan, and the end was unpremeditated, hurried on by mutual suspicions.—See Elphinstone's History of India, 767.

chief nobles, during which Gujarát not only lost its position of supremacy among the neighbouring kingdoms, but at home was a scene of general discontent and disorder.

Muhammad II., (A'siri) 1536.

On the death of king Bahádur in A. D. 1536, the nobles of Gujarát invited his nephew Muhammad Sháh A'siri to succeed him. Muhammad Sháh died shortly after his accession, and the nobles then conferred the crown on Muhammad Khán, son of Latif Khán, brother of Bahádur Sháh, and he ascended the throne in A.D. 1536, when only eleven years of age. The government of the country was now carried on by Daryá Khán and Imád-ul-Mulk, and the king was kept by them under a strict surveillance. Daryá Khán now resolved to overthrow Imád-ul-Mulk and acquired supreme power. He accordingly obtained an order from the king (whom on the pretence of hunting he withdrew from A'hmadábád) directing Imád-ul-Mulk to retire to his estates, and shortly after he expelled him from Gujarát. Daryá Khán now became absorbed in pleasure and luxury, and resigned the actual management of the kingdom to A'lam Khán Lodhi. The king, dissembling his dissatisfaction at the way he was treated, pretended to take no interest in affairs of state. A'lam Khán Lodhi, seeing the carelessness of Daryá Khán, began to entertain ambitious designs, and retired to his estate of Dhandhuká, whence he requested the king to join him. Muhammad Sháh, believing him to be in earnest, contrived to escape from surveillance and joined A'lam Khán. Daryá Khán, on discovering the king's flight, elevated to the throne a descendant of A'hmad Sháh by the title of Muzafar Sháh, and striking coin in his name set out with an army towards Dhandhuká. A'lam Khán and the king met him in the district of Dholká, and a battle was fought in which Muhammad Sháh and A'lam Khán were defeated. The king fled to Ránpur, and thence to Páliád, while A'lam Khán fled to Sádráh. Daryá Khán in the meantime occupied Dhandhuká; his men, however, dissatisfied at being placed in opposition to the king, rapidly deserted, some joining A'lam Khán and some Muhammad Sháh. Soon after the king joined A'lam Khán and marched on A'hmadábád, whither Daryá Khán had preceded them. The citizens closed the gates against Daryá Khán, and he only effected his entrance with difficulty, and, hearing of the king's approach, fled to Mubárak Sháh at Burhánpur, leaving his family and treasure in the fortress of Chámpáner.

Muhammad III., 1536-1554.

The king a minor, 1536.

Escapes from control and defeats Daryá Khán.

Chapter II.

A'hmad-a'ba'd Kings.

The king entered A'hmadábád, and soon after captured Chámpáner. A'lam Khán now obtained the recall of Imád-ul-Mulk, who received a grant of Broach and the port of Surat. Shortly afterwards Muhammad Sháh began to show great favour to men of low degree, especially to one Charji, a bird-catcher, whom he ennobled by the title of Muháfiz Khán. This man counselled him to put to death sultán Ala-ud-din Lodhi and Shujáat Khán, two of the principal nobles; and the king, without consulting his ministers, caused these men to be executed. The nobles now joining together besieged Muhammad Sháh in his palace, and demanded that Muháfiz Khán should be surrendered to them, but the king refused to give him up. Next the nobles demanded an audience, and this the king granted, Muháfiz Khán, though warned of his danger, being foolishly present. On entering the royal presence A'lam Khán signalled to his followers to slay Muháfiz, and he was killed in spite of the king's remonstrances. Muhammad Sháh then attempted to kill himself, but was prevented and placed under guard, and the chief nobles took it in turn to watch him; but after a little time strife arose between A'lam Khán and Mujáhid Khán and his brother, and the two latter nobles contrived the king's escape and sacked the houses of A'lam Khán and his followers. A'lam Khán himself escaped with difficulty. He then joined Daryá Khán, but after some fighting they were driven from Gujarát and forced to take shelter with the sovereign of Delhi. The king now appointed Afzal Khán, the minister of the late Bahádur Sháh, as his own minister, and though Afzal Khán lived in retirement, his counsel was taken on measures of importance. Other great nobles were Syad Mubárak, Fateh Khán Baloch, and Abdul Karim Khán, who received the title of Itimád Khán, and who enjoyed the king's entire confidence, so much so that he was admitted to the harem. The king now consulted A'saf Khán as to the propriety of conquering Málwá. A'saf Khán, however advised him rather to resume the lands granted to the Rájput chiefs and proprietors. Muhammad Sháh followed this advice, and consequently the chief men of Idar, Sirohi, Dungarpur, Bánswará, Lunáwárá, Rájpiplá, Dohad, and the banks of the Mahi, while defending their own possessions, commenced to disturb the country. The king, therefore, strengthened his line of outposts, establishing one at Sirohi, another at Idar, besides fresh posts in other places, and at the same time commenced persecuting the Hindus. In this reign the fort of Surat was built by Khudáwand

Quarrels among the nobles.

Disturbances among the Rájput chiefs, 1545.

Chapter II.

Ahmad-a'ba'd Kings.

Death of the King, 1554.

Khán, in spite of the intrigues and opposition of the Portuguese. In A.D. 1554 one Burhán, a servant of the king's, conceived the idea of killing him and reigning in his stead. He accordingly gave his master an intoxicating drug, and then while sleeping stabbed him to the heart, and in the king's name, summoning the principal nobles, put them also to death, and endeavoured himself to mount the throne. But no one joined him, and even his accomplices deserted him. He was attacked by Imád-ul-Mulk Rumi,[1] Alagh Khán, and others, and when marching against them was cut down by Shirwán Khán.

A'hmad II., King, 1554-1561.

Itimád Khán regent.

After the death of Burhán, the nobles took counsel together and elected as sovereign a descendant of the stock of A'hmad Sháh of the name of A'hmad Khán, and proclaimed him king by the title of A'hmad Sháh II. At the same time they agreed that, as the king was young, Itimád Khán should carry on the government, and they further divided the country among themselves, each one agreeing to protect the frontiers and preserve the public peace. Mubárak Sháh of Khándesh, considering this a good opportunity, preferred a claim to the crown and marched to the frontier. An army was sent against him, and by negotiation Mubárak Sháh was induced to withdraw his claim. Násir-ul-Mulk now aspired to supreme power, and gaining over several nobles to his side attacked the forces of Itimád Khán and Syad Mubárak, who suffered a defeat, after which the syad withdrew to his estate of Kapaḍwanj. Here he was joined by Itimád Khán, while Násir-ul-Mulk, taking Sultán A'hmad with him to A'hmadábád, assumed the entire government of the country. After a short time he assembled an army and marched against Syad Mubárak and Itimád Khán, with a view to expelling them from Gujarát. But Alagh Khán and Imád-ul-Mulk, disgusted with the assumption of Násir-ul-Mulk, deserted him and joined Syad Mubárak and Itimád Khán. Násir-ul-Mulk was forced to fly, and after a short time died in the

---

1 This Imád-ul-Mulk is a different man from the Imád-ul-Mulk mentioned above (p. 51) as receiving a grant of Broach and Surat. The latter had before this retired to Surat, and was killed there in A.D. 1545.—(Bird, 266.) Imád-ul-Mulk II., who attacked Burhán, was originally called Malik Arslán (Bird, 272.) He is also called the leader of the Turks, and Rumi. This Imád-ul-Mulk Rumi, who was the father of Changez Khán, was ultimately killed in A.D. 1560 at Surat by his own son-in-law, Khudawand or Iktyár Khan.

Chapter II.

A'hmad-a'ba'd Kings.

mountains of Pál.[1] Ikhtiyár-ul-Mulk, Fateh Khán Baloch, and Hasan Khán Dakhani now set up another king named Sháhu, and a battle was fought in which Sháhu and his supporters were defeated and Hasan Khán Dakhani slain. Previous to the battle Fateh Khán Baloch had been induced to forsake Sháhu, and Ikhtiyár-ul-Mulk, taking Sháhu with him, fled. The nobles now divided Gujarát between them as follows:—

Partition of the Province.

For A'hmad Sháh's private expenses.	A'hmadábád and the Daskrohi sub-division.
Itimád Khán and his party ...	Kadi, Jháláwár, Pitlád, Nadiád, Bhil, Rádhanpur, Sami, Munjpur, and Godhrá, and the country of Sorath.
Syad Mubárak and his party ...	Pátan, Cambay, with the Chorási, Dholká, Gogo, Dhandhuká. Chámpáner, Sarnál, Bálásinor, and Kapadwanj.
Imád-ul-Mulk Rumi and his party.	Broach, Baroda, Surat as far as the Sultánpur-Nandurbár frontier.
Gujarát nobles under Itimád Khán.	Morásá and similar districts.

Of these shares Itimád Khán bestowed the country of Sorath on Tatár Khán Ghori; the districts of Rádhanpur, Sami, and Munjpur on Fateh Khán Baloch; Nadiád on Malik-as-Shark, and some of the dependencies of Jháláwár on Alaf Khán Habshi. Syad Mubárak conferred the territory of Pátan on Musá Khán and Sher Khán Foládi. Imád-ul-Mulk Rumi bestowed the district of Baroda on Alaf Khán Habshi and the port of Surat on his own son-in-law Khudáwand Khán Rumi.

Dissensions among the nobles.

About this time A'lam Khán returned, and, through the influence of the syad Mubárak, was allowed to remain, and the syad gave to him and A'zam Humaiyun, Chámpáner, and Itimád Khán gave Godhrá to A'lp Khán Khatri, a follower of A'lam Khán. A'lam Khan and Itimád Khán shortly after expelled A'laf Khán Habshi from Jháláwár, and he fled to Imád-ul-Mulk Rumi at Broach, and at his intercession A'laf Khán received the Bhil district. A'lam Khán began now to

---

1 The mountains of Pál and the rájá of Pál, so frequently alluded to in this sketch, are probably the hills of Rájpiplá and the Khándesh frontier, and the rájá was probably the rájá of Rájpiplá. I say this, because in the account of the different territorial divisions of the country in the Mirat-i-A'hmadi, Pálwáráh is mentioned as comprising Rájpiplá, A'li Mohan, and Godhrá and their neighbourhood, and as Rájpiplá was the only one of these districts with any chief of importance, he is probably the rájá of Pál so frequently mentioned.

entertain ambitious designs, and desired to get rid of Itimád Khán and govern in his stead. Itimád Khán discovering this, made him leave the city and live in his own house in the Asáwal suburb. A'lam Khán now made overtures to Imád-ul-Mulk Rumi and became very friendly with him. One day A'lam Khán proposed to get rid of Itimád Khán; but seeing that Imád-ul-Mulk Rumi did not take to his proposal, he next endeavoured to ruin syad Mubárak. The syad, however, when the Gujarát army marched against him, made peace, and A'lam Khán's intrigues being apparent, he was attacked and compelled to fly. He now went to Berár and besought aid of Mubárak Sháh, who marched an army towards the Gujarát frontier. The Gujarát nobles, taking A'hmad Sháh with them, advanced to oppose him, and he retired. A'lam Khán now repaired to the Foládis at Pátan. Sher Khán uniting with him seized on Itimád Khán's district of Kaḍi. Imád-ul-Mulk Rumi and Itimád Khán now carried on the government, but dissension springing up between them, Itimád Khán fled to Mubárak Sháh in Khándesh, and induced him to lead an army against Gujarát. The nobles, fearing this combination, made peaceful overtures, and it was eventually settled that the lands of Sultánpur and Nandurbár should be given to Mubárak Sháh, and that Itimád Khán should be restored to his former position. Since this date the districts of Sultánpur and Nandurbár have been permanently severed from Gujarát and have formed a part of Khándesh, to which province they now belong. A'hmad Sháh, finding himself more strictly guarded than ever, contrived, one day, to flee to Syad Mubárak at Syadpur, who, though vexed at his coming, would not refuse him shelter. At this time Háji Khán, a noble of Delhi, came to Gujarát with a well equipped force and arrived at Pátan. The Gujarát nobles, especially Itimád Khán and Imád-ul-Mulk Rumi, conceiving that he came at the syad's invitation, and that the flight of the king was part of the plot, determined to crush the syad ere Háji Khán should join him, and marching to Syadpur defeated Syad Mubárak, who fell on the field of battle and was there buried. His estates also were resumed, though eventually Dholká was restored to his son syad Mirán.

Sultánpur and Nandurbár handed over to Khándesh, 1560.

Defeat and Death of Syad Mubárak.

Death of Imád-ul-Mulk Rumi.

The army and the two protectors returned to A'hmadábád, where dissensions again sprang up between them, and Imád-ul-Mulk Rumi summoned to his aid his son Changez Khán from Broach, while Itimád Khán sent for

Chapter II.

A'hmad-a ba'd Kings.

Tatár Khán Ghori from Sorath. Tatár Khán arrived first and Itimád Khán ordered Imád-ul-Mulk Rumi to return to his estate; and he, seeing it would be useless for him to contend against so overwhelming a force, retired to his possessions at Broach. Shortly afterwards, having marched against Surat at the request of the inhabitants, who were wearied of the tyranny of Khudáwand Khán, he was decoyed by that chief to an entertainment and was there assassinated. His son Changez Khán marched against Surat to take revenge for his father's death, and, finding the fortress too strong for him, summoned to his aid the Portuguese, to whom, as the price of their assistance, he surrendered the districts of Daman and Saján.[1] The Portuguese, bringing a strong fleet up the Tápti, cut off the supplies, and Khudáwand Khán was forced to surrender, and was slain by Changez Khán in revenge for his father's death. Changez Khán shortly afterwards quarrelled with the Habshis, who fought with him, but being defeated fled to Itimád Khan, who allotted them a grant of land. At this time Fateh Khán Baloch, the proprietor of Rádhanpur and Sami, was Itimád Khán's chief supporter, and with his assistance Itimád Khán marched to besiege Changez Khán in Broach. Tatár Khán Ghori and other nobles, fearing lest Itimád Khán should become too powerful, endeavoured to make peace; and failing, Tatár Khán wrote to the Foládis to attack Fateh Khán Baloch, when Itimád Khán would be forced to retire. They did so, and Fateh Khán, after being defeated near Rádhanpur, took refuge in the fort of Dhulkot, which is close to the town. Itimád Khán, on hearing this, raised the siege of Broach and came to A'hmadábád, where he busied himself in checking the intrigues of king A'hmad, who was doing all in his power to become independent. Finally, at the instigation of Waji-ul-Mulk and Razi-ul-Mulk in A.D. 1560-61, Itimád Khán caused A'hmad II. to be assassinated.

Damán district ceded to the Portuguese, 1560.

A'hmad II. assassinated, 1560.

---

[1] The fort of Damán was taken by the Portuguese in A.D. 1530, and, according to Portuguese accounts (Faria y Souza in Kerr's Voyages VI., 413) the country round was annexed by them in 1558. The districts surrendered by Changez Khán would seem, according to a statement given in Bird's History, 128, to have contained 700 towns (villages) yielding a yearly revenue of 430,000*l.* (Rs. 43,00,000). Sáján, since known as St. John's Head (N. Lat. 20° 13', E. Long. 72° 47'), between Damán and Bassein, is generally supposed to be the Sindan of the Arab geographers. In A.D. 842 Sindan, then a city of some size, is mentioned by Belador (Reinaud's Fragments, 216-217) as having been taken by a Musalmán slave of the name of Mansour. In the 12th century the town was great with a large import and export trade, well peopled, its inhabitants rich, warlike, and industrious. (Jaubert's Edrisi A.D. 1153, 172).

Chapter II.

A'hmad-a'ba'dKings.

Muzafar III. King 1561-1572.

The new sovereign a minor.

After this Itimád Khán raised to the throne a youth, whom he styled Muzafar Sháh III., and who, he asserted, was a posthumous son of Mahmud Sháh, and then marched towards Pátan to take his revenge on the Foládis for their attack on Fateh Khán Baloch. The nobles, however, were unwilling to crush the Foládis, fearing lest their turn might come next, and the Foládis entered into secret correspondence with them, and when battle was joined induced them to withdraw. In consequence of this, Itimád Khán was forced to retire and return unsuccessful to A'hmadábád, whither, with a view of again attacking the Foládis, he summoned Tatár Khán Ghori from Junágarh. The nobles, however, remained aloof, and even Tatár Khán Ghori made excuses, which so exasperated Itimád Khan that he sought to slay him. Tatár Khán, however, managed to escape to Sorath, and then openly sided with the Foládis. Syad Mirán also left A'hmadábád for his estate at Dholká, and entered into correspondence with the Foládis. Meanwhile Itimád Khán, again collecting an army, marched once more towards Pátan, but was met by the Foládis near the village of Jhotáná, about thirty miles from that town. Itimád Khán was defeated and compelled to return to A'hmadábád, while the Foládis encamped at Jhotáná. Syad Mirán now intervened and made peace. Itimád Khán, however, still thirsted for revenge on the Foládis, and for this purpose he invited Changez Khán, son of Imád-ul-Mulk Rumi, to the capital, and by much courteous treatment induced him to join him in another expedition against the Foládis. Changez Khán, however, like the other nobles, became lukewarm; and as Musá Khán Foládi died while Itimád Khán was marching on Pátan, Changez Khán assigned this as a reason for not proceeding further, averring that it was not fit to war with people in misfortune. Itimád Khán perforce returned to A'hmadábád.

Disputes between Itimád Khán and the Foládis of Pátan.

Now Itimád Khán had disgusted all the nobles, both by his causing the assassination of A'hmad Sháh and by his enmity with the Foládis, which the nobles suspected was merely the commencement of a general resumption of private estates. Nevertheless as he had charge of Muzafar Sháh and possession of the capital, the government of the country was in his hands. At this time the Mirzás,[1] who

[1] These Mirzás were the great grandsons of a Muhammad sultán Mirza, the ruler of Khorásan, who, driven out of his dominions, sought refuge in

Chapter II.

A'hmad-a'ba'd Kings.

Arrival of the Mirzás in Gujarát, 1571.

were the sons of sultán Husain of Khurásán, quarrelling with Jalál-ud-din Muhammad Akbar, entered Gujarát, as also did Mirzá Ashraf-ud-din, and they all joined Changez Khán. Changez Khán now proposed to Sher Khán Foládi, that they should expel Itimád Khán and divide Gujarát between them, the capital and the country south of the Sábarmati falling to the share of Changez Khán, and that to the north to Sher Khán Foládi. Sher Khán agreed, and Changez Khán joining him they marched on A'hmadábád. Syad Mirán, however, induced Sher Khán to stay in Kaḍi. Changez Khán, on the other hand, refused to listen to him, and a battle was fought between him, Itimád Khán and the syad about eight miles from A'hmadábád. Itimád Khán was defeated, and fled with the king to Morásá, while Changez Khán took possession of the capital. Sher Khán Foládi now advanced to the Sábarmati, and, after dividing the province as had been agreed, Sher Khán retired to Kaḍi. Itimád Khán entreated Mirán Muhammad Sháh, king of Khándesh, to march against Gujarát to his aid, and he did so. Changez Khán now invited Itimád Khán to return. He came accordingly to Mámurábád, where he heard that Muhammad Sháh had sustained a defeat and retired to his own country; he therefore, taking Muzafar Sháh with him, returned to Morásá, and thence went to Dungarpur. Changez Khán now remained in A'hmadábád, while Sher Khán withdrew to Kaḍi. After this success all the chief nobles of Gujarát, including the Habshis, joined Changez Khán, who was now at the zenith of his power, and began to think of subduing Sher Khán Foládi, who on his part was anxious and fearful. At this time a Habshi, named Bijli Khán, was offended with Changez Khán, because though he had once made him a grant of Cambay, he afterwards resumed it and bestowed it on his own mother. This man persuaded A'laf Khán and Jhujhár Khán Habshi that Changez Khán had determined on killing them. The Habshi Kháns, resolving to be beforehand with him, invited Changez Khán, with whom they were very intimate, to play a game of *chaugán*.[1] He went with them, when A'laf Khán,

They defeat Itimád Khán.

India. This prince and his descendants were, on the ground of their common descent from Taimur, entertained first by Bábar (A.D. 1526-1531), and afterwards by Humaiyun (A.D. 1531-1566). Before this quarrel Akbar had treated the Mirzás with great honour.—Elliot's History, VI., 122.

[1] A game resembling polo.

Chapter II.

A'hmada'ba'd Kings.

Death of Changez Khán.

after making Jhujhár Khán a signal, attracted Changez Khán's notice to the horse on which he was riding. Jhujhár Khán, as Changez Khán turned to look at the horse, cut him down. The Habshis now plundered Changez Khán's house, while the Mirzás, mounting, went south and took possession of Broach, Baroda, and Chámpáner. Sher Khán now advanced from Kaḍi, and demanded that the Habshis should hand over A'hmadábád to him. The Habshis treated with him, but secretly summoned Itimád Khán, who, returning with Muzafar Sháh, entered the city. It was now arranged that Itimád Khán should take the place of Changez Khán, and the old division of Gujarát between Changez Khán and Sher Khán should be maintained. Itimád Khán, however, found the Habshis so domineering that he withdrew from public affairs. Afterwards A'laf Khán and Jhujhár Khán, quarrelling over the division of Changez Khán's property, A'laf Khán left A'hmadábád and joined Sher Khán, who, advancing from Kaḍi, laid siege to A'hmadábád. Itimád Khán now besought aid from the Mirzás, and Mirzá Ibráhim Husain marched from Broach to help him and harassed Sher Khán's army with his Moghal archers.

Itimád Khán enters into terms with the emperor Akbar.

At the same time Itimád Khán turned for help to the emperor Akbar, who, glad of any pretext for driving the Mirzás from their place of refuge in Gujarát, was not slow in availing himself of Itimád Khán's proposal. He marched at once for A'hmadábád, and, with his arrival in the province, the history of Gujarát as a separate kingdom comes to an end.

CHAPTER III.

THE MOGHAL VICEROYS.

Chapter III.
Moghal Viceroys.
Akbar, Emperor, 1573-1605.

While the nobles were thus fighting among themselves news reached them that Akbar had advanced to Disá. Upon this Ibráhim Husain Mirzá returned to Broach, and the army of the Foládis dispersed. When the imperial army reached Kaḍi, Itimád Khán, Ikhtiyár Khán, A'laf Khán, and Jhujhár Khán met Akbar there, and Syad Hámid also was honoured with an audience at Hájipur. The emperor imprisoned A'laf Khán and Jhujhár Khán Habshi, while he encouraged the other Gujarát nobles. The emperor now advanced to A'hmadábád, where the mother of Changez Khán came and demanded justice on Jhujhár Khán for having wantonly slain her son. As her complaint was just, the emperor ordered Jhujhár Khán to be thrown under the feet of an elephant. Ikhtiyár-ul-Mulk now fled to Lunáwárá, and the emperor, fearing that other of the Gujarát nobles might follow his example, placed Itimád Khán under surveillance. Mirzá Ibráhim Husain, now evacuating Broach, fled to Hindustán, and both Broach and Surat fell into the hands of the emperor. Muhammad Khán, son of Sher Khán Foládi, who had fled to the mountains of Idar, now returned and took the city of Pátan, besieging the imperial governor, Syad A'hmad Khán Bárya, in the citadel. At this time Mirzá Muhammad Husain was at Ránpur near Dhandhuká. When Sher Khán Foládi, who had taken refuge in Sorath, heard of Muhammad Khán's return to Pátan, he met Mirzá Muhammad Husain, and they both uniting their forces joined Muhammad Khán at Pátan. Mirzá Aziz Kokaltash with other nobles marched against them, and after a hard fought battle, in which several of the Imperial nobles were slain, the Mirzá Aziz Kokaltásh was victorious. Sher Khán again took refuge in Sorath, and his son fled for safety to the Idar hills, while the Mirzá withdrew to the Khándesh frontier.

Akbar advances to A'hmadábád, 1573.

Captures Broach and Surat, 1573.

Chapter III.

Moghal Viceroys.

The conquest of Gujarát completed, Akbar returned to Agra. From A.D. 1573, the date of its annexation as a province of the Empire, to A.D. 1757, the year of the final capture of A'hmadábád by the Maráthás, Gujarát remained under the government of officers appointed by the Court of Delhi. As was the case with the rule of the A'hmadábád kings, this whole term of 184 years may conveniently be divided into two periods: the first,—lasting from A.D. 1573 to the death of Aurangzeb in A. D. 1707, or altogether about 134 years,—a time on the whole of public order and strong government; and the second,—lasting for 50 years, from A.D. 1707 to A.D. 1757,—the history of the decline of the viceroy's power and the spread of disorder throughout the province.

Section I.—A.D. 1573-1707.

Mirza' A'ziz 1st Viceroy, 1573-1575.

Before leaving Gujarát Akbar placed the charge of the province in the hands of Mirzá A'ziz Kokaltash. At the same time the emperor rewarded his supporters by grants of land, assigning A'hmadábád and several other districts to the viceroy, Mirzá A'ziz, and the territory of Pátan to the Khán Kilán Mir Muhammad Khán. Broach was given to Kutb-ud-din Muhammad, and Dholká, Khánpur, and Sami were confirmed to Syad Hámid and Syad Mahmud Bukhári.

Insurrection in Gujarát, 1573.

As soon as the departure of the emperor was known, Ikhtiyár-ul-Mulk and Muhammad Khán, son of Sher Khán, who had taken shelter in the Idar hills, issued forth, and the viceroy marched to Ahmadnagar to hold them in check. Mirzá Muhammad Husain, now advancing quickly from the Nandurbár frontier, took the fort of Broach, and went thence to Cambay. The viceroy on this ordered Syad Hámid Bukhári, Nawáb Naurang Khán, and others to join Kutb-ud-din Muhammad Khán, and they went and laid siege to Cambay, but the Mirzá managed to evacuate the town and join Ikhtiyár-ul-Mulk and Muhammad Khán. When the Mirzá joined these men the viceroy retired to A'hmadábád, and the rebels laid siege to the city. Kutb-ud-din Khán, Syad Mirán, and others of the imperial party succeeded, however, in entering the city and joining the garrison.

Quelled by Akbar, 1573.

The siege had lasted two months when Akbar, making forced marches, arrived before A'hmadábád and, at once engaging the enemy, totally defeated them. In this battle both Mirzá Muhammad Husain and Ikhtiyár-ul-Mulk were slain. Akbar, after but eleven days'

Chapter III.

Moghal Viceroys.

MIRZA KHA'N, 2nd Viceroy, 1575-1577.

stay, entrusted the government of Gujarát again to Mirzá Aziz Koká, and returned to Agra. Mirzá Aziz Koká did not, however, long continue to act as viceroy, for in A.D. 1575, in consequence of some dispute with the emperor, he retired into private life. On his resignation Akbar conferred the post of viceroy on Mirzá Khán, son of Beirám Khán, who afterwards rose to the high rank of khán khán, or chief of the nobles. As this was Mirzá Khán's first service, and as he was still a youth, he was ordered to follow the advice of the deputy viceroy, Wazir Khán, in whose hands the administration of the province during the two following years remained. Wazir Khán's government was not, however, successful. And the emperor, hearing that the country was not prosperous, sent Rájá Todar Mal to make the revenue settlement of the province, which he did in a most efficient and able manner. After this had been done, Wajih-ul-Mulk Gujaráti was, in A.D. 1575, appointed the first minister[1] of the province. Some historians say that Wazir Khán relieved Mirzá Aziz Koká as viceroy, A.D. 1576, but the author of the Mirat-i-A'hmadi,—and this is perhaps the more reliable account,—asserts that Mirzá Khán held office with Wazir Khán as his deputy.

Survey of the province by Rájá Todar Mal.

SHA'HA'B-UD-DIN, 3rd Viceroy, 1577-1583.

As Wazir Khán's management was not successful, the post of viceroy was, in the end of the year A.D. 1577, conferred upon Sháháb-ud-din A'hmad Khán, the governor of Málwá. Sháháb-ud-din's first step was to create new military posts and strengthen the old ones. At this time Fateh Khán Shirwáni, the commander of A'min Khán Ghori's army, quarrelled with his chief, and, coming to Sháháb-ud-din, offered to capture the port of Junágarh. Sháháb-ud-din entertained his proposals, and sent his nephew Mirzá Khán and 4,000 horse with him. When the troops crossed the Sorath frontier, they were met by envoys from A'min Khán, agreeing, in his name, to pay tribute and surrender the country, provided he were permitted to retain the fortress of Junágarh and were allotted a sufficient grant of land. Mirzá Khán, however, rejected these proposals, and continued his march against Junágarh. A'min Khán made a vigorous resistance, and applied for aid to the jám of Nawánagar. At this juncture Fateh Khán died, and Mirzá Khán went to Mángrol and besieged that town. The jám's

Sends a force against Junágarh.

---

1 The word used is *diwán*. This officer administered civil justice, subordinate to the viceroy. (See Introduction, p. 7.)

Chapter III.

Moghal Viceroys.

Mirzá Khán is defeated.

minister now joined A'min Khán with 4,000 horse, and he, quitting Junágarh, marched to Mángrol.[1] On their approach Mirzá Khán retired to the town of Kodinár[2] followed by A'min Khán. Here a pitched battle was fought, and Mirzá Khán defeated with the loss of all his baggage. Many of his men were slain, and he himself, being wounded, escaped with difficulty to A'hmadábád. Sháháb-ud-din, who had meanwhile been giving his attention to revenue matters, and to the more correct measurement of the lands of the province, was rudely recalled from these peaceful occupations by his nephew's defeat. At the same time, news was brought of the escape of the former king, Muzafar Sháh, who, eluding the vigilance of the imperial servants, appeared in Gujarát in A.D. 1583. Muzafar remained for some time in the Rájpiplá country, and thence came to Luná Káthi, at the village of Khiri, in the district of Sardhár in Sorath.

Return of Muzafar Sháh, 1583.

Itima'd Kha'n Guja-ra'ti, 4th Viceroy, 1583.

Before, however, he could march against Muzafar, Sháháb-ud-din was recalled, and in A.D. 1583 Itimád Khán Gujaráti was appointed viceroy. At this time a party of about 700 or 800 Moghals, called Wazir Khánis, separating from Sháháb-ud-din, remained behind in hope of being entertained by the new viceroy. As, however, Itimád Khán declared that he was unable to take them into his service, they went off in a body and joined Muzafar at Khiri, and he with them and three or four thousand Káthi horse marched at once on A'hmadábád. On hearing this Itimád Khán, leaving his son Sher Khán in A'hmadábád, followed Sháháb-ud-din to Kaḍi, and entreated him to return. Meanwhile Muzafar Sháh reached A'hmadábád, which was but weakly defended, and in A.D. 1583, after a brief struggle, took possession of the city. While the

Muzafar captures A'hmadabád, 1583.

---

1 Mángrol (N. Lat. 21°8', E. Long. 70°10'), a seaport on the south coast of Káthiáwár, about 20 miles west of Somnáth. This town, supposed to be the Monoglossium Emporium of Ptolemy (A.D. 150) (see Bird 115) is spelt Manglur by the Muhammadan historians. Barbosa (A.D. 1511-1514) under the name of Suratimangaler, calls it a "very good port where many ships from Malabár touch for horses, wheat, rice, cotton goods, and vegetables." In A.D. 1531 the city was taken by the Portuguese general Sylveria with a vast booty and a great number of prisoners (Churchill's Travels, III., 529). It is only incidentally mentioned in the Ain-i-Akbári (A.D. 1590); but in A.D. 1638 is again said, by Mandelslo, to be famous for its linen cloth, and in A.D. 1700 is mentioned by Hamilton (N. A. I. 136) as a place of some trade.

2 This has been rendered by Bird, 353, "the Mountain of Dinár" quasi Koh Dinár.

Chapter III.

Moghal Viceroys.

siege of A'hmadábád was going on, Sháháb-ud-din and Itimád Khán were returning, and were actually within a few miles of the city, when the intelligence of its capture reached them. They still continued their advance, but had barely arrived at A'hmadábád when they were attacked by Muzafar Sháh, and were totally defeated, losing all their baggage. Seeing the issue of the fight, most of their army went over to Muzafar Sháh, and the viceroy with but a few men fled to Pátan. Kutb-ud-din Muhammad Khán, one of the Imperial commanders who was on the Khándesh frontier, now advanced by forced marches to Baroda. Against him Muzafar marched with a large army. Kutb-ud-din, however, threw himself into Baroda, and, in spite of the treachery of his troops, defended the city for some time. At last, on an assurance, on the part of Muzafar, that his life should be spared, Kutb-ud-din repaired to the enemies camp to treat for peace. On his arrival he was imprisoned, and next day was treacherously put to death. The fort of Broach was also at this time traitorously surrendered to Muzafar by the garrison.

Mirza Kha'n Kha'n Kha-na'n, 5th Viceroy, 1583-1590.

On receiving the news of the insurrection in Gujarát the emperor, at the close of the year A.D. 1583, conferred the government of the province on Mirzá Khán, son of Beirám Khán, who had formerly (A.D. 1575) acted as viceroy. Muzafar, who was still at Broach, hearing of the advance of the new viceroy with a large army, returned rapidly to A'hmadábád,

Defeat of Muzafar, 1584.

and in A.D. 1584 a pitched battle was fought between him and Mirzá Khán before the city. In this engagement Muzafar was entirely defeated, and fled to Cambay pursued by Mirzá Khán. Muzafar now hearing that Mirzá Khán had been joined by Naurang Khán and other nobles with the imperial army from Málwá, quitting Cambay, fled to his old place of shelter in Rájpiplá, and being pursued there, after fighting and losing another battle in the Rájpiplá hills, again repaired to Luná Káthi in Khiri. As a reward for these two victories, the emperor bestowed on Mirzá Khán the title of khán khánán. Broach now submitted, and Muzafar sought shelter with A'min Khán Ghori at Junágarh, by whom he was allotted the waste town of Gondal as a residence. A'min Khán, however, seeing that his cause was hopeless, on pretence of aiding him, induced Muzafar to give him a sum of about 10,000*l.* [1]; but when he had

[1] Two lakhs of mahmudis. The *mahmudi* varied in value from about one-half to two-thirds of a rupee. (See Introduction, p. 19.)

Chapter III.

Moghal Viceroys.

obtained the money, on one pretext or another he withheld the promised aid. The khán khánán now marched an army into Sorath against Muzafar. The jám of Nawánagar and A'min Khán sent their envoys to meet the viceroy, declaring that they had not sheltered Muzafar, and that he was wandering about leading an outlaw's life, entirely unaided by them. The viceroy agreed not to molest them, on condition of their withholding all aid and shelter from Muzafar, and himself marched against him. When he reached Upletá, about 15 miles from the fortress of Junágarh, the viceroy heard that Muzafar had sought shelter in the Bardá [1] mountains. Repairing to Bardá, he halted his main force outside of the rough country, sending in skirmishing parties to examine the hills. Ere this, however, Muzafar, leaving the hills, had passed through the jám's country and again entered Gujarát. Here he was once more defeated, and a third time took refuge in the Rájpiplá country. The viceroy now marched on Nawánagar to punish the jám. The jám, however, sent in his submission, and the viceroy taking from him, by way of fine, an elephant and some valuable horses, returned to A'hmadábád.

Ismail Kuli Kha'n, 6th Viceroy, 1590.

Mirza' A'ziz Kokalta'sh, 7th Viceroy, 1590-1592.

Muzafar seeks refuge in Káthiáwár.

In A.D. 1580, the khán khánán was re-called and his place supplied by Ismáil Kuli Khán. Ismáil's government, however, lasted only for a few months, when he was superseded by Mirzá A'ziz Kokaltásh, who was a second time appointed viceroy. In A.D. 1591, Muzafar again returned to Sorath. The viceroy, hearing that he had been joined by the jám, the Cutch chief, and Daulat Khán Ghori, the son of A'min Khán, marched with a large army towards Sorath, and, halting at Viramgám, sent forward a detachment under Naurang Khán, Syad Kásim, and other officers. Advancing as far as Morbi,[2] Naurang Khán entered into negotiations with the jám, who, however, refused to accede to the demands of the imperial commander. On this the viceroy joined Naurang Khán with the bulk of his army, and after a short delay marched on Nawánagar. On his way thither Muzafar and the jám opposed him, and an obstinate battle was fought in which Muzafar was entirely defeated. The son and

---

1 The Bardá Hills are in the division of the province of Káthiáwár called Bardá, which includes the principality of Porbandar.

2 Morbi (N. Lat. 29° 48', E. Long. 70° 50'), a town in Káthiáwár, about 21 miles south of Cutch.

Chapter III.

Moghal Viceroys.

Is attacked by the imperial army.

minister of the jám were slain, and Muzafar, the jám, and Daulat Khán, who was wounded, fled to the fortress of Junágarh. The viceroy now advanced and plundered Nawánagar, and remaining there himself sent Naurang Khán, Syad Kásim, and Gujar Khán against Junágarh. The day the army arrived before the fortress Daulat Khán died of his wounds; nevertheless the nobles above mentioned were unable to take the fortress, and though the viceroy joined them they were still unsuccessful, and were in great straits from want of grain. The viceroy, therefore, returned to A'hmadábád, but after seven or eight months again marched against the Junágarh fortress. The jám, who was still a fugitive, now sent envoys and promised to aid the viceroy if his country were restored to him. The viceroy assented on condition that, during the operations against Junágarh, the jám should furnish his army with supplies of grain. The jám accordingly agreed to provide grain, and after a siege of three months the garrison surrendered the fortress.

Muzafar flies to Cutch.

News was next received that Muzafar had taken refuge at Jagat.[1] The viceroy at once sent Naurang Khán and others with an army in pursuit. But on reaching Jagat, it was found that Muzafar had already left that place for the village of Sewá Wádhel. Without halting Naurang Khán at once started in pursuit, nearly surprising Muzafar, who, however, escaping on horseback with a few followers, crossed over to Cutch. Sewá Wádhel covered his retreat, fighting gallantly with the imperial forces till he was slain. Naurang Khán then came to Arámrá, a village belonging to Singrám Wádhel, rájá of Jagat, and after frustrating a scheme devised by that chief to entrap a body of the troops on board ship, under pretence of pursuing Muzafar's family, led his men back to Junágarh. The viceroy, now hearing whither Muzafar had fled, marched to Morbi, where the jám of Nawánagar came and paid his respects. At the same time the Cutch chief, who is called Khengár in the Mirat-i-A'hmadi and Bhárá in the Mirat-i-Sikandri, sent a message to say that if the viceroy would refrain from invading his country and supply him with a detachment of troops, he would point out to them where Muzafar was concealed. He, accordingly, capturing Muzafar, handed him over to the force sent to

[1] Jagat (N. Lat. 22° 15', E. Long. 69°1'), the site of the temple of Dwárká, at the western extremity of the peninsula of Káthiáwár.

Chapter III.

Moghal Viceroys.

Commits suicide, 1591-92.

secure him. The detachment, strictly guarding the prisoner, were marching rapidly towards Morbi, when, on reaching Dhrol, under pretence of obeying a call of nature, Muzafar withdrew and cut his throat with a razor so that he died. This happened in A.D. 1591-92. The viceroy sent Muzafar's head to court, and though he was now recalled by the emperor he delayed on pretence of wishing to humble the Portuguese. His real object, however, was to make a pilgrimage to Mecca, and in A.D. 1592 he started from Verâwal[1] after obtaining the necessary permission from the Portuguese.

SULTAN MURA'D BAKHT, 8th Viceroy, 1592-1600.

The emperor, who was much vexed to hear of the departure of the viceroy, appointed prince sultán Murád Bakht in his stead. In A.D. 1593-94 Mirzá A'ziz Kokaltásh returned from his pilgrimage and repaired to court, and next year prince Murád Bakht going to the Deccan, Surajsingh was appointed his deputy. In A.D. 1594-95 Bahádur, son of the late Muzafar Sháh, excited a rebellion, but was defeated by Surajsingh. In A.D. 1600, owing to the death of sultán Morád, Mirzá A'ziz Kokaltásh was a third time appointed viceroy of Gujarát, and he sent Shams-ud-din Husain as his deputy to A'hmadábád. Further changes were made in A.D. 1602 when Mirzá A'ziz sent his eldest son Shádmán as deputy; his second son, Khurram, as governor of Junágarh; and Syad Bayázid, as minister. Khurram was afterwards relieved of the charge of Sorath and Junágarh by his brother Abdullah.

MIRZA' A'ZIZ KOKALTA'SH, 9th Viceroy, 1600-1606.

Jaha'ngir, Emperor, 1605-1627.

KALIJ KHA'N, 10th Viceroy, 1606.

SYAD MURTAZA', 11th Viceroy, 1606-1609.

In A.D. 1605 Nur-ud-din Muhammad Jahángir ascended the imperial throne. He appointed Kalij Khán to be viceroy of Gujarát; but Kalij Khán never joined his charge, allowing Mirzá A'ziz Kokaltásh to act in his place. Shortly afterwards, in A.D. 1606, on the transfer of Mirzá A'ziz to the Láhor viceroyalty, Syad Murtazá Khán Bukhári was entrusted with the charge of Gujarát, Syad Bayázid being continued as minister. Syad Murtazá, who, it is said, owed his appointment as viceroy to a present to the emperor of a magnificent ruby, appears to have been more of a scholar than a governor, and the only thing of note that he did was to repair the fort of Kaḍi.[2] During his tenure of power disturbances

---

[1] Verâwal (N. Lat. 20° 55', E. Long. 70° 21'), on the S.W. coast of Káthiáwár. On the south point of Verâwal bay stood the city of Dev, or Mungi Pátan, and within its walls the temple of Somnáth.

[2] Now belonging to His Highness the Gáekwár, about 27 miles N.W. of A'hmadábád.

Chapter III. — Moghal Viceroys.

broke out, and rái Gopináth, son of rájá Todar Mal, with rájá Sursingh of Jodhpur, were sent to Gujarát by way of Málwá, Surat, and Baroda. They overcame and imprisoned Kalián, chief of Belpár,[1] but were in turn defeated by the Mándwá[2] chieftain, and withdrew to A'hmadábád. Rái Gopináth, however, this time obtaining reinforcements, returned to Mándwá and succeeded in capturing the chief. He then marched against the rebellious Kolis of the Kánkrej, and took prisoner their leader, whom, on promising not to stir up future rebellions, he afterwards restored to liberty[3].

Mirza' A'ziz Kokalta'sh, 12th Viceroy, 1609-1611.

Sack of Surat by Malik A'mbar, 1609.

In A.D. 1609 the Khán A'zam Mirzá A'ziz Kokaltásh was appointed twelfth viceroy of Gujarát; he was, however, permitted to remain at court and send his son Jahángir Kuli Khán as his deputy. In this year Malik A'mbar, a noble of nizám Sháh's court and governor of Daulatábád, invaded Gujarát at the head of 50,000 horse, and plundered both Surat and Baroda, but retired as quickly as he came. To prevent such outrages in future, a body of 25,000 men was posted at Rámnagar[4] on the Deccan frontier, and remained there for four years. The following details, of the strength of the several contingents of which this force was composed, give some idea of the relative importance of the different chiefs at that time:—

The viceroy of A'hmadábád	4,000	men.
Nobles of his Court	5,000	,,
The chiefs of Sáler and Mulher (Báglán) ...	3,000	,,
The son of the Cutch chief	2,500	,,
The chief of Nawánagar	2,500	,,
The chief of Idar	2,000	,,
The chief of Dungarpur } Now under the Hilly Tracts Agency, Rajputáná.	2,000	,,
The chief of Bánswadá }	2,000	,,
The chief of Rámnagar (Dharampur)	1,000	,,
The chief of Rájpiplá	1,000	,,

---

1 Belpár, belonging to the Thákor of Umetá in the Rewá Kántá.

2 This Mándwá is probably the Mándwá under His Highness the Gáekwár in his district of Atarsumbá, but it may be Mándwá on the Narbadá in the Rewá Kántá. Atarsumbá is about 10 miles west of Kapaḍwanj in the British district of Kaira.

3 In A.D. 1608 Captain Hawkins, with the permission of the viceroy, sold some goods at Surat.

4 Now belonging to the rájá of Dharampur. East of the British district of Surat.

The chief of A'li (Alirájpur under the Bhopáwar Agency)...	300	men.
The chief of Mohan (Mohan a former capital of the State of Chotá Udyápur in the Rewá Kántá)	350	"
Total... ...	25,650	men.

Firoz Jang, 13th Viceroy, 1611-1616.

In A.D. 1611 Abdullah Khán Bahádur Firoz Jang was appointed thirteenth viceroy of Gujarát, with Gheiás-ud-din as his minister, under orders to proceed to the Deccan to avenge the recent inroad.[1] The viceroy marched accordingly, but, returning without effecting anything, was again, in A.D. 1616, this time in company with the prince Sháh Jahán,—directed to move against the Deccan. This second expedition was successful; the country was humbled, and, with the exception of Malik A'mbar, most of the princes submitted to the emperor. On their return to Delhi, Mukarab Khán was appointed fourteenth viceroy of Gujarát, with Muhammad Safi as his minister. At this time the emperor came to Gujarát to hunt elephants in the Dohad forests. He visited Cambay, and thence went to A'hmadábád. But as the climate of that place was disagreeable to him,[2] he retired to the banks of the Mahi river. Here the jám of Nawánagar came to pay his homage, and presented 50 Cutch horses as tribute. The emperor now returned to A'hmadábád, where he received a visit from the rái Bhárá of Cutch, who presented 100 Cutch horses, 100 *ashrafis*,[3] and 2,000 rupees. The rái

Mukarab Kha'n, 14th Viceroy, 1616.

Elephant hunting in the Panch Mahals, 1616.

1 In this year, (A.D. 1611) the English East India Company sent vessels to trade with Surat. The Portuguese made an armed resistance, but were defeated. The Moghal commander, who was not sorry to see the Portuguese beaten, gave the English a warm reception, and in A.D. 1612-13 a factory was opened in Surat by the English, and in A.D. 1614 a fleet was kept in the Tápti under Captain Downton to protect the factory. In A.D. 1615, Sir Thomas Roe came as ambassador to the emperor Jahángir, and obtained permission to establish factories, not only at Surat but also at Broach, Cambay, and Gogo. The factory at Gogo would seem to have been first established in A.D. 1613. The Dutch closely followed the English at Surat, and were established there in A.D. 1618.

2 At first Jahángir, who visited A'hmadábád in the hot weather, (March) contented himself with abusing its sandy streets, calling the city the "abode of dust," *gardábád*. After an attack of fever, however, his dislike grew stronger, and he was uncertain whether, the "home of the simoom," *samumistán;* the "place of sickness" *bimaristán;* the "thorn brake," *zakumdár*, or "hell," *jahannamábád*, was its most fitting name.—Elliot's Hist. of India, VI., 358.

3 This was probably the gold *ashrafi*, or seraph, of which Hawkins (1609-1611) says, "seraffins Ekberi, which be ten rupees a-piece."—Thomas Chron. Pat. Kings of Delhi, 425.

Chapter III.

Moghal Viceroys.

was then ninety years of age, and had never before paid his respects to any emperor. Jahángir, much pleased with the old chief, gave him his own horse, a male and female elephant, a dagger, a sword with diamond mounted hilt, and four rings of precious stones. As he still suffered from the climate, the emperor set out to return to Agra, and just at that time he heard of the birth of a grandson, afterwards the famous Abu'l Muzafar Mahya-ud-din Muhammad Aurangzeb. In honour of this event Sháh Jahán held a great festival at Ujain.

PRINCE SHA'H JAHA'N, 15th Viceroy, 1616-1622.

The emperor then started for Agra, appointing ere he left Sháh Jahán to be fifteenth viceroy of Gujarát. Muhammad Safi was continued as minister. As, however, the prince preferred remaining at Ujain, he chose Rustam Khán as his deputy; but the emperor, disapproving of this choice, selected rájá Vikramájit in Rustam Khán's stead. Shortly afterwards, in A.D. 1622-23, Sháh Jahán rebelled, and in one of the battles which took place rájá Vikramájit was killed. Sháh Jahán, during his tenure of the viceroyalty, built the Sháhi Bagh at A'hmadábád. After the death of Vikramájit, his brother succeeded as deputy viceroy. While Sháh Jahán was still in rebellion, the emperor appointed sultán Dáwar Baksh as sixteenth viceroy of Gujarát, Muhammad Safi being retained in his post of minister. Sháh Jahán, who was then at Mándu in Málwá, appointed on his part Abdullah Khán Bahádur Firoz Jang viceroy and Khwájah Sara Abdullah Khán minister. Sultán Dáwar Baksh, the emperor's nominee, was accompanied by Khán A'zam Mirzá A'ziz Kokaltásh to instruct him in the management of affairs. Now, the prince Sháh Jahán had instructed his minister to carry away all the treasure; but Muhammad Safi, who appears to have been a most able man, at once imprisoned the prince's partizans in A'hmadábád, and, among others, captured Khwájah Sara Abdullah Khán. When this news reached the prince at Mándu, he sent Abdullah Khán Bahádur with an army to Gujarát by way of Baroda. The minister, however, met and defeated him, and forced him to fly and rejoin the prince at Mándu. Muhammad Safi, for his gallant conduct, received the title of saif khán, while his monthly pay was increased from 200*l.* to 300*l.* (Rs. 2,000 to 3,000) and the command of 300 horsemen was conferred on him. In the meantime sultán Dáwar Baksh, with the Khán A'zam, arrived and assumed the charge of the government, but the

Sháh Jahán rebels, 1622-1623.

Builds the Sháhi Bágh at A'hmadábád.

SULTA'N DA'WAR BAKSH, 16th Viceroy, 1622-1624.

Sháh Jahán's party defeated, 1624.

Chapter III.

Moghal Viceroys.

Khán A'zám died soon afterwards, in A.D. 1624. Sultán Dáwar Baksh was now recalled, and Khán Jahán was appointed deputy viceroy with Yusuf Khán as his minister. On his arrival at A'hmadábád, however, prince Sháh Jahán employed Khán Jahán in his own service, and sent him as his ambassador to the emperor. Saif Khán, who acted for him, may be called the seventeenth viceroy, as indeed he had been the governing spirit for the last eight or ten years. He held the post of viceroy of Gujarát until the death of the emperor in A.D. 1627.

SAIF KHA'N, 17th Viceroy, 1624-1627.

On the death of the emperor Jahángir, his son Abúl Muzafar Sháháb-ud-din Sháh Jahán ascended the throne. He, remembering Saif Khán's hostility to him during his rebellion, at once caused him to be imprisoned, and appointed Sher Khán Tar as eighteenth viceroy with Khwájah Haiyát as his minister. In A.D. 1627, Sháh Jahán visited A'hmadábád, and encamped in tents outside of the city, near the Kánkryá tank. Sher Khán was advanced to the command of 5,000 men, and received an increase of salary and other gifts; while Khán Jahán was appointed his minister, and Mirzá Isá Tar Khán viceroy of Thatta in Sindh. In A.D. 1628 Khwájah Abúl Hasan was sent against the country of Násik, which he ravaged, and returned after taking the fort of Chándoḍ and levying tribute from the chief of Báglán. In A.D. 1630, Jamál Khán Karáwal came to the Gujarát-Khándesh frontier and captured 130 elephants in the Sultánpur forests, of which 70 were sent to Delhi. In A.D. 1631-32, there was a great famine in Gujarát, known as the *Satiásio Kál,* or the famine of Samvat 1687.

Death of Jahángir, 1627.

Sha'hJa'han Emperor, 1627-1658.

Elephant hunting in Sultánpur, 1630.

Year of famine, 1631-32.

Sher Khán was re-called in A.D. 1632, but died ere he could be relieved by the nineteenth viceroy of Gujarát, Islám Khán, along with whom Khwájah Jahán was chosen minister. The monthly salary of Islám Khán was 400*l.* (Rs. 4,000), and he was a commander of 5,000; and on his sending the emperor some valuable presents, he was raised to the rank of a commander of 6,000. In A.D. 1632 Khwájah Jahán went on a pilgrimage to Makká, and was succeeded as minister by A'gá Afzal with the title of Afzal Khán. Afzal Khán was soon appointed commander of Baroda, and Riáyat Khán succeeded him as minister. The post of viceroy of Gujarát, at this time, appears to have been granted to whichever of the nobles of the court was in a position to make the most valuable presents to the emperor.

ISLA'M KHA'N, 19th Viceroy, 1632.

Disordered state of the province, 1632.

Chapter III. Moghal Viceroys.

BA'KAR KHA'N, 20th Viceroy, 1632.

SIPA'HDA'R KHA'N, 21st Viceroy, 1633.

SAIF KHA'N, 22nd Viceroy, 1633-1635.

The province of Sorath waste, 1633.

Government consequently became lax, and, as will be seen hereafter, excesses were committed by the Kolis of the Kánkrej, while at the same time the jám of Nawánagar withheld his tribute. At this time Bákar Khán presented the emperor with a valuable gift, and was appointed viceroy, Riáyat Khán being continued as minister; and in A.D. 1633 Sipáhdár Khán was appointed viceroy, and presented the emperor with a costly velvet tent embroidered with gold, Riáyat Khán being continued as minister. In A.D. 1635 Saif Khán was appointed twenty-second viceroy, with Riáyat Khán as minister, but he was also changed within the year. During his tenure of power Mirzá Isa Tar Khán received a grant[1] of the province of Sorath, which had become waste through the laxity of its governors.

A'ZAM KHA'N, 23rd Viceroy, 1635-1642.

Governs with ability.

Punishes the Kolis, and

At the end of A.D. 1635 A'zam Khán was appointed twenty-third viceroy, with Riáyat Khán in the first instance, and afterwards with Mir Muhammad Sábar, as minister. The men who had recently been allowed to act as viceroys had shown themselves unfit to keep the rebellious chiefs and predatory tribes of Gujarát in order. For this reason the emperor's choice fell upon Azim Khán, a man of ability, who perceived the danger to the government in the existing state of affairs, and saw that to restore the province to order, firm, and even severe, measures were required. When A'zam Khán reached Sidhpur, the merchants complained bitterly to him of the outrages of one Kánji, a Chunwáliá Koli, who had of late been especially daring in plundering merchandize and committing highway robberies. A'zam Khán, desirous of commencing his rule with vigour, at once, before proceeding to A'hmadábád, marched against this chief and defeated him. Kánji fled to the Kherálu district, whither A'zam Khán pursued him so promptly that Kánji surrendered himself, and gave security not only that he would not again commit robberies, but that he would pay an annual tribute of 1,000*l.* (Rs. 10,000.) A'zam Khán then erected two fortified posts in the Koli country, one of which he named A'zamábád after himself, and one Khalilábád after his son. He next marched to Káthiáwár[2] and subdued

---

[1] The word used in the text is *tuyul.* In meaning it does not differ from *jágir.*

[2] This is one of the first mentions in history of Káthiáwár as such, or as anything other than Sorath or Sauráshtrá. It probably, however, only

Chapter III. Moghal Viceroys. The Káthis.

the Káthis, who were continually ravaging the country near Dhandhuká, and erected a fortified post to check them, called Sháhpur, not far distant from Chudá-Ránpur. Agá Afzal Fázal Khán, who had at one time held the post of minister, and had in A.D. 1636 been appointed governor of Baroda, was now selected to command the special cavalry composing the body-guard of prince Muhammad Aurangzeb. At the same time Syad Ilahdád was appointed governor of Surat Fort. Isá Tarkhán was still at Junágarh, and at this time, A.D. 1637, Mir Muhammad Sábar was chosen minister in place of Riáyat Khán, and in A.D. 1638 Moiz-ul-Mulk was reappointed to the command of Surat Fort. A'zam Khán was now high in favour, and his daughter was at this time sent to Delhi, and espoused to the emperor's son Muhammad Sujáh Bahádur. In A.D. 1639, A'zam Khán devoted his whole attention to placing fortified posts to check rebellion and robbery in the country of the Kolis and the Káthis, and he made such arrangements that people could travel safely in the districts of Káthiáwár, the country of the jám of Nawánagar, and in Cutch. The jám, however, who had been accustomed of late years to do much as he pleased, resented these arrangements, and in A.D. 1640 withheld payment of tribute, and set up a mint to coin *koris*.[1] When A'zam Khán heard of this, he marched with an army against Nawánagar, and, on arriving about three miles from the city, he sent the jám a peremptory order to pay the arrears of tribute and to close his mint, directing him in case of any disturbance occurring in that part of the country to send his son at once to the viceroy to learn his will. He further ordered the jám to dismiss to their own countries all refugees from other parts of Gujarát. The jám being unable to cope with A'zam Khán, acceded to these terms, and A'zam Khán, receiving the arrears of tribute, returned to A'hmadábád.

Restores order, 1639.

Revolt of the jám of Nawánagar, 1640.

Isatar Kha'n, 24th Viceroy, 1642-1644.

Though A'zam Khán had acted so firmly and well in the imperial interests, he necessarily made many enemies. These persons ceased not to traduce him to the weak emperor, who was at last induced to think that A'zam Khán's government

---

comprised the eastern possessions of the Kháchar Káthis and the division of the province known as the Panchál.

1 The author of the Mirat-i-A'hmadi says that in his time, A.D. 1746-1762, these Nawánagar *koris* were current even in A'hmadábád, two koris and two-thirds being equal to one imperial rupee.

Chapter III.

Moghal Viceroys.

was not beneficial, and, accordingly, recalling him, in A.D. 1662 he appointed in his place Mirzá Isa Tar Khán, the governor of Sorath, twenty-fourth viceroy of Gujarát. And as it was insinuated by his enemies that A'zam Khán might resist the message of recall, this order was written by the emperor with his own hand. The new viceroy, thanks to A'zam Khán's firm rule, found the province on the whole in good order, and was able to devote his attention to financial reforms, and introduced the system of levying revenue in kind known in Gujarát as Bhágwatái.[1] When Mirzá Isa Tar Khán was raised to be viceroy of Gujarát, he appointed his own son Inayat-ullah to be governor of Junágarh, and Moiz-ul-Mulk to fill the post of minister. Mirzá Isa Tar Khán's term of power was, however, brief, for in A.D. 1644 the emperor appointed prince Muhammad Aurangzeb to the charge of Gujarát, Moiz-ul-Mulk continuing to act as his minister. One of the events of interest recorded in the next year (A.D. 1645) is the capture of 73 elephants in the forests of Dohad and Chámpáner.

PRINCE MUHAMMAD AURANGZEB, 25th Viceroy, 1644-1646.

Prince Aurangzeb's rule in Gujarát was marked by religious disputes. One quarrel between the Hindus and the Musalmáns ended in the destruction, by the order of the prince, of a temple of Chintáman near Saraspur. In another case, both of the contending parties were Musalmáns, the orthodox believers rising against the representatives of the Mahdviyeh sect in A'hmadábád, who were then numerous. In consequence of these disturbances, prince Aurangzeb was relieved and Sháistah Khán appointed twenty-sixth viceroy of Gujarát. In the following year Moiz-ul-Mulk, who had till then continued to act as minister, was recalled, and his place supplied by Háfiz-Muhammad Násir. In A.D. 1648, prince Muhammad Dáráh Shekoh was chosen viceroy, with Ghairat Khán as his deputy and Hafiz Muhammad Násir as minister, while Sháistah Khán was sent to Málwá to relieve Sháh Nawáz Khán. In A.D. 1651, Mir Yahya was appointed minister in place of Háfiz Muhammad Násir, and in A.D. 1652 prince Dáráh was sent to Kandahár. Sháistah Khán now, for the second time, became viceroy, with Mir Yahya as minister; while sultán Yár was chosen governor of Baroda with the title of Himat Khán. In A.D. 1653, an imperial order was issued reducing the

SHA'ISTAH KHA'N, 26th Viceroy, 1646-1648.

PRINCE MUHAMMAD DA'RA'H, 27th Viceroy, 1648-1652.

SHA'ISTAH KHA'N, 28th Viceroy, 1652-1654.

1 Literally division into shares.

2 A suburb of A'hmadábád.

Mutiny among the troops, 1653.

pay of the troopers, as well as of the better class of horsemen, who brought with them a certain number of followers. This order created much discontent, and was most impolitic. During this year several changes were made in the charges of the different governors,—Muhammad Násir was sent to Surat, Himat Khán to Dholká, the governor of Dholká to Baroda, and Kutb-ud-din to Junágarh; while Syad Shekhan, son-in-law of Syad Diler Khán, was appointed governor of Tharád under Pátan, and Jagmál, the holder of Sánand, was deputed to Dholká as revenue collector.[1] At this time Sháistah Khán in person marched against and defeated the Chunwáliá Kolis, who, since A'zam Khán's time, had been ravaging the villages round A'hmadábád as well as those of Dholká, Kaḍi and Viramgám.

Prince Mora'd Baksh, 29th Viceroy, 1654-1657.

But though Sháistah Khán had, during these two years, restored some order in the province, the emperor seemed determined to neutralize the good effects of vigorous rule by continually changing his officers. Accordingly, in A.D. 1654, he appointed prince Muhammad Morád Baksh twenty-ninth viceroy of Gujarát, and Diánat Khán minister in place of Mir Záhya. Diánat Khán was, however, immediately superseded by Rehmat Khán. Mujáhid Khán Jhálori relieved Mir Shams-ud-din as governor of Pátan. At the same time the management of Godhrá was entrusted to Syad Hasan, son of Syad Diler Khán, and its revenues assigned to him. When prince Morád Baksh reached Jhábuá[2] on his way to A'hmadábád, the chief of that place presented him with 1,500*l.* (Rs. 15,000) as tribute; and when he reached A'hmadábád, Kánji, the notorious leader of the Chunwáliá Kolis, surrendered through Syad Shekhán, and promised to remain quiet and pay annually a tribute of 1,000*l.* (Rs. 10,000). Dildost, son of Sarfaráz Khán, was appointed to the charge of the post of Bijápur under Pátan; while Syad Shekhan was made governor of Sádrá, and Syad A'li paymaster, with the title of Radwi Khán. Many other changes were made at the same time, the prince receiving a grant of the district of Junágarh.

At the end of A.D. 1657, news arrived that Sháh Jahán was dangerously ill; and, on hearing this, prince Morád

[1] The word used is *amil*, a term applied both to a collector and to a farmer of the revenues.

[2] Jhábuá, now under the Bhopáwar Agency.

Chapter III.

Moghal Viceroys.

Morád proclaims himself emperor, 1657.

Baksh at once proclaimed himself emperor by the title of Murawwaj-ud-din. His next step was to put to death the minister Ali Naki, and direct his men to plunder and deprive of their estates the governor and Kudsi[1] Begam of Surat. He then borrowed 55,000*l.* (5½ lákhs of rupees) from the sons of Satidás Jhaveri; 4,000*l.* (Rs. 40,000) from Rohidás, partner of Satidás; and 8,800*l.* (Rs. 88,000) from Sánmal and others. With this sum he raised an army, arranging to meet his brother, prince Aurangzeb, and with him march against the máhárájá Jaswantsingh of Jodhpur and Kásam Khán, whom Sháh Jahán had appointed viceroys of Málwá and Gujarát, respectively, with orders to join together and march against the princes. Morád Baksh and Aurangzeb, on their side, uniting their forces, early in A.D. 1658 fought an obstinate battle with Jaswantsingh, in which they were at length victorious, and entered Ujain in triumph. It was from this city that prince Morád Baksh wrote the order allotting to Mánikchand priority of payment over his other creditors, and assigning to him 15,000*l.* (Rs. 1,50,000) from the revenues of Surat; 10,000*l.* (Rs. 1,00,000) from Cambay; 10,000*l.* (Rs. 1,00,000) from Pitlád; 7,500*l.* (Rs. 75,000) from Dholká; 5,000*l.* (Rs. 50,000) from Broach; 4,500*l.* (Rs. 45,000) from Viramgám, and 3,000*l.* (Rs. 30,000) from the salt works: in all 55,000*l.* (5½ lákhs of rupees). Further sums of 4,000*l.* (Rs. 40,000) are mentioned as due to Rohidás, partner of Satidás, and 8,800*l.* (Rs. 88,000) to Sánmal and others. The princes now advanced upon A'gra, and fought a still more obstinate battle with the imperial forces, commanded by prince Dáráh Shekoh, and after a long and doubtful contest were victorious, though Morád Baksh received several wounds. Prince Dáráh fled to Delhi, and the princes advanced and took possession of A'gra. After confining his father, Aurangzeb marched for Mathurá, and, having no further use of Morád, he there seized and imprisoned him. From Mathurá, Aurangzeb went to Delhi, but found it abandoned by Dáráh, who had meanwhile retired to Láhor.

KA'SAM KHA'N, 30th Viceroy, 1657-1659.

Morád with Aurangzeb victorious.

Morád is confined by Aurangzeb, 1658.

Aurangzeb, Emperor, 1658-1707.

In A.D. 1658, Aurangzeb, though his father was yet alive, assuming the Imperial titles ascended the throne, and in A.D. 1659 appointed Sháh Nawáz Khán Safávi thirty-first viceroy of Gujarát, with Rahmat Khán as minister. Sháh Nawáz

[1] Kudsi is a title; it means literally pure, holy.

Chapter III. Moghal Viceroys.

Khán was the father-in-law of both Aurangzeb and Morád Baksh, and it happened that, shortly after his appointment, while Morád's wife was paying a visit to her father, prince Dáráh, leaving Cutch, where he had been hospitably received by the ráv, made a sudden descent on Gujarát. The viceroy, won over by the entreaties of his daughter (who saw in the success of Dáráh a hope of release for her husband), joined the prince, who entered A'hmadábád, and thence, after collecting an army, and appointing Syad A'hmad deputy viceroy, marched towards A'jmer, once more to try his chance for empire. He was, however, defeated in A.D. 1659, and fled to A'hmadábád, where Sardár Khán, who had confined Syad A'hmad, closed the gates of the city in his face. The unhappy prince then retired to Cutch, but meeting with no support fled to Sindh, where he was treacherously seized and handed over to his brother by the chief of Jun. The emperor Aurangzeb, forgiving Jaswantsingh his opposition at Ujain, conferred on him the government of Gujarát, and in the place of Rahmat Khán appointed Makramat Khán to act as minister. Sardár Khán was thanked for his loyal conduct. Presents were also bestowed on Kutb-ud-din, the governor of Sorath, and shortly afterwards, for his refusal to help prince Dáráh, the chief of Cutch was rewarded. By these measures throughout Gujarát all signs of disaffection with the accession of Aurangzeb were removed.

SHA'H NAWA'Z KHA'N SAFA'VI, 31st Viceroy, 1659.

Rebellion of prince Dáráh, 1659.

Is defeated, 1659.

JASWANTSINGH, 32nd Viceroy, 1659-1662.

In A.D. 1662, Jaswantsingh received orders to march to the Deccan, and join prince Muazzam against Siváji the Maráthá leader; and Kutb-ud-din, governor of Sorath, was directed to act for him in his absence. In this year, Mahábat Khán was appointed thirty-third viceroy of Gujarát, and he joined his charge in A.D. 1663, while Sardár Khán, the governor of Broach, was sent to Idar to suppress certain disturbances that had arisen in that part of the country. About this time Ranmalji, jám of Nawánagar, died, leaving a spurious child named Lákhá, whom the late chief's brother Ráisinghji, with the aid of the ráv of Cutch and other Jádejás, set aside and himself mounted the throne. Lákhá was, however, taken to A'hmadábád by Malik Isá, a servant of the family, and the aid of the viceroy was invoked. Marching at once on Nawánagar, Kutb-ud-din defeated and slew Ráisingh, took possession of Nawánagar, and annexed the territory, changing the name of the city into Islámnagar. For the successful issue of this expedition, Kutb-ud-din received much praise from court. Ráisingh's son, Tamáchi, then an infant, however, escaped and

Jaswantsing sent against Siváji 1662.

MAHA'BAT KHA'N, 33rd Viceroy, 1662-1668.

Capture of Nawánagar (Islámnagar), 1664.

Chapter III. — Moghal Viceroys.

was sheltered in Cutch. This was about A.D. 1664; and in the same year a Baloch, personating Dáráh Shekoh, was joined by many Kolis, and disturbed the peace of the Chunwál, now a portion of the A'hmadábád collectorate north of Viramgám. Mahábat Khán, however, quelled these disturbances, and established two new military posts, one at Gájná under Cambay, and one at Belpár under Pitláḍ.

Rise of the Bábi family.

At this time we first hear of the celebrated Bábi family, one of whose members, Sher Khán Bábi, was sent with 700 men against Dudá Koli of the Chunwál.

Plunder of Surat by Siváji, 1664.

In the same year (A.D. 1664), Siváji made a rapid descent on Surat, and, by plundering the city created a great alarm over the whole province. The viceroy, Mahábat Khán, therefore marched to Surat with the following chiefs and officers: Jagmál, proprietor of Sánand; the governor of Dholká; Shádimal, chief of Idar; Syad Hasan Khán, governor of Idar; Muhammad Abid with 200 superior landholders of the district of Kaḍi; the rájá of Dungarpur; Sabalsingh, rájá of Wadhwán, in Káthiáwár, and other chiefs of Jháláwár; Lál Kalián, chief of Mándwá in the Gáekwár's dominions near Atarsumbá; the chief of Elol under Ahmadnagar; Prathiráj of Haldarwás, and the chief of Belpár. When they arrived at Surat there were no traces of Siváji, who had long since carried off his plunder safely to his head-quarters at Ráygarh.[1] The viceroy, therefore, after remaining three months at Surat levying tribute from the superior landholders of those parts, returned to A'hmadábád, and Ináyat Khán, the revenue collector,[2] Surat, built a wall round the town for its protection. About this time Kutb-ud-din Khán, governor of Sorath, was sent with an army to aid the máhárájá Jaswantsingh in the Deccan, and Sardár Khán was appointed in his place.

Second sack of Surat by the Maráthás, 1666.

The Maráthás in A.D. 1666 again attacked and plundered Surat, and in the same year the deposed emperor Sháh Jahán died, and Makramat Khán, minister of Gujarát, died also.

Copper coinage introduced, 1668.

In this year the viceroy, Mahábat Khán, in place of the old iron coins, introduced a copper coinage into Gujarát. Sardár Khán, the governor of Junágarh, was also put in charge of Islámnagar (Nawánagar), and 500 additional horsemen were placed under him.

---

1 Ráygarh (N. Lat. 18° 14', E. Long. 73° 30'), the name given in A.D. 1662 to Rairi, a hill fortress in the Mahád sub-division of the Kolábá collectorate. Siváji took the place and made it his capital in A.D. 1648.

2 The word is *mutsadi*, literally clerk.

Chapter III.

Moghal Viceroys.

KHA'NJAHA'N 34th Viceroy, 1668-1671.

In A.D. 1668, Bahádur Khán Khán Jahán, who had formerly been viceroy of Allahábád, was appointed viceroy of Gujarát, with Haji Shafia Khán, and afterwards Khwájah Muhammad Háshim, as his ministers. He joined his government in A.D. 1669, and in A.D. 1670 Siváji again plundered Surat. In A.D. 1670 Siváji made an attempt on Jhanjhirá,[1] the residence and stronghold of the admirals of Bijápur. Sidi Yákut, an Abyssinian, the commander of that fortress, applied to the governor of Surat for aid. On his consenting to become a vassal of the emperor and place his fleet at the emperor's disposal, Sidi Yákut received the title of Yákut Khán, and a yearly subsidy of 15,000*l.* (Rs. 1,50,000). About the same time Syad Diler Khán, who had accompanied máhárájá Jaswantsingh to the Deccan, was recalled by the viceroy Bahádur Khán and appointed governor of Sorath in place of Sardár Khán, who was sent to Idar. Syad Haidar, in charge of the military post of Haidarábád, reported that he had put down the rebellion in that part of the country, but, to preserve order in future, recommended that a small fort should be built. In A.D. 1670 Diler Khán was summoned by the emperor to discuss the state of affairs in the Deccan, and was afterwards sent to the seat of war, being replaced in the government of Sorath by Sardár Khán.

Third sack of Surat, 1670.

Sidi Yákut of Jhanjhirá becomes the Moghal admiral, 1670.

MA'HA'RA'JA' JASWANTSINGH, 35th Viceroy, 1671-1674.

In A.D. 1671, Bahádur Khán Khán Jahán was sent as viceroy to the Deccan. He was relieved by the máhárájá Jaswantsingh, who, viceroy of Gujarát for the second time, received an assignment of the districts of Dhandukà and Pitláḍ. Through the intercession of the viceroy, jám Tamáchi, the son of Raisingh, was, in A.D. 1673, on condition of serving the viceroy when required and of keeping order in that part of the country, restored to the throne of Nawánagar. At the same time the 25 small Jáḍejá principalities in the Hálár sub-division of the province of Káthiáwár were placed under his charge. Nevertheless, as long as the emperor Aurangzeb was alive, the city of Nawánagar (Islámnagar) was always kept in the hands of a Musalmán noble, the jám residing at Khambáliá, a town about 30 miles distant from the headquarters of the state. But in A.D. 1707, on Aurangzeb's death, the jám was allowed to return to his former capital.

---

1 Jhanjhirá (N. Lat. 18° to 18° 32′), on the western coast, about 44 miles south of Bombay. The Bijápur mentioned is the kingdom of that name in the Deccan.

Chapter III. Moghal Viceroys.

So, too, in regard to his pearl fisheries in the Gulf of Cutch. As long as Aurangzeb lived, the jám forbore to work them, but afterwards again made use of this source of revenue.

MUHAMMAD A'MIN KHA'N UMDAT-UL-MULK, 36th Viceroy, 1674.

About the year A.D. 1674, the máhárájá was relieved and sent to Kábul, and Muhammad A'min Khán Umdat-ul-Mulk, who had just been defeated at Kábul, was appointed thirty-sixth viceroy of Gujarát, receiving an assignment of the districts of Pátan and Viramgám. Among the military posts of which mention is made in the Mirat-i-A'hmadi is that of Sádráh,[1] at present the head-quarters of the Máhi Kántá Agency. This post, it would seem, was at that time called Islámábád,[2] and was under the command of Syad Kamál, son of Syad Kámil. At this time the Bábi family were rising into importance. Muhammad Muzafar, son of Sher Khán Bábi, was governor of the Kaḍi district, and Muhammad Mubáriz, another son of Sher Bábi, was in charge of one of the posts under Kaḍi. Kamál Khán Jhálori, who had been removed from the government of Pálanpur, and replaced by Muhammad Fateh, was now restored to his former post. In A.D. 1676, the Junágar, fortress was put into repair, and Shekh Nizám-ud-din A'hmad, minister of Gujarát, was sent to Málwá, and was succeeded by Muhammad Sharif. In this year the Kánkrej Kolis were again rebellious, and Muhammad A'min Khán Umdat-ul-Mulk went against them and remained four months in their country, subduing them and reducing them to order. In the end of A.D. 1678, the viceroy received instructions to join the emperor at A'jmir, and an officer of the same name, Muhammad A'min Khán, was appointed viceroy in his place. In this year an order was given to change the name of the Visalnagar district to that of Rasulnagar.

Increased power of the Bábi family.

MUHAMMAD A'MIN KHA'N, 37th Viceroy, 1678-1683.

The emperor Aurangzeb was at this time, A.D. 1679, using all his endeavours to crush both the rúná of Udyápur and the Ráthoḍs, but especially the former. Bhimsingh, the ráná's youngest son, made a descent into Gujarát and plundered

---

[1] Sádráh is always spelt Sháhdarah in the Mirat-i-A'hmadi.

[2] There was another post of the name of Islámábád, in Punádrá, which was situated in the pargana of A'zamábád. A'zamábád itself was a fort on the bank of the Wátrak, about 21 miles to the E.S.E. of A'hmadábád. A'zamábád was built by A'zam Khán during his viceroyalty, and was at his request erected into a pargana by permission of the emperor Sháh Jahán. 12 villages were attached to it, for the pay of the garrison from the neighbouring pargana of Bhil and Kapadwanj.

Chapter III. Moghal Viceroys.

Revolt of the Idar chief, 1679.

Wadnagar, A'hmadnagar, and other towns and villages. The chief of Idar, thinking this a favourable opportunity to recover his independence, expelled the Muhammadan garrison from Idar and regained possession of his capital. Muhammad A'min Khán and Muhammad Bahlol Khán, however, retook Idar, and the chief fled to the hills (pursued by Bahlól Khán), where he died, and his body was found by a wood-cutter, who, divesting him of his ornaments, brought the head to Bahlol Khán. As the chief's family had been captured, the head was shown to, and recognized by, his widow, who from that day put on mourning. Muhammad Bahlol Khán was much praised, and was appointed to the charge of Idar, and at the same time the minister Muhammad Sharif was succeeded by Abdul Latif, and in A.D. 1683 Muhammad A'min the viceroy died. Muhammad A'min was, according to the Mirat-i-A'hmadi, one of the best of the governors of Gujarát.

MUKHTA'R KHA'N, 38th Viceroy, 1683-1686.

He was succeeded by Mukhtár Khán as thirty-eighth viceroy, Abdul Latif continuing to hold the office of minister. In A.D. 1684, Abdur Rahmán Krori, the governor of Deva Pátan, was removed at the request of the inhabitants of that city, and in his place Muhammad Said was selected by Sardár Khán, governor of Sorath. In the following year Sardár Khán died at Thatta in Sindh, where he had gone as viceroy. Sardár Khán was, in the first instance, succeeded in the government of Sorath by Syad Muhammad Khán. But not long after Sorath was assigned as a personal estate to Prince Muhammad A'zam Sháh Bahádur, and during the prince's absence Sháhwardi Khán was sent to manage its affairs. In A.D. 1686 there was a great famine in Gujarát, and in the same year the viceroy died.

Year of famine, 1686.

SHUJA'AT KHA'N (KA'RTALAB KHA'N), 39th Viceroy, 1686-1703.

Prince Muhammad A'zam Sháh was now appointed viceroy, with Kártalab Khán, governor of Sorath, as his deputy. But almost immediately afterwards (A.D. 1686) Kártalab Khán was raised to the post of viceroy, and Muhammad Táhir appointed minister. In addition to his command, as viceroy of Gujarát, Kártalab Khán was afterwards placed in charge of Jodhpur. At the same time, besides his previous personal estate, the district of Pitlád was assigned to prince Muhammad A'zam Sháh, and Sher Afgan Khán, son of Sháhwardi Khán, was appointed governor of Sorath. In A.D. 1687, Sher Afgan Khán was relieved by Bahlol Sheráni, but in the following year was again restored to his former command. In A.D. 1689, on the news of the death of Ináyat

Chapter III. Moghal Viceroys.

The viceroy quells a mutiny of the troops, 1689.

Khán, governor of Jodhpur, Kártalab Khán started to settle the affairs of that state. As soon as he left A'hmadábád, a rumour was spread that a new viceroy was coming, and the troops grew mutinous. On hearing of this disturbance, Kártalab Khán promptly returned to A'hmadábád and quelled the mutiny. The firmness of his conduct on this occasion so pleased the emperor that he gave him the title of Shujáat Khán, and placed the governor of Jodhpur under his orders. Shujáat Khán now proceeded to Jodhpur, where Dargadás Ráthod, who had incited prince Akbar to rebellion, and Ajitsingh, the son of the máhárájáh Jaswantsingh, were causing much disturbance through the province. Finding that a strong resident governor was required to keep those insurgents in check, Shujáat Khán appointed Kásam Beg Muhammad A'min, a brave and resolute soldier, to be his deputy, and returned to A'hmadábád. In the year A.D. 1690, the minister, Amánat Khán, with the title of Itimád Khán, was made military governor of Surat, and Syad Mohsin chosen as minister in his place.

Revolt of Matiáhs and Momans, 1691.

In the following year (A.D. 1691) an attempt, on the part of the emperor, to suppress a body of Mussalmán sectarians, led to a somewhat serious insurrection. Hearing that Syad Sháhji, the religious preceptor of the Matiáhs of Khándesh and the Momans of Gujarát, two classes of converted Hindus, held heterodox views, the emperor ordered that he should be examined before the religious doctors[1] and the viceroy, and admonished. Disgusted with the treatment he received, the syad committed suicide. The loss of their leader so enraged his followers, that, collecting from all sides, they marched against Broach, seized the fort, and slew the governor. The insurgents held the fort of Broach against the governor of Baroda, who was sent to punish them, and for a time successfully resisted the efforts of his successor, Nazar Ali Khán. At last, at an unguarded spot, some of the besiegers stole over the city wall, and opening the gates admitted their companions. The Momans were attacked and defeated with great slaughter.

Disturbances in Káthiáwár, 1692.

In A.D. 1692 Shujáat Khán went to Jháláwár and Sorath to exact tribute, and on this occasion stormed the fort of

---

1 The class (called *mouldvis* or *mullahs*) from which judges, lawyers, and ministers of religion were generally or always taken, were rather graduates in law and divinity than ecclesiastics. (Elphinstone, 485.)

Moghal Viceroys.

Thán, the head-quarters of the plundering Káthis, and after destroying the fort returned to A'hmadábád. Shujáat Khán, one of the most able of the Gujarát viceroys, gave much of his attention to the management of affairs at Jodhpur, and, as a rule, used to spend about six months of every year in Márwár. At this time the emperor sent Shekh Ikvám-ud-din to levy the capitation tax from the Hindus of the Pálanpur and Jhálor districts. The viceroy, accordingly, deputed for this purpose Muhammad Mujáhid, son of Kamál Khán Jhálori, governor of Pálanpur. Dargadás Ráthod now again excited tumults and sedition in Márwár, so the viceroy went in person to Jodhpur, and there by a series of politic measures—one of which was on condition of service, confirming and guaranteeing their estates to the chief vassals and landholders[1] —he withdrew them from alliance with Dargadás, against whom he sent his deputy Kázam Beg, who expelled him from Márwár. Then, in place of Sajansingh, appointing Kunwar Mokamsingh as governor of Mertha in Márwár, Shujáat Khán returned to A'hmadábád. In A.D. 1693, at the request of Sher Afkan Khán, governor of Sorath, the walls of the fort of Jagat were restored. In this year also the viceroy himself went to Jhálá-wár to exact tribute, and on his return to A'hmadábád Safdár Khán Bábi, governor of Pátan, wrote to the viceroy, and at his request the forts of Khamboi and Sámprah were repaired. The viceroy now went to Jodhpur, and from that returned to A'hmadábád. In A.D. 1694 the wall of Azamábád was repaired. In this year the emperor, hearing that Ajitsingh and Dargadás were again contemplating rebellion, ordered the viceroy to go to Jodhpur. Muhammad Mubáriz Bábi was at the same time appointed deputy governor of Wadnagar, and an order was issued that the revenue of Pátan should be paid to Shujáat Khán instead of, as formerly, into the imperial treasury. In this year also Safdar Khán Bábi, governor of Pátan, was succeeded by Mubáriz Khán Bábi.

And in Márwár.

In A.D. 1696, Muhammad Bahlol Sheráni, governor of Baroda, died, and his place was supplied by Muhammad Beg Khán. During this year also the viceroy went to Jodhpur and remained there for some months. In A.D. 1697, an emissary arrived from the imperial court to settle the disputes

Dargadás Ráthod re-

[1] The word *patáwat* here used implies a holder of land on service tenure.

Chapter III. Moghal Viceroys.

conciled to the emperor, 1697.

about the Nawánagar succession,[1] and also to inquire into certain complaints made by the inhabitants of Sorath. About the same time Dargadás Ráthod, in whose charge were the son and daughter of prince Akbar, made an application to Shujáat Khán, proposing a truce, and saying that he wished personally to hand over the children to their grandfather. Shujáat Khán agreed, and Dargadás, accompanying him to Delhi, restored Akbar's children to the emperor. Aurangzeb was much pleased with Dargadás making peace with him, and assigning him as a personal estate the lands of Merthá in Jodhpur, and afterwards adding to this the grant of Dhanduká and other districts of Gujarát.

Year of scarcity. 1698.

In A.D. 1698, on the death of Itimád Khán, his son Muhammad Mohsan was made minister, and he was ordered to hand over to Dargadás Ráthod the district of Merthá. Amongst other changes made at that time Muhammad Munim was raised to the command of the fort of Jodhpur, and Khwájah Abdul Hamid was appointed minister. Owing to the failure of the rains, 1698 was a year of much scarcity in Márwár. The accounts of this year also notice a petition addressed by the Sihor Bráhmans to the viceroy, praying that they might not be seized as carriers or labourers. As, for some reason or other, a difference of opinion arose between Shujáat Khán and Safdar Khán Bábi, deputy governor of Pátan, Safdar Khán resigned office, and, until a successor was appointed, Muhammad Bahlol Sheráni was directed to administer the Pátan district. The government of Sorath was, during this year, bestowed by the emperor on Muhammad Beg Khán. In A.D. 1699, Dargadás Ráthod obtained from the emperor a pardon for Ajitsingh, son of the late máháráját Jaswantsingh. Lands in Jhálor and Sáchor in Márwár were assigned as a personal estate to Ajitsingh, who was at the same time placed in charge of these districts. Mujáhid Khán Jhálori, who had formerly held Jhálor and Sáchor, received in their stead the lands in Pálanpur and Disá, which they still hold. Afterwards, in the time of the emperor Ferakhsher (A.D. 1713-1719), Rahim Yár Khán was appointed governor of Pálanpur and Disá, and going to A'hmadábád collected men and summoned Firoz Khán Jhálori to give over charge. Firoz Khán however refused, and defeated Rahim Yár Khán, and afterwards, by sending large presents to the

[1] See above, p. 77.

Chapter III.

Moghal Viceroys.

emperor, was confirmed in his government. In this year also (A.D. 1699), Amánat Khán, governor of Surat, died, and the Maráthás, making a raid into the province, Shujáat Khán sent Nazar A'li Khán to drive them out.

Maráthá raid upon Surat, 1699.

In A.D. 1700, Firoz Khán Mewáti, deputy governor of Jodhpur, died, and the viceroy appointed Muhammad Záhid from Viramgám in his place. In the same year the manager of Dhandhuká, on behalf of Dargadás Ráthod, asked the viceroy for aid against the Káthis, who were plundering that district. The viceroy, therefore, ordered Muhammad Beg, governor of Sorath, to march against them. Shujáat Khán, who had so long and well held the office of viceroy in a most critical time, died in A.D. 1703. In his place prince Muhammad Azam Sháh, who was then at Dhár in Málwá, was appointed fortieth viceroy of Gujarát, as well as governor of Ajmer and Jodhpur; and until his arrival, the minister, Khwájah Abdul Hamid Khán, was ordered to administer the province.

Prince Muhammad, 40th Viceroy, 1703-1705.

On his way to A'hmadábád from the Deccan, the chief of Jhábuá, a state now under the Bhopáwar agency, paid his respects to the new viceroy, presenting him with a tribute of 1,600*l.* (Rs. 16,000). Among other arrangements the prince sent Jáfar Kuli, son of Kázam Beg, as deputy governor to Jodhpur, and appointed Dargadás Ráthod governor of Pátan. Shortly after this an order came from the emperor to decoy Dargadás to the prince's court, and there confine him, or else slay him wherever they could. Safdár Khán Bábi, who, in displeasure with Shujáat Khán, had retired to Málwá, now returned and offered to slay or capture Dargadás, who was accordingly invited to attend the prince's court. Dargadás came and pitched his camp near the capital, when suddenly discovering that treachery was contemplated, he burned his tents and fled. Safdar Khán Bábi was sent in pursuit, and, in spite of Dargadás' efforts, the imperial forces were gaining on him. Seeing this his grandson, who was with him, begged Dargadás to make good his escape, and himself staying behind with a band of his followers, charged the pursuers, and after a most gallant combat he and his Rájputs were slain. Meanwhile Dargadás had reached Unjah-Unáwá, and from there made his way to Pátan. Here, taking his family with him, he retired to Tharád, and from that proceeded to Márwár, where he was afterwards joined by Ajitsingh of Márwár, whom the emperor opposed on

Intrigue against Dargadás Ráthod, 1703.

Dargadás Ráthod escapes.

Chapter III. Moghal Viceroys.

the ground of illegitimacy. The imperial troops followed and took possession of Pátan, putting to death the head of the city police.

State of affairs in Surat, 1700-1703.

About this time news arrived that the Maráthás were threatening Surat, and the prince despatched a body of troops to guard that city against their incursions. Disputes between the government and the Portuguese were also, at this time, injuring the trade of the province. In A.D. 1703, at the request of the merchants of Gujarát, with the view of inducing the Portuguese to let ships from Surat pass unmolested, orders were issued that certain confiscated Portuguese merchandise should be restored to its owners. In A.D. 1704, Safdar Khán Bábi was raised to be governor of Bijápur, a district lying to the north of A'hmadábád, now under His Highness the Gáekwár. Sarandáz Khán was at the same time appointed to Sorath in place of Muhammad Beg Khán, who was placed in charge of the lands round A'hmadábád. The Maráthás again this year threatened Surat, and Mustafa Kuli, governor of Broach, was sent with 1,000 horsemen to defend that city.

Ibrahim Khan, 41st Viceroy, 1705.

In A.D. 1705, as the climate of Gujarát did not agree with the prince, Ibráhim Khán, viceroy of Káshmir, was appointed forty-first viceroy of Gujarát, and his son Zabardast Khán, viceroy of Láhor, was appointed to the government of A'jmer and Jodhpur. The prince at once went to Burhánpur in Khándesh, handing over charge of Gujarát to the minister, Abdul Hamid Khán, until the new viceroy should arrive. Dargadás Ráthod now asked for and received pardon. Abdul Hamid Khán was ordered to restore the lands formerly granted to Dargadás, and he was directed to act under Abdul Hamid's orders.

The Maráthás enter Gujarát.

About this time (A.D. 1705) the Maráthás, who had long been hovering on the frontiers of the province, bursting into Southern Gujarát with an army 15,000 strong, defeated the local forces and laid the country waste. Abdul Hamid Khán, on hearing of this invasion, ordered all governors of districts and officers in charge of posts to collect their men and advance to Surat. Between Nazar A'li Khán and Safdar Khán Bábi, the officers in command of this army, an unfortunate jealousy existed. Not knowing where the Maráthás were to be found, they halted on the Narbadá near the Bábá Piáráh ford. Here they remained for a month and a half, the leaders contenting themselves with sending out spies to search for the enemy. At last, hearing of the approach of the Maráthás, they sent to head-quarters asking for artillery and other reinforcements. In reply, Abdul Hamid Khán, a man of hasty temper, upbraided them for their inactivity and for allowing so much time to pass without making their way to Surat. Orders were, accordingly, at once issued for an advance, and the army next halted at Ratanpur in Rájpiplá. Here, apparently from the jealousy of the commanders, the different chiefs pitched their camps at some distance from each other. Finding the enemy's forces thus scattered, the Maráthás, under the command of Dhaná Jáda, lost no time in advancing against them. First attacking the camp of Safdar Khán Bábi, they defeated his troops, killed his son, and took prisoner the chief himself. Only a few of his men, with his nephew Muhammad A'zam, escaped to the camp of Nazar A'li Khán. Next, the Maráthás attacked the army under Muhammad Pardil Sheráni; and it also they defeated. Of the Musalmán army, those who were not slain, drowned in the Narbadá, or captured, reached Broach in miserable plight, where they were well treated by Akbar A'li Khán. Nazar A'li Khán burned his tents and fled to Broach without fighting.

Battle of Ratanpur; defeat of the Musalmáns, 1705.

The Maráthás now heard that Abdul Hamid Khán, then in charge of the province, was coming with an army to oppose them; but thinking he would not risk a battle, they went to the Bábá Piáráh ford, and there crossed the Narbadá. That very day Abdul Hamid Khán, with Muhammad Sher and Muhammad Salábat, sons of Safdar Khán Bábi, and others came to the spot where the Maráthás were encamped. All night long they were harassed by the Maráthás, and next morning found the enemy prepared for a general attack. The Muhammadans, weary with watching, dispirited from the defeats of Safdar Khán, and inferior in number to their assailants, were repulsed and surrounded. The two sons of Safdar Khán Bábi, and two other nobles, seeing that the day was lost, cut their way through the enemy and escaped, though not without difficulty. Abdul Hamid Khán, Nazar A'li Khán, and many others were taken prisoners. The Maráthás now plundered the Muhammadan camp, declared that they had a right to tribute, and extorted heavy ransoms from their prisoners. The Kolis, seeing the disorganized state of Gujarát, also commenced ravaging the country, and actually plundered

Battle of the Bábá Piáráh ford; second defeat of the Musalmáns, 1705.

Koli disturbances.

Chapter III.
Moghal Viceroys.

Baroda for two days. At A'hmadábád Muhammad Beg Khán, who had been appointed Koli governor of Sorath, was recalled to defend the capital, and when the news of the defeat reached Delhi, the emperor despatched prince Muhammad Bedar Bakht with a large army to drive out the invaders. But before this force reached Gujarát the Maráthás had already retired to their own country.

PRINCE MUHAMMAD BEDAR BAKHT, 42nd Viceroy, 1705-1706.

The prince arrived in A.D. 1705 as forty-second viceroy, and appointed Amánat Khán governor of the ports of Surat and Cambay. News was now received that Ajitsingh of Jodhpur and Verisálji of Rájpiplá were about to rebel, and the prince took measures to check them. About this time the emperor, hearing that an attack had been made on the Muhammadan post at Dwárká, ordered the temple there to be levelled to the ground; but it seems doubtful whether this order was actually carried out. Nazar A'li Khán, who had formerly enjoyed a grant of Halwad in Jháláwár, had been driven out by Chandrasingh, chief of Wánkáner; but on condition of his expelling Chandrasingh, these lands were again granted to him. Dargadás Ráthoḍ now took advantage of the general confusion to rejoin Ajitsingh, and an army was sent to Tharád against them. Ajitsingh, at first forced to retire, finally succeeded in defeating Kunwar Mokamsingh, and then marching on Jodhpur recovered possession of it from Jáfar Kuli, son of Kázam Beg. Dargadás meanwhile had taken shelter with the Kolis. At the head of a band of robbers of this class, meeting Shah Kuli, the son of Kásam Beg, on his way to join his appointment as deputy governor of Pátan, he attacked and killed him; and soon afterwards, at Chaniár in the Chunwál, laying in wait for Másum Kuli, the governor of Viramgám, he routed his escort, Másum Kuli escaping with difficulty. Safdar Khán Bábi now offered, on condition of his being appointed governor of Pátan, to kill or capture Dargadás. His offer was accepted, and as from this time Dargadás is no more heard of, it seems probable that Safdár Khán succeeded in killing him. In consequence of the disturbed state of the province a change of government seemed necessary, and Ibráhim Khán, who had been appointed viceroy in the previous year, was now ordered to join his post; this order he reluctantly obeyed in A.D. 1706.

Dargadás Ráthod again in rebellion.

IBRA'HIM KHA'N, 43rd Viceroy, 1706.

SECTION II.—FIFTY YEARS OF DISORDER, 1707-1757.

Chapter III.

Moghal Viceroys.

Death of the emperor Aurangzeb, 1707.

Shortly before this, early in A.D. 1707, the emperor Aurangzeb died, and with his death the period of strong government, which had latterly from year to year been growing weaker, came to an end. As soon as the news of Aurangzeb's death became known, the Maráthás under Báláji Vishwánáth entered Gujarát, marching by Jhábuá and Godhrá, where they were ineffectually opposed by the governor, Morád Baksh. Thence they went to Mundá, and proposed marching on A'hmadábád by way of Nadiád. The viceroy made preparations to resist them, and, enlisting special troops, camped outside of the city near the Kánkarya lake. The Maráthás did much mischief, plundering even as far as Bátwá, only four-and-a-half miles from the viceroy's camp. The viceroy, now thoroughly alarmed, concluded a treaty with Báláji, and on receiving a tribute of 21,000*l*. (Rs. 2,10,000) the Maráthás withdrew. Meanwhile, in the contest between the princes for the throne of Delhi, prince Muhammad A'zam Sháh was defeated and slain, and prince Muhammad Muazzam Sháh mounted the throne with the title of Bahádur Sháh. Ibráhim Khán was confirmed in the post of viceroy of Gujarát, but, fearing that the emperor might be displeased at his concession of tribute to the Maráthás, he went to Delhi to explain his conduct, and there resigned office.

The Maráthá advance to A'hmadábád and levy tribute, 1707.

Bahádur Sháh, emperor, 1708-1712.

GHA'ZI'-UDDIN, 44th Viceroy, 1708-1710.

In consequence of Ibráhim Khan's resignation, in A.D. 1708, Gház-i-ud-din Khán Bahádur Firoz Jang was appointed forty-fourth viceroy of Gujarát. In A.D. 1709, Shariat Khán, brother of Abdul Hamid Khán, was appointed minister in place of his brother, who obtained the office of chief Kázi. The viceroy, in A.D. 1710, when on tour exacting tribute, fell ill at Dántá and was brought to A'hmadábád, where he died. As this viceroy had not submitted satisfactory accounts, his property was confiscated; and Amánat Khán, governor of Surat, was appointed deputy viceroy in A.D. 1711 by the title of Sháhámat Khán. When Sháhámat Khán was levying tribute from the Kadi and Bijápur districts, he heard that a Maráthá force had advanced to the Bábá Piárah ford on the Narbadá. He at once marched to oppose them, summoning Syad A'hmad Gilání, governor of Sorath, to his assistance. When he reached Ankleshwar, the Maráthás met him, and a battle was fought in which the Maráthás were

Maráthá invasion, 1711.

Battle of Ankleshwar; defeat of the Maráthás, 1711.

Chapter III. Moghal Viceroys.

defeated. Sháhámat Khán then proceeded to Surat, and, after providing for its safety, returned to A'hmadábád.

Jaha'nda'r Sha'h, Emperor, 1712-1713. ASAF-UD-DAULA, 45th Viceroy, 1712-1713.

In A.D. 1712, the emperor died, and was succeeded by his son Abul Fateh Maghr-ud-din Jahándár Sháh, and Asaf-ud-daula Asad Khán Bahádur was appointed forty-fifth viceroy of Gujarát. As Muhammad Beg Khán, who was then at Kharkol, was a favourite of the new viceroy, he was through the viceroy's interest appointed his deputy. He accordingly went to A'hmadábád, and Sháhámat Khán was transferred to Málwá as viceroy. In the meantime Muhammad Beg Khán was appointed governor of Surat, and Sarbuland Khán Bahádur was sent to A'hmadábád as deputy viceroy. As Sarbuland Khán was coming to Gujarát, he was robbed in the Ságwárá district, now under Rájpiplá. On his arrival he promptly marched against the rebellious Kolis of the Chunwál and subdued them. At the end of the year, as Farukhsher, son of Azim-us-Shán, second son of the late emperor, was marching with a large army on the capital, Sarbuland Khán returned to Delhi.

Farukhsher, Emperor, 1713-1719.

This expedition of Farukhsher's was successful, and, putting Jahándár Sháh to death, he mounted the throne in A.D. 1713. This prince, who had been elevated to the throne principally through the aid of syads Husain A'li and Abdullah Khán, fell under the power of these nobles. Husain A'li was sent against Ajitsingh of Márwár, and concluded a treaty with that chief, whereby he engaged to send his son to court and give his daughter to the emperor in marriage: and the marriage was solemnized in A.D. 1715. In A.D. 1714, shortly after this treaty was concluded, A'jitsingh sent his son Abhyesingh to court, and on him was conferred the post of governor of Sorath in place of Syad A'hmad Gilání. He, however, remaining at court, sent to Junágarh his deputy, Káyat Fatehsingh. Before this, in A.D. 1713, Sháhámat Khán was appointed forty-sixth viceroy of Gujarát, but was, early in A.D. 1714, superseded by Dáud Khán Panni as forty-seventh viceroy. During this year, on the security of rájá Mokamsingh of Nágor, a sum of 5,000*l.* (Rs. 50,000) was granted to the brother of Dargadás Ráthod. In this year there was a great conflict between the Maslim and Hindu population of A'hmadábád, and many of the banker's houses were sacked, and about the same time there was also a great flood in the Sábarmati. Abdul Hamid Khán was

SHA'HA'MAT KHA'N, 46th Viceroy, 1713.

DA'UD KHA'N PANNI, 47th Viceroy, 1714-1715.

Religious riots in A'hmadábád, 1714.

now chosen governor of Sorath in place of Abhyesingh, and Momin Khán was appointed from Delhi, governor of Surat, and was at the same time placed in charge of Baroda, Broach, Dholká, Pitlád and Nadiád. Dáud Khán, the viceroy, now went into Káthiáwár and Nawánagar to collect tribute, and on his return to A'hmadábád, married the daughter[1] of the chief of Halwad in the Jháláwár subdivision of the Káthiáwár peninsula.

About this time Momin Khán, governor of Surat, arrived in Gujarát, and placing his deputies in Pitlád, Dholká, Baroda, and Nadiád, went himself to Surat in A.D. 1715. Here he was opposed by the commandant of the fort, Ziá Khán, who, however, was obliged to give way, his subordinate, Syad Kásam, being defeated by Fidá-ud-din Khán.

Further riots in A'hmadábád, 1715.

At this time some of the shops of Hindu merchants in A'hmadábád were again plundered by the Muhammadan troops, and much ill-blood arose. On this account, and for other reasons, the viceroy was recalled, and Ghazni Khán Jhálori was directed to act in his place until the arrival of a new viceroy.

MA'HA'RA'JA' AJITSINGH, 48th Viceroy, 1715-1716.

In this year, A.D. 1715, the máhárájá Ajitsingh was appointed forty-eighth viceroy of Gujarát, and his son, Kunwar Abhyesingh, was appointed governor of Sorath. Ajitsingh sent Wajeráj Bhandári to act as his deputy until his arrival, and Fatehsingh Káyat was chosen deputy governor of Sorath.

Haidar Kuli Khán, governor of Surat and Cambay.

Perhaps one of the most remarkable appointments of this time was that of Haidar Kuli Khán as minister of Baroda, Nándod the capital of the Rajpipla State, Arhar Mátar,[2] as well as of the ports of minis- Surat and Cambay. He chose an officer to act for him as ter, and after appointing deputies in his different charges himself went to Surat.

The máhárájá Ajitsingh, on reaching A'hmadábád, appointed Ghazni Khán Jhálori to be the governor of Pálanpur Dántiwárá, and Jawán Mard Khán Bábi to be governor of Rádhanpur. During this year an imperial order was received conferring on Haidar Kuli Khán, Sorath and Gohelwár,[3] then in the charge of Fatehsingh, the

---

1 Probably Jaswantsinghji's daughter.

2 Arhar Mátar now belongs to His Highness the Gáekwár.

3 This is the first mention of Gohelwár as the name of a separate district in any written history. Gohelwár is the south-eastern portion of the province of Káthiáwár, and is so called as comprising the possessions of the Gohels, a tribe of Rajputs.

Chapter III.

Moghal Viceroys.

viceroy's deputy. On receiving this order Haidar sent syad Akil as his deputy, and that officer went to Jámbusar, and, collecting men, set out to join his appointment. He first came and camped at Loliánáh, where the province of Sorath begins. Syad Akil thence marched his men against Pálitáná, and plundered the town. The viceroy, who was by no means well disposed towards Haidar Kuli Khán, sent a threatening message, that if any injury was done in Sorath he would take vengeance on the aggressors; and as neither Ajitsingh nor Haidar Kuli Khán was of a very compliant temper, civil war was on the point of breaking out. By the help of Salábat Khán Bábi, the deputy in Gohelwár, matters were, however, arranged, and syad Akil returned from Sorath. Haidar was anxious to send Salábat Khán as deputy to Sorath. But as he demanded too high a salary, Rozá Kuli, brother of the late governor of Baroda, was chosen. When this officer, with his brother Másum Kuli, reached Amreli, Fatehsingh, the viceroy's deputy, evacuated Junágarh. After this Haidar Kuli Khán, in company with Kázam Beg, governor of Baroda, marched against and defeated the chief of Munjpur, now under Rádhanpur, who had refused to pay the usual tribute The viceroy went to Sorath to collect the imperial revenue and, owing to his excessive demands, met with armed resistance from the jám of Nawánagar. Finally, however, the matter of the tribute was settled, and the viceroy, after paying a visit to the shrine of Dwárká, returned to A'hmadábád.

Disagreement between the viceroy and Haider Kuli Khán, 1715.

BASA'RAT JANG BAHADUR, 49th Viceroy, 1716-1719.

While the viceroy was at Dwárká, the emperor, in consequence of numerous complaints against him and his Márwári followers, in A.D. 1716 sent Samsám-ud-daula Basárat Jang Báhádur as forty-ninth viceroy of Gujarát. As it was expected that Ajitsingh would not give up his government without a contest, an army was prepared to compel him to leave. On hearing of this he marched straight on A'hmadábád, and encamped at Sarkhej, but was persuaded by Nahar Khán to retire to Jodhpur without giving battle. In A.D. 1717, after the departure of Ajitsingh, Haidar Kuli Khán, who had been appointed deputy viceroy, leaving Surat set out for A'hmadábád. When he arrived at Pitlád, some of the A'hmadábád nobles, among whom was Safdar Khán Bábi, went out to meet him. A dispute arose between one of Haidar's officers and a water-carrier in the army of the Bábi, which increased to a serious affray, and the baggage of the Bábi was plundered. Safdar Khán took serious offence

Contest between Háidar Kuli Khán and the Bábis, 1717.

Year of famine, 1718.

at this, and returning to A'hmadábád collected his kinsmen and followers and marched against Haidar Kuli Khán. Next day a battle was fought, in which Safdar Khán was defeated. The other Bábis escaped to Pálanpur, and Safdar Khán, who in the first instance had fled to Átar Sumba, afterwards joined his party at Pálanpur. Mahummad Firoz Jhálori, governor of Pálanpur, with the title of Ghazni Khán, afterwards succeeded in reconciling the Bábis and Háidar Kuli Khán. In A.D. 1718 there was a great famine in Gujarát. Abdul Hamid Khán, a noble of the Delhi court, at this time went to Gujarát and obtained the appointment of governor of Sorath. Háidar Kuli Khán now marched against the Kolis, who lived on the banks of the Mahi. In the meantime news was received of the appointment of a new viceroy, and Ghazni Khán, governor of Pálanpur, was ordered to stay at A'hmadábád for the defence of the city.

Death of the emperor Farukhsher, 1719.

Early in A.D. 1719, the emperor Farukhsher was deposed, and put to death by the syads; and a prince named Rafia-ud-Darját, a grandson of the emperor, was raised to the imperial throne. He was put to death by the syads after a reign of three months, and his brother, Rafia-ud-daulah, who succeeded him, also died after a few days'[1] reign; and then the syads elevated to the throne prince Roshan Akhtar by the title of Muhammad Sháh. After the murder of Farukhsher, the most powerful vassal in the neighbourhood of Delhi was Ajitsingh of Márwár, and, accordingly, to enlist him on their side, the syads granted him the viceroyalty of Gujarát, and Mihr A'li Khán was appointed to act for him until his arrival, while Muhammad Bahádur Bábi, son of Salábat Muhammad Khán Bábi, was placed in charge of the police of the district immediately round A'hmadábád. Shortly afterwards, through the influence of the máhárájá Ajitsingh, Nahár Khán superseded Mihr A'li Khán as deputy viceroy. He was also appointed to the charge of Dholká, Dohad, and Pitlád, and made superintendent of the customs. About this time the capitation tax was repealed, and orders were issued that it should cease to be levied in Gujarát.

Muhammad Sha'h, Emperor, **1721-1748.**

MA'HA'RA'JA' AJITSINGH, 50th Viceroy, 1719-1721.

Piláji Gáekwár established at Songad, 1719.

In this year Piláji Gáekwár marched on Surat with a large army, and defeated the imperial troops commanded by Syad Akil and Muhammad Panah, the latter commander being taken prisoner and forced to pay a heavy ransom. Piláji, now finding Gujarát an easy prey, made frequent in-

Chapter III. Moghal Viceroys.

cursions, and conquering Songarh established himself there. In this year Mihr A'li Khán, who had been acting for Nahar Khán, marched against and subdued the Kolis, who were committing piracy in the Mahi estuary. From this year it may be said that the rule of the Moghal emperors in Gujarát was finally doomed. Piláji Gáekwár was established at Songarh, and in the anarchy that ensued, the great Gujarát Houses of Bábis and Jháloris, as well as the newly arrived Momin Khán, turned their thoughts to gain independence, or usurp supreme power. Ajitsingh was imbued with a hatred to the Muhammadan rule, and secretly favoured the Maráthás while he was himself anxious to establish his own authority, if not over all Gujarát at least over such portions as bordered on his own territory of Márwár. And though in after years, under Sarbuland Khán, a vigorous attempt was made to reassert the imperial dominion, the final seeds of dissolution were already sown, and all efforts at recovery were vain.

Decay of imperial power, 1720.

In A.D. 1720, Ajitsingh the viceroy sent Anopsingh Bhandári to Gujarát as his deputy, and many changes were made. In this year the viceroy of Ujain, Nizám-ul-Mulk, was superseded by syad Diláwar Khán. The nizám retired to Burhánpur, whither Syad Diláwar Khán was ordered to pursue him. A battle ensued, in which the syad was killed, and the nizám retired to Aurangábád in the Deccan. A'lam A'li Khán, viceroy of the Deccan, was directed to march against him, while from Gujarát Anopsingh Bhandári was ordered to send 10,000 horse to Surat, and Nahar Khán, the deputy-viceroy, was instructed to proceed thither in person. A battle was fought between the nizám and A'lam A'li, in which the latter was killed. At this time Anopsingh Bhandári committed many oppressive acts, foremost amongst which was the murder of Kapurchand Bhansáli, the chief merchant of A'hmadábád. In A.D. 1721 Nizám-ul-Mulk was appointed prime minister of the empire. About this time Abdul Hamid Khán was recalled from Sorath, and Asad Kuli Khán, with the title of A'mir-ul-Umrao, was appointed governor of Sorath in his place. Asád Kuli Khán did not, however, proceed to his charge, but sent Muhammad Sharif Khán into Sorath as his deputy.

Nizám-ul-Mulk, Prime-minister of the Empire, 1721.

HAIDAR KULI KHA'N, 51st Viceroy, 1721-1722.

In this year Haidar Kuli Khán had, in conjunction with Muhammad A'min and Sáadat Khán, freed the emperor from the tyranny of the syads, and was rewarded by the title of Moiz-ud-daulah Haidar Kuli Khán Bahádur Zafar Jang and the viceroyalty of Gujarát. He obtained the appointment of minister for his brother Jaafar Kuli Khán. Másum Kuli Khán was dignified by the title of Shuját Khán Bahádur and appointed deputy viceroy. As soon as this change was notified, the people of A'hmadábád, who were discontented with the rule of Anopsingh, attacked his palace, the Bhadar, and he escaped with difficulty with his life. There had always been enmity between Haidar Kuli Khán and the Márwáris, and Shuját Khán, the deputy viceroy, attacked the house of Nahar Khán who had been Ajitsingh's minister. Nahar Khán was, however, permitted to leave the city on paying a sum of 10,000*l.* (Rs. 1,00,000). After this Shuját Khán ventured to interfere with the lands of Safdar Khán Bábi, the deputy governor of Godhrá, and his brothers. But on one of them repairing to Delhi and remonstrating, Haidar Kuli, who, above all things, was a Muhammadan and anxious to strengthen himself with the Muhammadan nobility of Gujarát, restored their lands to the Bábis. In consequence of this decision ill-feeling sprung up between Shuját Khán and the Bábis, and when the former went to exact tribute he was opposed by Muhammad Khán Bábi, governor of Kaira, who, however, was obliged to pay him 1,000*l.* (Rs. 10,000). Shortly afterwards one of the viceroy's officers, Kásam A'li Khán, while employed against the Kolis of that part of the country, was killed at Pithápur. Against this place Shuját Khán advanced, and revenged Kásam A'li's death by burning the town. Next, he passed into Sorath, and, after exacting tribute, crossed over to Cutch. Here the chief opposed him, and a battle was fought, the result of which was that the chief was beaten and agreed to pay a tribute of about 22,500*l.*[1] In A.D. 1721, a syad was sent to Sorath as deputy governor in place of Muhammad Sharif, and Haidar Kuli was appointed governor of Kaḍi, the Chunwál and Halwad (called Muhammadnagar) and put in charge of Tharád, Arjanpur, Bhámnárli, Pithápur and Kherálu in place of Wakhatsingh, son of the máhárájá Ajitsingh.

Disorder in A'hmadábád, 1721.

Haidar Kuli Khán leaves

Early in A.D. 1722 Nizám-ul-Mulk took up the office of prime-minister of the empire, to which he had been appoint-

1 The sum is 675,000 *mahmudis.* Like the *changzi* (see above, p. 64) the *mahmudi* would seem to have varied in value from one-third to two-thirds of a rupee.

Chapter III. Moghal Viceroys. Delhi for Gujarát, 1722.

ed the year previously, and strenuous efforts were made to embroil him with Haidar Kuli Khán; as the nizám's austerity and craft were a source of not less anxiety to the Delhi court than Haidar Kuli's more daring and restless ambition. Haidar Kuli Khán, unable to contend with the nizám leaving Delhi, retired to his command in Gujarát. About this time, amongst other changes, Muhammad Bahádur, son of Salábat Khán Bábi, was placed in charge of Sádrá and Virpur, with the title of Sher Khán. The viceroy shortly after his arrival, marched against and subdued the rebellious Kolis of the Chunwál, appointing Rustám A'li Khán his governor there; and then, returning to A'hmadábád, took up his sidence in the Bhadar. There is little doubt, but that Haidar Kuli at this time desired to become independent and to bring all Gujarát under his rule. Marching to collect tribute from the chiefs in the Dungarpur direction, he levied 8,000*l.* (Rs. 80,000) from the state of Lunáwárá; but through the mediation of the Udyapur ráná the ráwal of Dungarpur escaped. He next proceeded to Bijápur, north of A'hmadábád; but hearing that the emperor was displeased at his assumption of the power of giving and changing grants of land, he returned to A'hmadábád and restored several estates which he had confiscated. The court, however, continued to distrust him, and at the close of A.D. 1722 appointed Jumlat-ul-Muluk Nizám-ul-Mulk fifty-second viceroy.

Shows sign of independence and is recalled, 1722.

NIZA'M-UL-MULK, 52nd Viceroy, 1722.

Haidar Kuli Khán was very indignant, but, finding himself no match for the nizám, he was induced by his friends to retire quietly, and accordingly left Gujarát by way of Dungarpur. Shuját Khán and Rustam Ali Khán accompanied him as far as Dungarpur, and then returned to A'hmadábád. In the meantime the nizám had reached Ujain, and thence directed Safdar Khán Bábi to carry on the government till he should arrive, appointing at the same time Hámid Khán his minister. Subsequently the nizám came to Gujarát and selected officers of his own for places of trust, amongst whom it is here necessary to notice Momin Khán, who was appointed governor of Surat. He then returned to Delhi, but after a short time, disgusted with his treatment at court, he retired to the Deccan, where, making Háidárábád his capital, he began gradually to act as an independent ruler. Meanwhile in Gujarát, dissensions sprung up between Hámid Khán and other officers, but matters were arranged without any actual outbreak of hostility. Tribute was exacted from the chiefs on the banks of the Wátrak and from Modheyrá

Hámid Khán deputy-viceroy; Momin Khán governor of Surat, 1722.

and an insubordinate Koli village was burned down, and garrisons placed in the Koli country. In A.D. 1723, Rustam Ali Khán and Shuját Khán were ordered from Delhi to march upon Jodhpur, which place they captured and plundered, and then returned to A'hmadábád.

Increase of the Maráthá power, 1723.

In this year Piláji Gáekwár, who had been long hovering on the frontier, marched upon Surat and was opposed by Momin Khán, whom he defeated. After levying contributions from the surrounding country, he returned to his old head-quarters at Songarh, and from this overran a considerable portion of the Surat territory, building at the same time several forts in the Rájpiplá country. Kantáji Kadam Bánde, too, invading Gujarát from the side of Dohad, commenced to levy fixed contributions. Though occasional demands had before this often been made, it was in A.D. 1723, for the first time, that the Maráthás imposed a regular tribute on Gujarát. Momin Khán was now appointed minister, and as the nizám had gone to the Deccan without leave from the emperor, Mubáriz-ul-Mulk Sarbuland Khán Bahádur Diláwar Jang was appointed fifty-third viceroy of Gujarát. He selected Shuját Khán as his deputy, and made other arrangements for the government of the province. Hámid Khán, uncle and deputy of the nizám, prepared to oppose Shuját Khán, but through the intervention of Bábis Salábat Khán, Safdar Khán, and Jáwan Mard Khán, Hámid Khán evacuated the Bhaddar, and withdrew to Dohad. Shuját Khán now went to collect tribute, leaving Ibráhim Kuli at A'hmadábád, while Rámrái was posted at Mahudhá in Kaira, with strict injunctions to watch the movements of Hámid Khá n. As the viceroy was in need of money, he farmed to one Jivan Jugal the districts of Jambusar, Makbulábád, Dholká, and Broach; and after this, in A.D. 1724, he came in person to A'hmadábád with A'li Muhammad Khán, father of the author of the Mirat-i-A'hmadi, as his private minister.

SARBULAND KHA'N, 53rd Viceroy, 1723-1730.

Shuját Khán his deputy.

Contest between Nizám-ul-Mulk and Sárbuland Khan.

Rustam A'li, governor of Surat, having succeeded twice or thrice in defeating the Maráthás under Piláji Gáekwár, now offered, in conjuction with his brother Shuját Khán, that if 20,000 men were placed under their orders, they would march against the nizám. The emperor accepted this offer, allowing Rustam A'li to draw on the Surat Treasury to the extent of 20,000*l.* (Rs. 2,00,000). He accordingly, with the aid of A'hmad Kuli, his brother's son, equipped an army. In the meantime the nizám was not idle. He

Chapter III. Moghal Viceroys.

promised to Kantáji Kadam Bánde a one-fourth share of the revenue of Gujarát, provided he should be able, in concert with Hámid Khán, to reconquer the province from Mubáriz-ul-Mulk. Shuját Khán, who was now at Kaḍi, instead of following the advice of his minister and carefully watching Hámid Khán's movements from Kapaḍwanj, went to a distant part of the province. Hámid Khán, seeing his opportunity, united his forces with those of Kantáji Kadam, and marched to Kapaḍwanj. Shuját Khán, hearing of this, advanced towards A'hmadábád and encamped at Dabhorá, and thence proceeded to Mota Medrá, about six miles from the capital. When he came so near the city of A'hmadábád, many of his soldiers returned there, without leave, to visit their families, and at this time the Maráthás attacked his rear guard, and his men, giving way, took to flight. Hámid Khán, seeing that Shuját Khán had but a small force with him, marched between him and the capital. A battle was fought, in which Shuját Khán was slain, and his two sons, Hasan Kuli and Mustafa Kuli, were taken prisoners. Shuját Khán's head was cut off and sent to Safdar Khán Bábi, to be sent to Ibráhim Kuli, his son, commandant at A'hmadábád. Hámid Khán took up his quarters in the Sháhi Bágh, and got possession of all the country round A'hmadábád, except the city. Hámid Khán now sent a message to the emperor, that the Maráthás had been successful in defeating Shuját Khán and conquering Gujarát, but that he had defended A'hmadábád against them. The emperor, on this, sent him a dress of honour, but after a few days the falsity of his message became known. The Maráthás now marched through the country collecting their one-fourth[1] and one-tenth shares of the revenue. Kantáji first went to Viramgám and besieged the town, but on the promise of one of the chief inhabitants to raise a sum of 35,000*l.* (Rs. 3,50,000) the Maráthás retired. Hámid Khán, who had now rendered himself independent, commenced to bestow lands and districts; and many of the grants made at this time remained in the hands of the grantees, and were never recovered by future governors. Ibráhim Kuli, son of Shuját Khán, in revenge for his father's death, determined to assassinate Hámid Khán. The attempt, however,

Sarbuland Khán's deputy defeated, 1724.

Hámid Khán, the nizám's deputy, practically independent.

---

[1] The one-fourth share was called the *chauth*, and the one-tenth the *sardeshmukhi*.

failed: Hámid Khán escaped, and Ibráhim Kuli himself was slain.

The Maráthás engaged as allies on both sides.

Rustam A'li Khán, governor of Surat, was now anxious to be revenged on Hámid Khán, and therefore invited the aid of Piláji Gáekwár, and it was agreed that they should meet on the north bank of the Narbadá. Piláji promised to aid Rustam Khán, and the allied armies, crossing the Mahi, encamped at Arás.[1] Hearing of this, Hámid Khán, accompanied by Mir Nathu, Muhammad Salábat Rohilla, and Kantáji Kadam, marched to oppose Rustam Khán. Hámid Khán also entered into secret negotiations with Piláji Gáekwár, who resolved to remain neutral and side with the conqueror. A battle was fought, in which Piláji took no part, but Hámid Khán was defeated and put to flight, and Mir Nathu was killed. After the fight was over Rustam A'li remained on the field of battle and liberated his nephews, plundering Hámid Khán's camp. In the meantime, Piláji plundered Rustam A'li's camp and then moved off, while Kantáji carried away what was left in the camp of Hámid Khán. Hámid Khán reproached Kantáji for his inactivity; but he pleaded in excuse that he was watching the mode of warfare amongst Muhammadans, and promised to attack Rustam A'li shortly. Now, as the Maráthás really desired to ruin Rustam A'li, who was their bitter foe, they after a few days surrounded him and cut off his supplies; Rustam A'li stood a blockade of eight days, and then forced his way through his enemies and went to Nápáḍ[2] in Cambay, marching from that to near Kalamsar, and thence to Nápá Pitláḍ. The Maráthás still pursuing him, he retired to Wasu, about 25 miles from A'hmadábád, where he gave battle, and by a furious charge broke the Maráthá array; they however rallied, and finally Rustam Khán and his men were defeated, and Rustam Khán himself slain. He was buried on the field of battle, and his head was sent to A'hmadábád, and his nephews were again taken prisoners.

Battle of Arás; Hámid Khán defeated by Rustam A'li, 1723.

Maráthás join Hámid Khán against Rustam A'li.

Battle of Basu; defeat and death of Rustam A'li.

Hámid Khán shares the revenue with the Maratha chiefs, 1724.

Hámid Khán returned to A'hmadábád with the Maráthás, who saw that their only means of effecting a permanent footing in the province was by supporting him. Hámid Khán then assigned a one-fourth share of the revenue of the territory north of the Mahi to Kantáji, and to Piláji a cor-

---

[1] Arás, in the Anand sub-division of the British district of Kaira.

[2] Nápád is now under the British district of Kaira.

Chapter III.

Moghal Viceroys.

responding interest in the territory south of the Mahi, including Surat and Baroda. After this Hámid Khán acted tyrannically, and commenced to extort large sums from rich persons, and he poisoned the two sons of Shujāt Khán. When the news of the success of Kantáji and Piláji reached the Deccan, Trimbakráv Dhábáre, son of Khanderáv Senápati, came with a large army and laid siege to Cambay, but the Maráthás were forced to retire. At this time Salábat Khán, leaving A'hmadábád, went to Viramgám, and after some time, placing his nephew at Viramgám, he went into Gohelwár. When the news of the defeat and death of Rustam A'li reached Delhi, the emperor ordered Mubáriz-ul-Mulk to take a strong army and proceed in person to Gujarát and expel Hámid Khán and the Maráthás. Mubáriz-ul-Mulk accordingly marched on Gujarát with a large army, assisted by máháráját Abhyesingh of Jodhpur, Chatarsingh rájá of Narur, Gandrapsingh, and the máháráná of Udyapur. On his arrival at A'jmer he was received by his private minister. A'li Muhammad Khán, who afterwards joining Jawán Mard Khán Bábi in Rádhanpur, they together marched and united their troops with those under Mubáriz-ul-Mulk. At that time Salábat Khán was removed from his government, and Safdar Khán Bábi died. Agreeably to the imperial order, Mubáriz-ul-Mulk marched from A'jmer and came to the Gujarát frontier. On his approach Hámid Khán returned to A'hmadábád, and, placing Rupsingh and Sardár Muhammad Ghorni in charge of the city, he himself withdrew to Mahmudábád. Mubáriz-ul-Mulk now sent Shekh Aliyár in advance with an army against A'hmadábád. When Shekh Aliyár arrived before the city, Muhammad Ghorni, who was dissatisfied with Hámid Khán for bringing in the Maráthás, persuaded Rupsingh to fly. In the meantime Mubáriz-ul-Mulk with the main body of his forces reached Sidhpur. Hámid Khán, accompanied by a detachment of Maráthá horse, now returned to A'hmadábád; but Muhammad Ghorni closed the gates, and would not suffer him to enter the city. Mubáriz-ul-Mulk now marched to Mesáná. About this time, A'li Muhammad Khán, the father of the author of the Mirat-i-A'hmadi, who was now with Mubáriz-ul-Mulk at Mesáná, advised him to conciliate the influential Muhammadan family of Bábi; and, accordingly, by his advice, Salábat Muhammad Khán Bábi was appointed governor of Viramgám, and Jawán Mard Khán governor of Pátan. Shortly afterwards Morlidhardás, the Gujaráti minister of Hámid Khán, seeing his

Mubáriz-ul-Mulk sent against the Maráthás, 1725.

Hámid Khán and other Maráthás retire.

master's cause declining, deserted him. When Kantáji heard that Mubáriz-ul-Mulk had arrived at Pithápur, only eighteen miles from A'hmadábád, he retired to Mahmudábád. Before the close of the year A.D. 1725, Mubáriz-ul-Mulk arrived at A'hmadábád, and was well received by the officials and merchants of the city. On this occasion he conferred on Momin Khán the title of Najam-ud-daulah.

Mubáriz-ul-Mulk enters A'hmadábád, 1725.

Hámid Khán and Kantáji, who had by this time reached the banks of the Mahi, were now joined by Piláji Gáekwár. The Maráthá leaders, seeing that their only way to preserve their footing in the province was to espouse the cause of Hámid Khán, they united their forces with his, and prepared to march on A'hmadábád. Mubáriz-ul-Mulk deputed his son Khánahzád Khán with an army to oppose them, and made several appointments, amongst other changes raising A'li Muhammad Khán to the post of minister. Khánahzád Khán met the Maráthás near Sojitrá, about ten miles to the north-west of Pitlád, and defeated them, pursuing them as far as the Mahi. Then returning, he was reinforced by his brother Sháh Nawáz Khán, and marched against the Maráthás, who were encamped at Kapadwanj. Another battle was fought, and the Maráthás were again defeated and pursued as far as the hills of A'li-Mohan. Khánahzád Khán now appointed Hasan-ud-din governor of Baroda, Broach, Jambusar, and Makbulábád. In the meantime Antáji Bháskar, a Maráthá noble, entering Gujarát from the side of Idar, laid siege to the town of Wadnagar. This town was inhabited by wealthy Bráhmans of the Nágar caste, who requested Mubáriz-ul-Mulk to help them and relieve the town; but as both his sons were at that time in pursuit of the other Maráthá bands defeated at Kapadwanj, the viceroy had no troops to spare from the A'hmadábád garrison. The Nágars accordingly, seeing no prospect of help, paid a sum of 40,000*l.* (Rs. 4,00,000). On receiving this tribute Antáji Bháskar retired. Kantáji and Piláji, encouraged by this raid of Antáji's, entered Gujarát from different quarters. Kantáji again laid siege to Wadnagar, but the Nágars this time were unable to pay the contribution demanded, and consequently escaped at night, leaving their property and house furniture behind them. Kantáji, entering, burned down the town, and the Nágars fled in all directions. Shortly afterwards Umreth, in the Kairá district, suffered a similar fate at the hands of Kantáji. In one of his raids Piláji Gáekwár advancing as far as Baroda was there met by Khánahzád Khán, the son of

Defeat of the Maráthás at Sojitrá and Kapadwanj, 1725.

Maráthá expedition against Wadnagar, 1725.

Chapter III.

Moghal Viceroys.

the viceroy. Distrusting the issue of a battle Piláji fled to Cambay, and from that withdrew to Sorath. For these services the emperor raised Khánahzád Khán to the rank of a noble, bestowing on him the title of Ghálib Jang. About this time several changes were made among the imperial officers in Gujarát. A'li Muhammad Khán was dismissed from the post of minister, and in his stead first Muhammad Sáid Beg and afterwards Muhammad Sulimán were appointed. Not long afterwards A'li Muhammad Khán was again entrusted with a command and raised to be governor of Dholká.

Mubárid-ul-Mulk a mits the Maráthá claim to tribute, 1726.

The Maráthás for a time retired to the Deccan, but returning in A.D. 1726, compelled Mubáriz-ul-Mulk to confirm his predecessor's grants in their favour. The emperor, however, refused to acknowledge any cessions of revenue to the Maráthás; and the viceroy, hard pressed for money, unable to obtain any support from court, and receiving but little help from his impoverished districts, was forced to impose fresh taxes on the citizens of A'hmadábád and, at the same time, send an army to collect their tribute from the chiefs on the banks of the Mahi. It was part of the agreement between Mubáriz-ul-Mulk and the Maráthá chiefs that Piláji should receive a share in the revenue of the districts south of the Mahi. But the Peshwá, Bájiráv Balál, to whom, as agent of his rival Khanderáv Dhábáre, Piláji was obnoxious, sent Udáji Puár to drive Piláji away. In this Udáji was successful, and defeating Piláji forced him to seek the aid of Kantáji. Kantáji, perceiving that if the Peshwá became supreme his own independence would suffer, joined Piláji, and marching together upon Baroda they endeavoured, but without success, to prevent the Musalmán governor, Sadr-ud-din Khán, from entering that city. Mubáriz-ul-Mulk, in straits for want of funds, was, about this time, forced to sell the greater part of the Dholká district to different landholders.

Rivalry between the peshwá and Piláji Gáekwár.

Alliance of the viceroy and the Peshwá, 1727.

In the following year, A.D. 1727, the Peshwá, Bájiráv, began to negotiate with Mubáriz-ul-Mulk, undertaking that if the one-fourth and one-tenth shares in the revenue of the province were guaranteed to him, he would protect Gujarát from other invaders. The viceroy, though he did not consent to these proposals, so far accepted the alliance of the Peshwá, as to allow the governor of Baroda to aid Udáji Puár against Piláji. Piláji and Kantáji, however, outmanœuvred Udáji and prevented him from effecting a junction with the governor of Baroda, who finally was forced

Chapter III.

Moghal Viceroys.

Piláji Gáekwár obtains Baroda and Dabhoi, 1727.

to abandon both that city and the stronghold of Dabhoi, while Udáji retired to Málwá. Piláji Gáekwár now obtained possession of Baroda. Mubáriz-ul-Mulk, still sorely pressed for funds, marched into Sorath to exact tribute from the chiefs. On reaching Viramgám, Salábat Muhammad Khán Bábi, on behalf of the jám of Nawánagar, presented the viceroy with a sum of 10,000*l.* (Rs. 1,00,000), and for this service was rewarded by the gift of an elephant. Mubáriz-ul-Mulk then marched against Chhayá, the capital of the chief of Porbandar in the west of Káthiáwár. This chief, by putting to sea, hoped to escape the payment of tribute. But on hearing that the viceroy proposed to annex his territory and appoint an officer to govern it, he returned and agreed to pay a tribute of about 4,000*l.*[1] On his way back to A'hmadábád, Mubáriz-ul-Mulk passed through Halwad in Jháláwár, and there married the daughter of Jhálá Pratápsingh, the chief of that district, whom he accordingly exempted from the payment of tribute. About this time the viceroy received orders from the emperor to restore certain land which he had confiscated, and as the viceroy neglected to obey, certain estates of his in the Panjáb were resumed. In the meantime Krishnáji, foster son of Kantáji, made a sudden attack upon Chámpáner and captured that fortress, and from that time Kantáji's agents remained permanently in Gujarát to collect his share of the tribute.

Capture of Chámpáner by the Maráthás, 1728.

Grant of tribute to the Peshwá, 1729.

In A.D. 1728 the minister, Momin Khán, died, and in his place the emperor selected his brother Abd-ul-Ghani Khán. About this time Asad A'li, governor of Junágarh, also died, and on his deathbed appointed Salábat Muhammad Khán Bábi deputy governor of that fortress. Salábat Muhammad Khán sent his son Sher Khán Bábi to act on his behalf. When the emperor heard of the death of Asad A'li, he appointed Ghulám Mahy-ud-din Khán, son of the late Asad A'li, as governor. Ghulam did not, however, himself proceed to Junágarh, but continued Sher Khán Bábi as his deputy. Mubáriz-ul-Mulk, now perceiving that neither Piláji nor Kantáji afforded any protection to Gujarát, but rather pillaged it, closed with the offers of Bájiráv Peshwá, and in A.D. 1729 formally granted to him the one-fourth and one-tenth shares of the revenue of the province. The Peshwá accordingly sent his brother Chimnájiráv to

[1] The amount was 1,25,000 *mahmudis.*

Chapter III.

Moghal Viceroys.

collect the tribute. Chimnáji plundered Dholká and the country near Chámpáner, while Mubáriz-ul-Mulk exacted tribute from the chiefs on the banks of the Wátrak. Kantáji now entered Gujarát and prepared for war in case Chimnáji and the viceroy should unite against him. His movements were not, however, interfered with, and, after collecting his share of the tribute, he retired to Sorath. The viceroy now marched against the Kolis, and after destroying many of them, together with their wives and children, returned to A'hmadábád by way of Morásá and Ahmadnagar. Ghulám Mahy-ud-din Khán, governor of Junágarh, who had not yet proceeded to his command, appointed about this time a second deputy. Through the influence of the viceroy this appointment was not, however, confirmed, and instead Sher Khán Bábi, son of Salábat Muhammad Khán, was placed in charge of that fortress.

Mullá Muhammad A'li raises a disturbance at Surat, 1729.

The year A.D. 1729 was a year of some mark in the records of the city of Surat. There was a severe flood in the Tápti and a local disturbance of some consequence. The chief cause of the disturbance was a rich Musalmán trader of Surat of the name of Mullá Muhammad A'li. This man, who, as chief of the merchants, had already a special rank in that city, was tempted to take advantage of the disorders of the time to raise himself to the position of an independent ruler. With this object, he chose as his head-quarters the island of Piram, in the Gulf of Cambay, near the port of Gogo, and there spent considerable sums of money in strengthening the island and tempting settlers to place themselves under his protection. Piram was not, however, a popular colony, and, giving it up, Mullá Muhammad fixed on the village of Athwá, on the left bank of the Tápti, about twelve miles from its mouth. Here he began to build a fort, but was ordered to desist by Sohráb Khán, the governor of Surat, from which city the proposed stronghold was only three miles distant. Mullá Muhammad, however, so far from obeying, persuaded the commander of the fort of Surat to side with him. Accordingly, next day, the commander of the fort bombarded Sohráb Khán's residence, proclaiming that Teg-bakht Khán brothe. was appointed governor. It was finally agreed that the matter in dispute should be referred to the emperor for settlement.

Nadiád given out in farm, 1729.

In the same year, A.D. 1729, several changes were made in the management of the different districts of the province. Jawán Mard Khán Bábi was chosen governor of Pitlád, A'li

Chapter III

Moghal Viceroys.

Muhammad Khán made collector of the revenue of the country round A'hmadábád; his son, the author of the Mirat-i-A'hmadi, and his brother being respectively appointed governor and superintendent of the customs of that district. A'li Muhammad Khán, however, shortly resigned, and was succeeded by Zambil Khán. At this time Jawán Mard Khán Bábi, while subduing the Kolis of Balor, was killed by a man of that tribe, and in revenge for his death the town of Balor was plundered. On the death of Jawán Mard Khán, at the request of Salábat Muhammad Khán Bábi, his eldest son Kamál-ud-din Khán Bábi received the districts of Sami and Munjpur and the title of Jawán Mard Khán; and at the same time, the second son, Muhammad Anwar, with the title of Safdar Khán, was appointed to the government of Rádhanpur. The viceroy now went to Naḍiád, where Rái Kishandás, agent of Jawán Mard Khán, received the district of Pitláḍ in farm. From Naḍiad Mubáriz-ul-Mulk went to collect tribute from Sardársingh, the chief of Bhádarwá,[1] on the banks of the Mahi, who, after some fighting, agreed to pay a sum of 2,000*l.* (Rs. 20,000). On his way back to A'hmadábád the viceroy levied tribute from the chief of Umetá.[2] As Rái Kishandás failed to pay the sum agreed on for the farm of Pitláḍ, an order was issued for his imprisonment; but to save himself from such an indignity, he committed suicide.

The Maráthás carry off the viceroy's elephants. A fort built at Athwá near Surát, 1730.

When Kantáji returned from Soráth he came and camped at Sánand, and his advanced guard carried off some of the viceroy's elephants which were grazing there. Men were sent in pursuit, but in vain, and the Maráthás escaped. Meanwhile, at Surat, Mullá Muhammad A'li had, by his intrigues, continued the building of the Athwá fort. At last his accomplice, the commander of the Surat fort, began to perceive that if the Athwá fort were completed, the mullá would be in a position to obstruct the trade of the port of Surat. He consequently ordered him to discontinue his building. The mullá, however, succeeded in persuading Sohráb Khán to allow him to continue building his fort, promising in return to get him confirmed as governor of Surat. Sohráb Khán agreed, and the fort was completed. As, however it was at the entrance of the harbour, the revenue of

---

1 Under the Rewá Kántá Agency.

2 In the British district of Kaira.

Chapter III.

Moghal Viceroys.

Surat was thereby greatly diminished, and Sohráb Khán, when it was too late, saw his mistake.

The viceroy levies tribute in Káthiáwár and Cutch, 1730.

In A.D. 1730, Mubáriz-ul-Mulk went into Gohelwár in the province of Káthiáwár, and levied tribute from Bháosingh, chief of Sihor; thence he proceeded to Mádhupur, a town under Porbandar, and laid it waste. While engaged at Mádhupur, Momin Khán, son-in-law of the late Momin Khán, had some misunderstanding with the viceroy, and in consequence left at once for A'hmadábád, and from that proceeded to the court at A'grá. The viceroy now marched in the direction of Cutch, and, refusing the offer of a yearly tribute of about 33,000*l.* (1,000,000 *mahmudis*), advanced against Bhuj. He, however, experienced great difficulty in crossing the Ran, and as the ráo had cut off all supplies, and as at the same time news arrived of disturbances in A'hmadábád, he was obliged, after a month and a half, to retire to Rádhanpur. The author of the Mirát-i-A'hmadi was ordered to suppress the A'hmadábád riots, which had arisen out of the levy of some fresh taxes, and was invested with the title of Hasan Muhammad Khán. In this year, Udikaran, the Desái [1] of Viramgám, was murdered by a Kasbáti [2] of that town named A'li, and Salábát Muhammad Khán Bábi, who was sent to investigate this murder, died on his way at Páldi, a village on the bank of the Sábarmati.

Riots at A'hmadábád.

MA'HA'RA'JA', ABHEYSINGH 54th Viceroy, 1730.

Mubáriz-ul-Mulk resists the new viceroy.

News was now (A.D. 1730) received that máhárájá Abhyesingh of Jodhpur had been appointed viceroy and had reached Pálanpur. The friends of order endeavoured to arrange the transfer peaceably between the máhárájá and the late viceroy, but Mubáriz-ul-Mulk determined to try the chances of war, and prepared for resistance. At this time Mir Ismáil, deputy of Ghulám Mahy-ud-din Khán, arrived and took charge of the government of Junágarh from Sher Khán Bábi. Máhá-

---

[1] The Desáis were local collectors of revenue under the Moghals; they were appointed by rájá Todar Mal in his revenue settlement of Gujarát. Shortly after Akbar's conquest he allowed them to levy from the ryots 2½ per cent on every hundred rupees they collected of imperial revenue. But when Mirz Azéz Kokaltáah was viceroy, he diminished their duties by one half, and afterwards they were again reduced by one half, so that but ten annas per hundred rupees eventually remained.

[2] Kasbátis are descended from certain Musalmán soldiers who settled in some of the towns of Northern Gujarát.

The Kasbátis of Viramgám were Tánks.

rájá Abhyesingh, after making various appointments, set out with his brother Wakhatsingh and 20,000 men to take up the government of Gujarát. When he reached Pálanpur and saw that Mubáriz-ul-Mulk was determined on resistance, he sent an order to Sardár Muhammad Ghorni appointing him his minister, and directing him to take possession of the city of A'hmadábád and drive out the late viceroy. This, however, the Sardár Muhammad was not strong enough to effect; so he awaited the máhárájá's arrival. When the máhárájá reached Sidhpur he was joined by Safdar Khán Bábi and Jawán Mard Khán Bábi from Rádhanpur. They then advanced together to Aḍálaj, distant only about eight miles from the capital, their army increasing daily. Mubáriz-ul-Mulk was already encamped between Aḍálaj and the city, and on the approach of the máhárájá a battle was fought in which the máhárájá was defeated. Abhyesingh changed his position, and another and bloodier engagement took place, in which either side tried to kill the opposing commander. But as both Mubáriz-ul-Mulk and the máhárájá fought disguised as common soldiers, neither party succeeded in its attempt. At first the máhárájá, who had the advantage in position, succeeded in repulsing the enemy, but Mubáriz-ul-Mulk fought so desperately in the river bed that the Ráthoḍs gave way. Rallying, however, they made one more desperate charge, but were met, repulsed, and finally pursued as far as Sarkhej. The máhárájá, who had not expected so determined an opposition, now sent Momin Khán and Amarsingh to negotiate with Mubáriz-ul-Mulk, who was still determined to resist to the uttermost. It was finally agreed that Mubáriz-ul-Mulk should receive a sum of 10,000*l*. (Rs. 1,00,000) and should surrender A'hmadábád to the máhárájá. Mubáriz-ul-Mulk accordingly quitted the city, and left for A'grá by way of Udeypur.

Battle of Aḍálaj; the máhárájá defeated by Mubáriz-ul-Mulk, 1730.

Mubáriz-ul-Mulk retires.

The máhárájá then entering A'hmadábád, appointed Ratansingh Bhandári his deputy, and placed Fidá-ud-din Khán, cousin of Momin Khán, in charge of the police of the city. Shortly afterwards took place the death of Karimdád Khán Jhálori, governor of Pálanpur, who had accompanied the máhárája into Gujarát. After the death of Salábat Muhammad Khán Bábi, his son, Sher Khán Bábi, was dismissed from the government of Junágarh. He therefore went and lived in his estate of Gogo, and when the máhárájá arrived in A'hmadábád he went there and paid his respects, presenting him with an elephant and some

Government of Abhyesingh

Chapter III.

Moghal Viceroys.

horses. The máhárájá confirmed to him the lands assigned to his father, and reported concerning this to the emperor. Momin Khán was made ruler of Cambay, and Fidá-ud-din Khán, his cousin, was made governor of the lands near that city, the revenue of which had been assigned to the máhárájá. So great fear was at this time entertained of the Maráthás, that Mustafid Khán, the governor elect of Surat, instead of proceeding to that city direct by land, went to Cambay. From Cambay he moved on to Broach, and from that city entered into negotiations with Piláji Gáekwár, promising, if allowed to retain possession of Surat, to pay Piláji the one-fourth share of its revenues. Piláji agreed to these proposals, but Sohráb Khán, who was still in possession of Surat, refused to hand it over to Mustafid Khán. In this year, also, Wakhatsingh, brother of the máhárájá Abhyesingh, was appointed governor of Pátan, and sent a deputy there to act for him. About the same time Mir Fakhr-ud-din, a follower of the late viceroy, leaving him secretly, came to A'hmadábád, and in an interview with the máhárájá obtained for himself the post of deputy-governor of Junágarh. When, however, shortly afterwards, he proceeded to take up his appointment, he was opposed by Mir Ismáil, and in a battle fought near Amreli[1] was killed. Muhammad Pahár, son of Karimdád Khán Jhálori, was now appointed governor of Pálanpur in succession to his father, and Jawán Mard Khán was sent to Waḍnagar.

Momin Khán, ruler of Cambay, 1730.

League of the Peshwá and viceroy against Piláji Gáekwár, 1731.

In the following year, A.D. 1731, Bájiráv Peshwá, entering Gujarát at the head of an army, advanced against Baroda, then in the possession of Piláji Gáekwár. Afterwards, at the invitation of the máhárájá, he visited A'hmadábád and had a meeting with the viceroy in the Sháhi Bágh. At this meeting it was agreed that Bájiráv should assist Azmatullah, the governor of Baroda, in taking possession of that town and in expelling Piláji Gáekwár. By this arrangement the viceroy, on his part, hoped by playing off the Peshwá against Piláji, to succeed in getting rid of the latter, while the Peshwá, intended that if Piláji was forced to give up Baroda, he himself should gain possession of that city.

---

[1] Amreli (N. Lat. 21° 36'; E. Long. 71° 15'), a town in the peninsula of Káthiáwár, 132 miles S. W. of A'hmadábád.

Accordingly the Peshwá, together with an army from the viceroy, marched on Baroda, but had scarcely laid siege to that city when he heard that Nizám-ul-Mulk was advancing on Gujarát against him. Abandoning all further operations against Baroda, the Peshwá on receiving this news withdrew, with all speed, to the Deccan. On his way he encountered the army of Trimbakráv Senápati, who, together with Piláji Kantáji and Udáji Puár, had united to resist the pretensions of the Peshwá in Gujarát, and were also secretly leagued with the nizám. An engagement was fought in which the Peshwá was victorious and Trimbakráv was slain. Without halting the Peshwá then pushed on to the Deccan, contriving on the way to avoid the nizám, though his baggage was plundered by that chief, who had camped at Ghaḷá Kámḷej, on the Tápti, about ten miles above Surat.

The Peshwá recalled to the Deccan.

Defeats his opponents.

During these changes the city of Broach, which, on account of the strength of its fort, the Maráthás had failed to gain possession of, was governed by Abdullá Beg, an officer originally appointed to that command by Mubáriz-ul-Mulk. Dissatisfied that the government of Gujarát should be in the hands of Abhyesingh, Abdullá Beg, in A.D. 1731, entered into negotiations with the nizám, offering in future to hold Broach as the nizám's deputy. Nizám-ul-Mulk agreed to these proposals, appointed Abdullá his deputy, and ennobled him with the title of Nek A'lam Khán. About the same time Wakhatsingh, brother of the viceroy, withdrew to his chiefship of Nágor, in Jodhpur, and Azmat-ullah went to A'grá. Bájiráv Peshwá meanwhile, reaching the Deccan in safety, entered into an agreement with the nizám under the terms of which the grants of Dholká, Broach, Jambusar, and Makbulábád were continued to the nizám. Momin Khán received the farm of Pitláḍ, and Kantáji was confirmed in the share he had acquired of the revenues of Gujarát. In A.D. 1732 the paymaster, Amánatdár Khán, died, and was succeeded by Ghulám Hasan Khán, who sent Mujáhid-ud-din Khán to act as his deputy. Through the influence of Mullá Muhammad A'li, Sohráb A'li was now confirmed as governor of Surat, and Mustafid Khán was obliged to return to A'hmadábád.

Abdullá Beg appointed the nizám's deputy at Broach.

Piláji Gáekwár as the agent of the deceased Khanderáv Dhábáre Senápati, as the owner of the fort of Songarh, and as the ally of the Bhils and Kolis, was naturally a thorn in the

Chapter III.

Moghal Viceroys.

The viceroy procures the death of Piláji Gáekwár, 1732;

side of the viceroy Abhyesingh. Of late, too, by the acquisition of the town of Baroda and the strong fortress of Dabhoi, he had made himself still more formidable. Under these circumstances, Abhyesingh, who had long wished to recover Baroda and Dabhoi, determined to assassinate Piláji, and this was effected by a Márwádi at Dákor,[1] a village in the Thásra sub-division. The Maráthás slew the assassin and hastily withdrew across the Mahi, burning the body of Piláji at the village of Sánoli or Sáwali.[2] They then evacuated the district of Baroda, retiring to the fortress of Dabhoi. The viceroy on hearing of the death of Piláji immediately advanced against the Maráthás, and, after taking possession of Baroda, laid siege to Dabhoi. He failed, however, to capture this fortress, and as the rainy season had set in and provisions were scarce, he was obliged to retire. He then went to Baroda, and after placing Sher Khán Bábi in charge of the city returned to A'hmadábád. This year, A.D. 1732, was a year of great famine in Gujarát.

and takes Baroda.

Year of famine, 1732.

Affairs at Surat, 1732.

Meanwhile at Surat Mullá Muhammad A'li of Athwá was again the cause of disturbances. Resisting with force the demand of a sum of 10,000*l*. (Rs. 1,00,000) by Sohráb Khán, the governor of Surat, he succeeded in the end in driving Sohráb Khán out of the city, and the government of Surat was then usurped by Tegbakht Khán, a brother of the mullá. On hearing of these contests, the emperor ordered that the mullá should be imprisoned; and Tegbakht Khán, inviting him to an entertainment, placed him in confinement, and after keeping him in prison for two years, in A.D. 1734 put him to death. He also took possession of the fort of Athwá, and plundered it. Sohráb Khán, seeing that he could not recover Surat, went with Syad Wali to Gogo, where his relatives lived, and from that, proceeding to Bhávnagar, settled there. When the emperor heard what had happened, he appointed Momin Khán to Surat and Tegbakht Khán to Cambay. Momin Khán sent Syad Nurullah to act for him, but he was defeated by Tegbakht Khán, who afterwards contrived, in A.D. 1733, to

Tegbakht Khán, governor of Surat.

---

[1] Dákor.—This is a well-known place of pilgrimage, now in the British district of Kairá.

[2] Sáwali is a Mahál under His Highness the Gáekwár, about 14 miles north of Baroda.

Chapter III.

Moghal Viceroys.

be formally appointed governor of Surat with the title of Bahádur.

Advance of the Maráthás to avenge the death of Pilájí, 1733.

When Umábái, widow of Khanderáo Senápati, heard of the assassination of Piláji Gáekwár, she determined to avenge his death. Collecting an army and taking with her Kantáji Kadam and Dámáji Gáekwár, son of Piláji, she marched upon A'hmadábád, where, however, they were unable to gain any signal advantage, though they slew a Rájput leader named Jivaráj. Nevertheless the máhárájá found it politic to come to terms, and eventually it was agreed that in addition to the one-fourth and one-tenth share of the revenue a sum of 8,000*l.* (Rs. 80,000) should be paid from the A'hmadábád treasury, Jawán Mard Khán being kept as a hostage till the payments were made. For his services on this occasion Jawán Mard Khán was made governor of Viramgám. During this year Khushalchand Seth was, by an imperial order, appointed to be chief of the merchants,[1] of A'hmadábád.. Umábái now marched upon Baroda, and the governor, Sher Khán Bábi, prepared to oppose the Maráthás. But Umábái, sending to Sher Khán, explained that she had just concluded a peace with the máhárájá, and was suffered to pass unmolested. The emperor, satisfied with the arrangements made by the máhárájá, presented him with a dress of honour. In this year the máhárájá went to court by way of Jodhpur, and appointed Ratansingh Bhandári as his deputy, and the author of the Mirat-i-A'hmadi as daily recorder. In the same year, A. D. 1733, Ghulám Mahya-ud-din Khán, governor of Junágarh, died, and his son Mir Hazabar Khán was selected to fill his place.

Former cession of revenue confirmed.

Ratansingh Bhanda'ri, Deputy-Viceroy in charge, 1733-1737.

Return of the Maráthás to collect tribute.

Meanwhile as the Maráthás had not received their rights, Jádoji Dhábáre, son of Umábái, returned to Gujarát. Peace was, however, concluded on the former basis, and Jádoji then marched into Sorath to exact tribute from the chiefs of that province. In this year the Kolis of the Chunwál and Kánkrej committed many excesses, and one of the Rájput nobles was robbed in the Pátan district. In the meantime Sohráb Khán, the former governor of Surat who had been kindly received by Bháosinghji, the chief of Sihor, began to raise

1 The title was *Nagar Seth.* The name is still kept up, though it has ceased to carry with it the position and respect which the holder formerly enjoyed.

Chapter III.

Moghal Viceroys.

a following and was appointed collector of arrears in Sorath. He chose Syad Nurullah as his deputy, and sent him to recover the revenue for the current year.

Contest for the Government of Gogo.

Now on the death of Salábat Khán Bábi, though the máhárájá had endeavoured to get Sher Khán Bábi appointed in place of his father, Gogo had been granted to Burhán-ul-Mulk, who chose Sohráb Khán as his deputy. At this time Sher Khán Bábi was at Baroda, and his younger brother, though he resisted, was compelled to leave Gogo. Now the deputy-governor of Sorath complained to the governor of the conduct of Sohráb Khán. But Burhán-ul-Mulk supporting him, obtained for himself the government of Sorath, and sent Sohráb Khán as his deputy to Junágarh. In A.D. 1734, Ratansingh Bhandári, the deputy-viceroy, who had a great enmity against Bháosingh, son of Udikaran, the hereditary officer of Viramgam, persuaded Jawán Mard Khán to imprison him and send him to A'hmadábád. Jawán Mard Khán went so far as to arrest Bháosingh, but was forced by his supporters to release him.[1]

Disturbance at Viramgám, 1734.

Baroda recovered by the Maráthás, 1734.

In this year Sher Khán Bábi, governor of Baroda, went to visit his lands at Bálásinor, leaving Muhammad Sarbáz in command at Baroda. Máhadáji Gáekwár, brother of Piláji, who then held Jambusar, sending to Songarh to Dámáji for aid, marched on Baroda with a strong force. The garrison made a brave defence, and Sher Khán hearing of this, at Bálásinor, demanded aid from Ratansingh Bhandári, the deputy-viceroy, who directed Momin Khán the governor of Cambay to join Sher Khán and drive back the Maráthás. Sher Khán himself started at once for Baroda; but Máhadáji, leaving a sufficient force before the town, pushed on with the bulk of his army to meet Sher Khán, and, though he and his men fought bravely, defeated him, and then returned to Baroda, Sher Khán retiring to Bálásinor. Momin Khán, who arrived after Sher Khán's defeat, did not deem it prudent to engage the Maráthás, and retired to Cambay. In the meantime the garrison of Baroda, hopeless of succour, surrendered the town, and since that day Baroda has continued to be the head-quarters of the Gáekwár family.

Change of governor at Viramgám.

Since Jawán Mard Khán's capture of Bhávsingh of Viramgám, he had become much disliked in that town, and accordingly Ratansingh Bhandári, the deputy-viceroy, trans-

---

1 Grant Duff says that this event took place in A.D. 1732.

ferring him to the charge of Kaḍi and Bijápur, appointed in his place Sher Khán Bábi, whose father Salábát Muhammad Khán Bábi had been a popular governor of Viramgám. At this time Dhanrup Bhandári, governor of Pitláḍ, died, and the farm of the districts of Naḍiád, Arhar Mátar, Pitláḍ and Mahudhá was given to Momin Khán. Khushálchand, the chief of the merchants of A'hmadábád, having had a difference with Ratansingh, was forced to leave the city, and eventually sought shelter at A'hmadábád. Jawán Mard Khán, who was of an ambitious temperament, now conceived the design of conquering Idar from A'nandsingh and Ráisingh, brothers of the máhárájá Abhyesingh. He accordingly marched upon Idar, taking with him as allies Aghráji Koli of Katosan and Koli Amrá of Elol Kánrah. In this strait, Anandsingh and Ráisingh sought the aid of Malhárráv Holkár and Ranoji Sindiá, who were at this time in Málwá. The Maráthá Chiefs at once marched to the help of Idar, and Jawán Mard Khán, disbelieving the report of the Maráthá aid, continued to advance until he found himself opposed by an overwhelming force. Negotiations were, however, entered into, and Jawán Mard Khán agreed to pay a sum of 17,500*l.* (Rs. 1,75,000). Of the total amount 2,500*l.* (Rs. 25,000) were paid at once, and Zoráwár Khán, brother of Jawán Mard Khán, and Ajabsingh, agent of Aghráji Koli, were kept as hostages until the balance should be paid.

Chapter III.

Moghal Viceroys.

Jawán Mard Khán fails in an attempt on Idar.

Rivalry of Ratansingh Bhandári and Sohráb Khán, 1735.

In the following year, A.D. 1735, Dholká was assigned to Ratansingh Bhandári, and Sohráb Khán, through the influence of Burhán-ul-Mulk, was appointed governor of Viramgám. Ratansingh, however, resented this, and eventually Viramgám was conferred on the máhárájá Abhyesingh. When this order reached Sohráb Khán, he forwarded it to Burhán-ul-Mulk, and in consequence of Burhán-ul-Mulk's remonstrances the arrangements were changed and Sohráb Khán appointed governor. Upon this, Sohráb Khán, leaving Sádák A'li as his deputy in Junágarh, marched himself for Viramgám; while Ratansingh Bhandári, hearing of Sohráb Khán's approach, summoned Momin Khán and others to his assistance, and with his own army proceeded to Dholká and plundered Kot. From Kot he advanced and pitched at Harálah, about ten miles from Sohráb Khán's camp, and here he was joined by Momin Khán and others whom he had summoned to support him. After the union of these forces he marched to Dholi, six miles from Dhandhuká, at which place Sohráb Khán was then en-

Chapter III.

Moghal Viceroys.

Battle of Dholi; defeat and death of Sohráb Khán, 1735.

camped. Ratansingh Bhandári now proposed that peace should be concluded, and that Sohráb Khán should enjoy possession of Viramgám until final orders were passed in the matter by the emperor. Safdár Khán Bábi and others went to Sohráb Khán and endeavoured to bring him to consent to these; terms but he would not listen to them, and preparations were made on both sides for battle. During the following night Ratansingh Bhandári planned an attack on Sohráb Khán's camp. The surprise was complete: Sohráb Khan's troops fled, and himself, mortally wounded, shortly afterwards died. By the death of Sohráb Khán the family of Kázam Beg Khán became extinct.

Rivalry between Ratansingh Bhandári and Momin Khán, 1735.

After this success a single horseman attacked and wounded Ratansingh Bhandári in two places; the horseman was at once slain, but no one was able to recognize him. Ratansingh, who in two months had recovered from his injuries, now determined to attack Momin Khán, as that officer in the recent struggle had taken part on the side of Sohráb Khán. Momin Khán, however, hearing of Ratansingh's intentions, withdrew to Cambay. In the course of this year, on the expiry of the period of the farm of Mahudhá, Árhar Mátár, and Naḍiád, these districts were transferred from Momin Khán to Safdar Khán Bábi. Kalánchand, a man of low origin, was appointed to Viramgám in place of Sher Khán Bábi, and instead of Sohráb Khán, Mohsan Khán Khalvi was appointed deputy governor of Sorath.

MARA'THA' AFFAIRS.

Contest between Dámáji Gáekwár and Kantáji, 1735.

Battle of Anand Mogri; defeat of Kantáji.

About this time Dámáji Gáekwár, who had been chosen by Umábái as her representative in Gujarát, appointed Rangoji to act as his agent. Kantáji was dissatisfied with this arrangement, in which his rights were ignored, and marched into Gujarát. Rangoji met him, and a battle was fought near Anand-Mogri,[1] in which Kantáji was defeated and his son killed. On suffering this reverse, Kantáji retired to Pitláḍ. Momin Khán with his army was drawn up near Pitláḍ to oppose Rangoji, but was compelled to retire to Cambay, where peace was concluded on condition that Dámáji should receive the one-fourth share of the revenues of the country north of the Mahi. As the districts where these battles were fought were held in farm by Safdar Khán Bábi, he suffered much loss, and consequently retired to Rádhanpur.

---

[1] The sub-division of that name in the British district of Kairá.

Chapter III.

Moghal Viceroys.

The Maráthás help Bháosingh to expel the Viramgám Kasbátis.

Rangoji was joined by Dámáji Gáekwár, and these two leaders went together to Dholká. While they were there, Bháosingh of Viramgám, invited them to come to that town, both on account of the annoyance he suffered from the Márwáḍis and that he might take vengeance on the Kasbátis for the murder of his father Udikaran. He accordingly treacherously admitted the Maráthás and slew Daulat Muhammad Tánk, brother of the murderer of his father, and expelled the rest of the Kasbátis, while Kahân Kámdár was permitted to go to A'hmadábád. Leaving Rangoji at Viramgám, Dámáji now marched into Sorath to levy tribute from the chiefs, and after collecting his dues he returned to the Deccan, Rangoji staying in Gujarát to levy the remainder of the tribute. In the following year, A.D. 1736, Rangoji advanced as far as Báola near Dholká and commenced harassing the country. Upon this Ratansingh Bhandári, the deputy viceroy, marched with an army against him, and compelled him to retire to Viramgám. Pursuing the Maráthás to Viramgám, Ratansingh attacked and defeated them, capturing their baggage. The Maráthás, however, made good their retreat into the fort. About this time some Marâthá horse who were at Sarnál, otherwise called Thásrah, joining the Kolis of those parts, advanced with them against Kapaḍwanj, and after but a slight resistance succeeded in capturing the town. In the meantime, though Mòmin Khán had been summoned to his aid by Ratansingh, he delayed coming, as he began to entertain the desire of becoming independent at Cambay.

Battle of Viramgám; Rangoji defeated by Ratansingh, 1736.

The Maráthás capture Kapadwanj.

Troops from the Gáekwár and the Peshwá plunder the country.

News was now received by Ratansingh Bhandári that Pratáprâv, brother of Dámáji and Deváji Tákpar, were advancing on A'hmadábád with 10,000 horse. At first he thought this was a device to draw him away from Viramgám, to the walls of which city his mines had now reached; but on ascertaining from trusty spies the truth of the report, he raised the siege of Viramgám, returned rapidly to A'hmadábád, and thence pushing forward to meet Pratáprâv,—who, having crossed the Mahi, had advanced as far as the Wátrak,—exacted tribute from the chiefs on the banks of that river. As Pratáprâv drew near, the governor of the Bhil District retired before him, and he continuing his advance passed through Valad and Pithápur, and so by way of Chhálá reached Dholká. Here, through Muhammad Ismáil, the governor of that place, he demanded from the Bhandári his

Chapter III

Moghal Viceroys.

share of the revenue. Afterwards, leaving 2,000 horse in Dholká, he himself went to Dhandhuká. In the meantime Kantáji, who was a follower of Bájiráv Peshwá, joining with Malhárráv Holkar, advanced upon Idar, and, coming against Dántá, plundered that town. Some Nágar Bráhmans of the town of Waḍnagar, who were settled in Dántá, tried to escape to the hills, but were intercepted and pillaged. The Maráthás then proceeded to Waḍnagar and plundered the town. From Waḍnagar they went as far as Pálanpur, where Pahar Khán Jhálori, being unable to oppose them, agreed to pay a tribute of 10,000*l.* (Rs. 1,00,000). Kantáji and Malhárráv Holkar then marched into Márwár, while Pratápráv and Rangoji crossed over from Dhandhuká into[1] Káthiáwár and Gohelwár. About this time Muhammad Páhar Khán Jhálori was appointed deputy-governor of Pátan on behalf of Wakhatsingh. As no settlement of his demands on the revenues of Dholká had yet been made, Pratápráv returned to that town and sent Narhar Pandit to receive the tribute due to him. Afterwards proceeding onwards to Baroda with Rangoji they were summoned to Sorath by Dámáji to assist him. Sher Khán Bábi, who up to this time had been at Kaira, now came to A'hmadábád, and as the Bhandári was displeased with Momin Khán's conduct when Viramgám was besieged, he appointed Sher Khán as his own deputy at Pitláḍ, Arhar Mátar, and Naḍiád; but afterwards, on Momin Khán's remonstrance, Subhachand Márwáḍi was appointed to examine the accounts and receive the revenue in place of Sher Khán. In A.D. 1737 Dámáji's brother Pratápráv, returning to his country, after exacting tribute from the chiefs of Sorath, died of small-pox at Kánkar near Dholká. Momin Khán, seeing that Sher Khán had not yet left Kairá, collected some men and came to Pitláḍ, while Sher Khán went to Dehgám and awaited the departure of Rangoji. On the Bhandári making preparations to assist Sher Khán, Momin Khán returned to Cambay.

MOMIN KHA'N, 55th Viceroy, 1737.

At this time, however, as the máhárájá Abhyesingh was not in favour at court, Momin Khán was appointed fifty-fifth viceroy. He was, however, unable to effect anything by himself; but, persuading Jawán Mard Khán Bábi to join him by a promise of the government of Pátan, directed him to pro-

---

1 This shows that there was even then a distinction between Káthiáwár and Gohelwár.

Chapter III.

Moghal Viceroys.

Contest between Momin Khán and the supporters of the late viceroy.

ceed and take up that appointment. Now the Jháloris were allies of the Ráthoḍs, and Páhar Khán Jhálori, then in command of Pátan, refused to surrender charge and repulsed Jawán Mard Khán. Momin Khán, who hitherto had not produced the order appointing him viceroy, now made it public and began to act as viceroy with the title of Najm-ud-daulah Momin Khán Bahádur Firoz Jang, and in A.D. 1737 sent a copy of this order to Abdul Husain Khán, the deputy minister, and to Mustafid Khán, who held the office of kázi.

Momin Khán allies himself with the Maráthás,

Sher Khán Bábi, wishing to remain neutral, retired to Bálásinor. Momin Khán now summoned Rangoji, who was in the neighbourhood of Cambay, to his assistance. Rangoji agreed to aid him in expelling the Márwáḍis, on condition that if successful, he should be granted one-half of the produce of Gujarát, excepting that of the city of A'hmadábád, the lands in the immediate neighbourhood of the city, and the port of Cambay. The ambition of Momin Khán and his disastrous alliance with the Maráthás gave the last blow to the already expiring power of the Moghals in Gujarát, which otherwise might have lingered on for at least a quarter of a century, and he himself lived to repent his conduct. About this time the government of Junágarh was conferred on Mir Hazabar A'li Khán in place of Mohsen Khán.

When Ratansingh Bhandári heard of the appointment of Momin Khán to be viceroy he wrote to the máhárájá for orders, and in the meantime sent Muhammadan officials to Cambay with the view of persuading Momin Khán to take no further steps until a reply should be received to the reference he Momin Khán had made to Agrá. The reply of the máhárájá was to resist Momin Khán if he could. Ratansingh Bhandári therefore prepared to defend A'hmadábád. Momin Khán, on his part, collecting an army, camped at the Náransar lake. He then advanced to Sojitrá, where he was joined by Jawán Mard Khán Bábi; then proceeding together they came to Basu under Pitláḍ, about 26 miles from A'hmadábád, and from that to Kairá, about 18 miles from the capital. At Kairá they encamped on the banks of the Wátrak, and owing to the incessant rain were forced to remain there for about a month. When the rain abated and the rivers were fordable, Momin Khán, moving on to A'hmadábád, encamped in front of the city on the Kánkria Tank and prepared for a siege. About the same time Momin Khán's manager, Vajerám, whom

And lays siege to A'hmadábád.

Chapter III. Moghal Viceroys.

he had sent to Songarh to solicit Dámáji to march in person to his assistance, arrived and informed him that Dámáji would join him shortly. Jorávar Khán, who had been left at the Maráthá camp as security for the payment of the tribute, was recalled, and instead the district of Prántej was formally assigned to the Maráthás in payment of their demands. Some of the máhárájá's guns, which were being sent by his agents at Surat, were about this time captured by a party of Momin Khán's men. When the Bhandári wrote to the máhárája of Momin Khán's advance upon A'hmadábád, the máhárájá was much displeased, and went from the emperor's presence in anger. The nobles, however, fearing the consequences, recalled him, and persuaded the emperor to reappoint him as viceroy of Gujarát.

MA'HA'RA'JA' ABHYESINGH, 56th Viceroy, 1737.

Momin Khán continues the siege of A'hmadábád.

Momin Khán was, however, secretly enjoined to disregard this appointment and persevere in expelling the Ráthods, and was assured of the emperor's approbation of this line of conduct. Momin Khán, therefore, continued to prosecute the siege with vigour. In the meantime another order was received from the imperial court confirming the reappointment of the máhárájá and appointing Fidá-ud-din Khán to guard the city with 500 men, directing also that Momin Khán should return to Cambay. It was further stated that, as Ratansingh Bhandári had acted oppressively, some other person should be appointed deputy to fill his place, and that in the meantime a Rájput noble, named Abhikaran, was to carry on the government. Shortly before this Muhammad Bákar Khán, son of Mutamid Khán, joined Momin Khán from Surat, while Sádak A'li Khán and his nephew reinforced him from Junágarh. When Momin Khán was informed of the purport of the imperial order he agreed to return to Cambay provided Ratansingh Bhandári would quit the city, hand over charge to Abhikaran, and admit Fidá-ud-din Khán and his men into the city.

Defence of the City by Ratansingh Bhandári.

Ratansingh Bhandári, however, determined not to leave the city, and prepared to defend himself to the last. Dámáji Gáekwár now joined Momin Khán from Songarh. Momin Khán met him at Isanpur, three miles from A'hmadábád, and made great show of friendship for him, calling him his brother. When Ratansingh Bhandári heard of the arrangements made between Dámáji and Momin Khán, he sent a message to Dámáji saying, "Momin Khán has promised Rangoji half of the revenues of Gujarát excepting the city of

A'hmadábád the lands immediately round it, and Cambay; but if you will join me, I will give you half of everything not excepting the city nor Cambay, and will send to your camp some of my chief landholders, as security if you agree." Dámáji showed this to Momin Khán, and asked him what he proposed to do. Momin Khán now perforce agreed to do the same; but instead of Cambay offered to make over to the Maráthás the whole district of Viramgám. Dámáji, accepting these terms, ceased to negotiate with the Bhandári. He then proceeded on a pilgrimage to Dudesar, and returning thence in the same year, A.D. 1738, he and Rangoji commenced active operations against A'hmadábád. They bombarded the city and did so much damage that Momin Khán repented having called them to his aid, and foresaw that when the Maráthás were once in possession of any portion of the city, their expulsion would be a difficult matter. Momin Khán now sent the writer of the Mirat-i-A'hmadi to the Bhandári, in hopes that he might withdraw peaceably, but Ratansingh refused to listen to any terms. After some time the Mussulmans under Kázam A'li Khán and others, and the Maráthás under Baburáv endeavoured to take the city by storm, but after a bloody contest were forced to retire. Next day however Ratansingh, seeing that he could not long hold the city, entered into a negotiation with Momin Khán, and, on receiving a sum of money for his expenses, and on being allowed to retire with the honours of war, left the city.

Momin Khán with the aid of Dámáji Gáekwár captures A'hmadábád, 1738.

Momin Khán then entered A'hmadábád. On the capture of the city half of it was, in accordance with Momin Khán's engagement, handed over to the Maráthás. Momin Khán now sent news of what had taken place to the emperor, and appointed Fidá-ud-din Khán his deputy. Dámáji, who in the meantime had been to Sorath, now returned and was met by Rangoji, who accompanied him as far as the banks of the Mahi, whence Rangoji proceeded to Dholká. After spending a few days at Dholká, Rangoji returned to A'hmadábád and took charge of his share of the city, which comprised the Ráikhar, Khánjahán, Jamálpur, Band, Asheriá, and Ráipur gates. The city was thus equally divided, and the gates mentioned were guarded by the Maráthás. At that time the inhabitants of A'hmadábád were chiefly Muhammadans, and the Maráthás, accustomed to extortion, attempting to oppress them, they rose against the strangers and after a severe affray expelled the greater part of them from the city. Momin Khán, though

The Maráthás expelled 1738.

Chapter III. Moghal Viceroys.

secretly pleased, affected ignorance and sent Fidá-ud-din Khán to reassure Rangoji, who had remained in the city; and this with some difficulty was effected. Jawán Mard Khán was now sent to Pátan, and, instead of Prántej, the district of Kherálu was granted to Zoráwar Khán Bábi.

MOMIN KHA'N 57th Viceroy, 1738-1743.

Prosperity of Ahmadábád, 1738.

Now that the Maráthá oppressions ceased, the city began to recover its former splendour and opulence. The emperor, on hearing what had happened, was much pleased with Momin Khán, and raising his rank presented him with a dress of honour, a sword, and other articles of value. At the close of the rainy season Momin Khán went to levy tribute from the chiefs on the banks of the Sábarmati, and Rangoji was asked to accompany him. They marched to Adálej, whence Fidá-ud-din Khán, the deputy viceroy, returned to the city accompained by Rámáji as deputy of Rangoji. Jawán Mard Khán and Sher Khán Bábi now joined the viceroy's camp, and, about the same time, Hathisingh, chief of Pithápur, paying a visit to the viceroy, settled the amount of his tribute. From Adálej they advanced to Mánsá, and here were visited by the chief of that place. From Mánsá they proceeded to Kaḍi, and from that to Bijápur. After Momin Khán's departure much oppression was practised on the inhabitants of A'hmadábád; and Rangoji, leaving his brother Akoji in the camp, returned to the capital, whence he marched towards Viramgám and Sorath. Momin Khán went from Bijápur to Idar, and there levied tribute from the chiefs of Mohanpur and Ranásan.

Expedition of the Viceroy to collect tribute, 1738.

When Momin Khán arrived at Idar, A'nandsingh and Ráisingh, brothers of máhárájá Abhyesingh, went to him and claimed the tribute of Mohanpur and Ranásan as being within the limits of the Idar territory. The matter was amicably settled, and the two brothers accompanied the viceroy as far as the Idar frontier, when A'nandsingh returned to Idar, and Ráisingh, at Momin Khán's request, remained with him, Momin Khán agreeing to pay the expenses of his men. At this time Sher Muhammad Khán Bábi was appointed to succeed Mir Dost A'li as deputy governor of Sorath. The Maráthás, who had attempted to deprive some of the Rasulábád and Bátwá syads of their land, were now attacked by the Muhammadan population, and a few men were wounded on either side. Momin Khán, receiving tribute from various chiefs, had now reached Pálanpur, and Páhar Khán Jhálori, the governor of that place, was introduced to

Chapter III.
Moghal Viceroys.

the viceroy by Sher Khán Bábi. News was now received that Devoji Tákpar was advancing through the Baroda districts, so Momin Khán marched towards A'hmadábád, dismissing Páhar Khán Jhálori on the Pálanpur frontier. Jawán Mard Khán Bábi, appointing his brother Safdar Khán Bábi as his deputy at Pátan, pushed forward in advance for A'hmadábád. Mámu Khán, who had been chosen by Mir Hazabar A'li as his deputy in Sorath, now arrived and complained to Momin Khán regarding Sher Khán Bábi's appointment. Momin Khán said, that as neither had assumed charge of their duties, they should await a final order from the emperor. He then advanced to Hájipur, and thence encamped on the side of the city near Bahrámpur, and occupied himself in strengthening the city defences; and from that camp he proceeded to Isanpur on the banks of the Wátrak, and commenced levying tribute from the chiefs of that neighbourhood. After this he proceeded to Kapulej, where he heard that Dámáji had left Songarh, and crossing the Mahi had gone to A'rás. Next he returned to the city, while Dámáji going to Dholká marched from that to Sorath. Momin Khán now permitted Sher Khán to return to his lands in Gogo, whence he proceeded to Junágarh and took charge of the office of deputy governor.

Sher Khán Bábi, deputy governor of Sorath, 1738.

In the meantime, in A.D. 1738, Mir Hazabar Khán, the governor of Sorath, died, and as Sher Khán had occupied the city, and taken into his employ all the troops of Mir Dost Ali, Mámur Khán was obliged to resign his pretensions and return. The emperor now appointed Himat A'li Khán, nephew of Momin Khán, governor of Sorath, and he wrote to his uncle to appoint a fitting deputy. Momin Khán, as the Maráthá incursions into Sorath increased yearly, and as Sher Khán Bábi was a man able to hold his own with them, suffered him to remain as deputy. When Dámáji returned to Viramgám after levying tribute from the chiefs of Sorath, on account of the excesses of the Kolis he was obliged to march against Kánji Koli, the chief of Chaniár in the Chunwál. He could not, however, prevail against them, and was forced to call on Momin Khán for aid. Momin Khán sent Fidá-ud-din Khán at the head of a well-equipped army, and on their approach the Kolis fled, and the village was burned down, and Fidá-ud-din Khán returned to the capital. Dámáji now leaving Rangoji as his deputy, returned to Songarh. About this time, A.D. 1738, occurred the invasion of Hindustán by

Nádir Sháh, the sack of Delhi, and the surrender of the emperor. But except that coin was struck in Nádir's name, —and even this ceased as soon as he withdrew—these events had but little effect on the politics of Gujarát.

Expedition of the deputy viceroy to collect tribute, 1739.

In A.D. 1739 Fidá-ud-din Khán was sent to levy tribute from the chiefs on the banks of the Sábarmati, and, accompanied by Jawán Mard Khán Bábi and rajá Ráisingh of Idar, marched to Charárah. About this time the village of Pánmul under Bijápur was assigned to the author of the Mirat-i-A'hmadi. He, therefore, also accompanied Fidá-ud-din Khán, who now marched to Ahmadnagar, and thence demanded tribute from Jitsingh of Mohanpur, and Ranásan. Jitsingh made armed resistance and a doubtful battle was fought. Next day Fidá-ud-din Khán changed his position and again attacked him, and the chief being defeated agreed to pay 1,000*l*. (Rs. 10,000.) Thence they went to Idar, where they were hospitably received by rájá Ráisingh, who presented the leaders of the force with horses. From Idar they proceeded to Waḍnagar, which was under Jawán Mard Khán, who also received them courteously and presented horses; the army then marched to Visalnagar. On the arrival of the troops at Visalnagar, Jawán Mard Khán requested Fidá-ud-din Khán to subdue Jámoji the Koli Chief of Thará Jámpur in the Kánkrej, who was then at Balásaná, and who was continually plundering the country. Fidá-ud-din Khán marched therefore to Balásaná, but Jámoji would not risk a battle and fled, and the Muhammadans plundered the town. From Balásaná he marched to Kaḍi, and at this point, allowing Jawán Mard Khán to return to Pátan, he himself proceeded to A'hmadábád.

Maráthás regain their share in A'hmadábád, 1739.

At A'hmadábád, disputes frequently occurred, between Rangoji and Momin Khán, regarding the government of the city; and on one occasion a serious disturbance arose, when Momin Khán was worsted and forced to sue for peace and grant Rangoji his half share both in the government and revenue, which had, since the affray in A.D. 1738, been in abeyance. This year, A.D. 1739, was marked by two events—a disastrous flood in the Sábarmati, and the capture of the city of Bassein from the Portuguese, by the Maráthás under Chimnáji A'ppá.

Capture of Bassein by Maráthás, 1739.

Tribute expedition, 1740.

In the following year Dámáji, on his return from his progress in Sorath, took Rangoji with him to the Deccan and appointed Malhárráv Khuni as his deputy at A'hmadábád.

Fidá-ud-din Khán met the new deputy at Isanpur and escorted him to the city. Fidá-ud-din Khán and Nazar A'li Khán now marched to collect tribute, and Jawán Mard Khán sent his brother Zoráwar Khán Bábi to accompany them. They advanced against Dabhorá in the Bhil District and fought with the chief, who agreed to pay tribute. Thence they went to Autarsumbá, where the Kolis tried to surprise their cannon; they also eventually agreed to pay tribute, and the force then proceeded to Mándwá and levied a contribution from that chief. They then went to Kapadwanj, and passing through Bálásinor reached Virpur under Lunáwárá. Here, from Sultánsingh, agent of the Lunáwárá chief, they received two horses and 300*l*. (Rs. 3,000) as tribute. While they were engaged at Lunáwárá an order of recall came from Momin Khán, who intimated that Malhár Khuni had laid up large stores of grain and contemplated war. He, therefore, desired them to return quickly to A'hmadábád. Fidá-ud-din Khán at once pushed forward through Bálásinor and Kapadwanj, advancing rapidly towards the capital. On the way, however, he received a second despatch from Momin Khán saying that, as the risk of war had for the present passed over, they should advance to Pitlád, where they would find Malhár Khuni and settle with him about the revenue accounts. They then continued their march, and in two days reached Kairá, being joined on their way by Muhammad Kuli Khán, who was charged with some messages for them from Momin Khán. On arriving at Kairá they found that Muhammad Husain, nephew of Fidá-ud-din Khán, who had been sent with a force to Máhudhá, had reached there two days before his uncle. As Malhárráv Khuni was at Piuj near Kairá, Fidá-ud-din Khán expressed a desire to meet him, and it was agreed that both sides should go to the Pitlád district and there settle the disputes about the revenue collection. Shortly afterwards they met and arrangements were being made when the Kolis of the Bhil District rebelled and Abdul Husain Khán and Wajerám were sent against them. After burning two or three villages this detachment rejoined the main body of the force, and not long after all returned to A'hmadábád. During the following year, A.D. 1740, Bájiráv Peshwá died.

Death of Bájiráv Peshwá, 1740.

The viceroy engaged at Cambay, 1741.

In A.D. 1741 Momin Khán went to Cambay, and while residing at Gheiáspur near that city received information that Dámáji had again appointed Rangoji as his deputy in place of Malhárráv Khuni, and shortly afterwards

Chapter III. Moghal Viceroys.

Rangoji arrived at Pitlád. At this time Momin Khán turned his attention to the falling off in the customs revenue of the port of Cambay and appointed Ismáil Muhammad collector of customs. As he was anxious to clear away some misunderstanding that had arisen between Rangoji and himself, Momin Khán set out to visit Rangoji and assure him of his good wishes. At this time Bhávsingh, of Viramgám, who found the Maráthás even more troublesome than the Muhammadans, as soon as he heard of Malhárráv's recall, suddenly attacked the fort of Viramgám, and with the aid of some Arabs and Rohillás expelled the Maráthá garrison and prepared to hold it on his own account. Shortly afterwards Rangoji demanded that a tower in A'hmadábád, which had been raised a storey by Momin Khán so as to command the residence of the Maráthá deputy at the Jamálpur gate, should be restored to its original height. At the same time he suggested that Momin Khán and he, uniting their forces, should advance and expel Bhávsingh from Viramgám. Momin Khán agreed to both proposals. The addition to the tower was pulled down, and Momin Khán and Rangoji, marching against Viramgám, laid siege to the town. Bhávsingh made a gallant defence, and Momin Khán, who was not sorry to see the Maráthás in difficulties, after a time left them and marched to Kaḍi and Bijápur to levy tribute. Rangoji, however, continued the siege, and as Bhávsingh saw that the Maráthá army was sufficient even without Momin Khán to reduce the place, he came to terms and agreed to surrender Viramgám provided the fort of Pátri and its dependent villages should be granted to him. Rangoji agreed, and thus the Maráthás again obtained possession of Viramgám, while Bhávsingh acquired Pátri,[1] a property which his descendants hold to this day.

Bhávsingh forced to surrender Viramgám to the Maráthás.

Receives instead the district of Pátri.

Momin Khán meanwhile had arrived at Bánsah, about 26 miles from Ahmadábád, but hearing that Dámáji had crossed the Mahi with 10,000 men, he at once returned to the capital. Dámáji in the meantime arrived at Bánsah and besieged it. The chiefs and Kolis defended the place bravely for about a month, when it fell into Dámáji's hands, who not only removed the prickly-pear stockade which surrounded it, but also burned down the town.

[1] Pátri (N. Lat. 23°10', E. Long. 71°44'), at the south-east angle of the Ran of Cutch, distant 52 miles west of A'hmadábád.

Chapter III.

Moghal Viceroys.

Siege of Broach by the Maráthás, 1741.

After this Dámáji marched to Sorath, and on his return from Sorath he laid siege to Broach, a port which, from its natural strength as well as from its favourable position on the banks of the Narbadá, it had been the constant ambition both of Dámáji and his father Piláji to capture. As has been already mentioned, Broach was, at this time, held in the interests of the nizám by Nek A'lam Khán. On the approach of Dámáji this officer prepared to defend the fort, and wrote to the nizám for aid. In reply the nizám addressed Dámáji, warning him not to attack his possessions. On receiving this letter Dámáji raised the siege and returned to Songarh. It seems probable, however, that some concessions were made with the view of tempting Dámáji to retire from Broach, and that the Gáekwár's share in the customs of that city dates from this siege.

Battle of Dholká; defeat of the Maráthás, 1741.

At this time a battle was fought between Káim Kuli Khán, governor of Dholká, and Rangoji's deputy, in which the Maráthás were defeated. Momin Khán, however, at the request of Rangoji, made peace between them. Fidá-ud-din Khán, who had recently been raised in rank with the title of Bahádur, starting to collect tribute burned down the refractory Koli village of Dabhorá, and placing a post there he passed to Sátumbá Bálásinor and Thásrá. After the battle at Dholká Rangoji built the fort of Borsad, and another fight took place between the Muhammadans and Maráthás there. Upon this Muhammad Hádi Khán, governor of Dholká, begged Fidá-ud-din Khán to come to Borsad. Fidá-ud-din accordingly, passing through Mahudhá to Pitlád, pushed forward to help him. In the meantime a battle was fought, in which the Maráthás under Malhárráv attacked Muhammad Hádi Khán, and after a short contest withdrew. Next day the Muhammadans, strengthened by the arrival of Fidá-ud-din Khán, besieged Sojitrá. A letter was now written to Rangoji, asking the meaning of this attack, and he replied excusing himself and attributing it to the ignorance of Malhárráv. Muhammad Hádi Khán and the author of the Mirat-i-A'hmadi eventually met Rangoji at Borsad, and there it was settled that he and Fidá-ud-din Khán should come together and arrange matters; but as Rangoji in his heart intended to fight, he wrote to his deputy Rámáji at A'hmadábád to be ready for war. Malhárráv now joined Rangoji at Borsad. About this time there were many misunderstandings and several fights between the Maráthás and the Muhammadans; but they were appeased by Momin Khán and Rangoji,

Contests between the Musalmáns and Maráthás.

Chapter III.

Moghal Viceroys.

who, in spite of the ill-feeling among their subordinates and a certain distrust of each other's designs, appear throughout to have retained a warm mutual regard. Dámáji from his stronghold at Songarh was too much occupied in the course of politics in the Deccan to give much attention to Gujarát affairs. Rangoji, on the other hand, gained so much influence with the Gujarát chiefs, that at one time he succeeded in engaging Sajansingh Hazári in his service, and also induced rájá Ráisingh of Idar to join him; but Momin Khán soon detached Ráisingh from this alliance, by placing him in charge of the post of Amliárá, and making him a grant of the districts of Morásá, Mánkrej, Ahmadnagar, Prántej and Harsol.

Disturbance at A'hmadábád, 1742

In the year A.D. 1742 another fight took place in the city of A'hmadábád, between the Maráthás and Muhammadans, in which the Muhammadans gained a slight advantage. Rangoji now leaving the city appointed, as before, Rámáji as his deputy, and joining Jagjiwan Puár went to Borsad, where he had built a fort. At this time one Jivandás came with authority from the nizám to act as manager[1] of Dholká, part of the lands assigned to the nizám as a personal grant. Jivandás was not, however, able to take up the appointment. About this time rájá A'nandsingh of Idar was killed, and his brother Ráisingh, taking leave, went to Idar to settle matters. Differences again broke out between Momin Khán and Rangoji, and again matters were settled by a friendly meeting between these two chiefs at Borsad, at which place Rangoji had taken up his residence. Momin Khán now went to Pitláḍ, and from that to Cambay, where he was taken ill, but after six weeks came to Wasu, where Rangoji visited him. Here he was again unwell, but nevertheless went to Dholká, and shortly afterwards he and Rangoji marched upon Limbḍi, which at this time is mentioned as being under Viramgám. While before this town, Rangoji was summoned by Dámáji to help him against Bábu Náik, and at once started to his assistance. Momin Khán now marched into Gohelwár, and proceeded by Loliáná to Gogo, then under the charge of a resident deputy of Sher Khán Bábi. Here he received tribute from the chief of Sihor, and from that, marching into Hállár, went against Nowánagar. The jám resisted for 20 days, but eventually

The viceroy collects tribute in Káthiáwár.

[1] The word is *amil*, or revenue collector.

on his agreeing to pay 5,000*l.* (Rs. 50,000) as tribute, Momin Khán returned to A'hmadábád. During his absence Nazar A'li Khán and Wajerám had collected tribute from the Koli chiefs, but had met with a stubborn resistance. Rangoji, who had now left Dámáji, joined battle with Bábu Náik ere he crossed the Mahi, and Bábu Náik turned back. Rangoji therefore remained at Borsad, but hearing of Momin Khán's illness, which had now become very serious, he went once or twice to A'hmadábád to visit him.

Death of Momin Khán, 1743.

Fida-ud-din acts as viceroy, 1743.

In A.D. 1743 Momin Khán died. His wife, fearing lest Fidá-ud-din Khán and Muftakhir Khán, Momin Khan's son, would deprive her of her estate, sought the protection of Rangoji. In the meantime Fidá-ud-din Khán and Muftakhir Khán received an imperial order to carry on the government until a new viceroy should be appointed. At this time a man named A'nandrám, who had been disgraced by Momin Khán, went over to Rangoji and incited him to murder Fidá-ud-din Khán and Muftakhir Khán. Rangoji with this intention invited them both to his house, but his heart failed him, and shortly afterwards Fidá-ud-din Khán went to Cambay. Rangoji now determined at all events to assassinate Muftakhir Khán, and with this object took Muftakhir Khán's associates, Wajerám and Káim Kuli Khán, into his confidence. Muftákhir Khán, however, accidentally heard of his designs, and remained on his guard. Rangoji in the meantime had promised Sher Khán Bábi the post of deputy viceroy, and he accordingly had advanced to Dholká and commenced plundering some of the Cambay villages. Rangoji, after another futile attempt to assassinate Muftakhir Khán, sent for his deputy Rámáji, who was then in the neighbourhood, and prepared to fight.

Defeats the Maráthás.

Muftakhir Khán, on his part, summoned Fidá-ud-din Khán from Cambay, and in a few days they succeeded in uniting their forces. Sher Khán Bábi now deserted the cause of Rangoji, and fighting commenced; but the Maráthás were worsted, and Rangoji's house was besieged. Rangoji, being hard pressed, eventually agreed to give up A'nandrám and to surrender both Borsad and Viramgám, Sher Khán Bábi becoming his security. In this way Fidá-ud-din Khán became sole master of Gujarát.

At this time Dámáji Gáekwár returned from Sátárá and came to Cambay. In the meantime Rangoji, who had been living with Sher Khán Bábi his security, contrived, with the connivance of Sher Khán, to escape together with his family. Fidá-ud-din Khán was much enraged with Sher Khán

Chapter III.

Moghal Viceroys.

Dámáji Gáekwár returns to Gujarát.

on this account, and he accordingly, leaving the city on pretence of hunting, escaped to Bálásinor, where his wife joined him. Fidá-ud-din Khán now put A'nandrám to death, while Rangoji, on his part, made good his escape to Borsad. Fidá-ud-din Khán had set out to collect tribute, when news arrived that Khanderáv Gáekwár, brother of Dámáji, had crossed the Mahi and joining Rangoji had laid siege to Pitláḍ. On hearing this, he at once returned to Ahmadábád, and sent Valabhdás Kotwál to Khanderáv to complain of the misconduct of Rangoji.

Abdul Aziz Khán of Juner, viceroy (by a forged order).

About this time Jawán Mard Khán Bábi, after the death of Momin Khán, the most powerful noble in Gujarát, began to aspire to power, and Fidá-ud-din, who was not good in the field, had thoughts of appointing him to act for him. Matters were in this state, and Jawán Mard Khán was already laying claim to the revenue of the district round A'hmadábád, when an order was received appointing Abdul Aziz Khán the commander of Juner, near Poona, to be viceroy of Gujarát. This order was really forged by Abdul Aziz Khán in Jawán Mard Khán's interests, whom he appointed his deputy. Fidá-ud-din Khán doubted the genuineness of the order, but was not sufficiently powerful to remove Jawán Mard Khán, who now proclaimed himself deputy viceroy. At this time the troops, clamorous on account of arrears, placed both Fidá-ud-din Khán and Muftakhir Khán under confinement. Jawán Mard Khán assumed charge of the city and placed his own men on guard. While Fidá-ud-din Khán and Muftakhir Khán were still in confinement, Khanderáv Gáekwár sent them a message that if they would cause the fort of Pitláḍ to be surrendered to him, he would help them. But to this they returned no answer. Fidá-ud-din Khán now entreated Jawán Mard Khán to interfere between him and his troops. Jawán Mard Khán accordingly persuaded the mutineers to release Fidá-ud-din Khán, who eventually escaped from the city and went to A'gra.

Mutiny of the troops.

Maráthás capture Pitláḍ.

Meanwhile Rangoji continued to press the siege of Pitláḍ, and the commander, Agá Muhammad Husain, after in vain appealing for help to Jawán Mard Khán, was forced to surrender. Rangoji now demolished the fort of Pitláḍ and marched upon A'hmadábád. As he approached the city Jawán Mard Khán sent the writer of the Mirat-i-A'hmadi and Ajabsingh to negotiate with Rangoji, who demanded all his former rights and possessions.

Chapter III.

Moghal Viceroys.

MUFTAKHIR KHA'N, 58th Viceroy, 1743-1744.

News had now reached Delhi that a false viceroy was governing Gujarát, and, accordingly, Muftakhir Khán was chosen fifty-eighth viceroy, the order explaining that Abdul Aziz had never been appointed viceroy, and directing Jawán Mard Khán to withdraw from the conduct of affairs. Muftakhir Khán was perplexed how to act. He succeeded, however, in persuading his troops that now he would be able to pay them their arrears, and he sent a copy of the order to Jawán Mard Khán; and, as he dared not displace him, he informed him that he had appointed him as his deputy, and that he himself would shortly leave A'hmadábád. Jawan Mard Khán, however, so far from obeying, ordered Muftakhir Khán's house to be surrounded. Eventually, Muftakhir Khán, leaving the city, joined Rangoji, and then retired to Cambay.

Appoints Jawán Mard Khán his deputy.

The Maráthás enforce their right to leave A'hmadábád.

Khanderáv Gáekwár now returned, and, with the view of enforcing his claims, uniting with Rangoji marched to Banjar, about five miles from A'hmadábád. Jawán Mard Khán also issuing from the city camped near the Kánkriyá tank. Narhar Pandit and Krishnáji were, on behalf of the Maráthá leaders, sent to Jawán Mard Khán to demand their former rights and possessions. He at first refused, but eventually consented, and Dádu Morar was appointed deputy of the city by the Maráthás. Sher Khán Bábi now returned to Bálásinor. Khanderáv and Kánáji then went to Dholká, and Rangoji to Pitlád. Shortly afterwards Khanderáv Gáekwár left for Sorath. Fidá-ud-din Khán now requested Rangoji to help Muftakhir Khán; he replied that he was willing to help him, but that he had no money. Rangoji then accompanied Fidá-ud-din Khán to Cambay, where Muftakhir Khán then was. Negotiations were entered into,' When Rangoji offered to advance them 10,000 L (Rs. 1,00,000) to carry on the war provided that he was granted his half share as before in all Gujarat not excluding Cambay, as well as his former possessions; but to these terms neither Fida-u-din Khan nor Muftakhir Khan would consent.

In the year A.D. 1744 Jawán Mard Khán, after appointing one of his brothers, Zoráwar Khán, as his deputy at Pátan, and keeping his other brother, Safdar Khán, at A'hmadábád, advanced from the city to Kadi to collect tribute. His next step was to invite Abdul Aziz Khán, the commander of Juner, near Poona, to join him in Gujarát. Abdul Aziz accordingly set out from Juner, taking with him Fatehyáb Khán, commander of the fort of Mulher in Báglán

Abdul Aziz Khán of Juner comes to Gujarát, 1744.

Chapter III.

Moghal Viceroys.

and Rustamráv Maráthá. Directing his march in the first instance to Surat, he was there watched, in the interests of Dámáji Gáekwár, by Devaji Tákpar, the lieutenant of that chief, who, seeing that on leaving Surat, Abdul Aziz continued to advance northwards to A'hmadábád, pursued him to Kim Kathodrá, about 15 miles from Surat, and there attacked him. In the engagement that followed Devaji Tákpar, who had gained over to his side Rustamráv Maráthá, one of the leading men in Abdul Aziz' army, was victorious. Abdul Aziz Khán retired from the battle, but so closely was he followed by the Maráthás, that at Panoli he was forced to leave his elephant, and, mounting a horse, fled with all speed towards Broach. On reaching the Narbadá he failed to find any boats, and, as his pursuers were now close upon him, putting his horse at the water he tried to swim across the river; but sticking fast in the mud the Maráthás overtook him, and he was slain.

Battle of Kim Kathodrá, defeat and death of Abdul Aziz Khán.

FAKHR-UD-DAULAH, 59th Viceroy, 1744-1748.

On hearing of the death of Abdul Aziz, Jawán Mard Khán thought of joining Muftakhir Khán. But, ere he could carry this plan into effect, the emperor receiving, it is said, a present of 20,000*l.* (Rs. 2,00,000) for the nomination, appointed Fakhr-ud-daulah Fakhr-ud-din Khán Shuját Jang Bahádur fifty-ninth viceroy of Gujarát. The new viceroy forwarded a blank paper to a banker of his acquaintance named Sitárám, asking him to enter in it the name of a fitting deputy. Sitárám filled in the name of Jawán Mard Khán, and Fakhr-ud-daulah was proclaimed viceroy. About this time Safdar Khán Bábi, after levying tribute from the chiefs on the banks of the Sábarmati, returned to A'hmadábád, and Khanderáv Gáekwár, as he passed through from Sorath to Songarh, appointed Rangoji as his deputy. On being raised to this post Rangoji sent Krishnáji instead of Morár Náik as his deputy to A'hmadábád, and proceeded himself to Arhar Mátar on the Wátrak, and from that moved to Kaira to visit Jawán Mard Khán, with whom he established friendly relations. In the same year A'li Muhammad Khán, superintendent of customs, died, and in his place the author of the Mirat-i-A'hmadi was appointed. In this year, too, Pahár Khán Jhálori died, and his uncle, Muhammad Bahádur, was appointed governor of Pálanpur in his stead.

Jawán Mard Khán Bábi, deputy viceroy.

Khanderáv Gáekwár called away to Sáttárá.

Khanderáv Gáekwár was, about this time, summoned by Umábái, widow of Khanderáv Dhábáre, to help her in her attempt to lessen the power of the Peshwá, and

Chapter III.

Moghal Viceroys.

Rámáji, who was sent in his place to Gujarát, appointed one Rámchandra as his deputy at A'hmadábád. Fakhr-ud-daulah, now advancing to join his appointment as viceroy, was received by Sher Khán Bábi with much respect at Bálásinor. Jawán Mard Khán Bábi, on the other hand, determined to resist Fakhr-ud-daulah to the utmost of his power, summoned Gangádhar with a body of Maráthá horse from Pitlád, and, posting them at Isanpur, about ten miles to the south-west of the city, himself leaving the fortifications of A'hmadábád, encamped at Asárwá, about a mile and a half from the city. The new viceroy was, as he continued to advance towards the capital, joined by Ráisinghji of Idar at Kapaḍwanj, and, advancing together, arrived at Bhilpur, eighteen miles east of A'hmadábád. On their approach Jawán Mard Khán sent Safdar Khán and Gangádhar to oppose them, and the two armies met at about six miles from the capital. After some fighting Fakhr-ud-daulah succeeded in forcing his way to the suburb of Rájpurá, and next day continuing to drive back the enemy occupied the suburb of Bahrámpurá and began the actual siege of the city. At this point, however, affairs took a turn. Fakhr-ud-daulah was wounded and returned to his camp, while Jawán Mard Khán succeeded in winning over to his side Sher Khán Bábi and Raisinghji of Idar, two of the viceroy's chief supporters. Next day Fakhr-ud-daulah was surrounded by Safdár Khán Bábi, and the Maráthás and himself, with one wife and some of his children, were taken prisoners, while another of his wives and his son, who had managed to escape to Sidhpur, were captured and brought back to A'hmadábád.

Defeat and capture of the Jawán Mard Khán Bábi.

Rangoji disgraced by Khanderáv Gáekwár.

After this Khanderáv Gáekwár returned to Gujarát to receive his share of the spoil, taken from Fakhr-ud-daulah. Reaching Borsad, he took Rangoji with him as far as Ahmadábád, where he met Jawán Mard Khán, and obtained from Rangoji his share of the tribute. Khanderáv was not, however, satisfied with the state of Rangoji's accounts, and shortly afterwards, appointing a fresh deputy, he attached all Rangoji's property, and finally, before leaving A'hmadábád for Sorath, put him in confinement at Borsad. Meanwhile in consequence of some misunderstanding between Jawán Mard Khán Bábi and his brother Safdar Khán, the latter retired to Udyapur, and Jawán Mard Khán went to Visalnagar, then in the hands of his brother Moráwar Khán. From Visalnagar, Jawán Mard Khán now proceeded to Rádhanpur, and meeting his bro-

Chapter III.

Moghal Viceroys.

Is restored by Umábái.

ther Safdar Khán there, they became reconciled, and returned together to A'hmadábád. Khanderáv Gáekwár, who had in the meantime returned from Soráth, encamping at Dholká appointed Trimbakráv Pandit as his deputy at A'hmadábád in place of Moro Pandit. Umábái, on hearing that Rangoji had been thrown into confinement, sent for him; and he along with Khanderáv Gáekwár repaired to the Deccan.

Punáji Vithal and Fakhr-ud-daulah oppose Rangoji and Jawán Mard Khán.

Shortly afterwards Punáji Vithal, in concert with Trimbak Pandit, being dissatisfied with Jawán Mard Khán, began to intrigue with Fakhr-ud-daulah. But, in the meantime, Umábái appointed Rangoji as her deputy, and, as he was a staunch friend of Jawán Mard Khán, he expelled Trimbakráv from A'hmadábád, and himself collected the Maráthás' share of the city revenues. Upon this Punáji Vithal sent Gungádhar and Krishnáji with an army, and, expelling the Muhammadan officers from the districts from which the Maráthás levied the one-fourth share of the revenue, took the management of them into their own hands. Rangoji now asked Sher Khán Bábi to help him. To this Sher Khán agreed; but not having funds enough to pay his troops, at first delayed much, and afterwards plundered Mahudhá and Naḍiád. As he was not now joined by Rangoji, Sher Khán proceeded by himself to Kapaḍwanj, and from that marched against the camp of the Maráthá force, with which Fakhr-ud-daulah was then associated. On the night after his arrival in their neighbourhood, the Maráthás made an attack on Sher Khán's camp, in which many men on both sides were slain. Next morning the battle was renewed, but on Sher Khán suggesting certain terms the fighting ceased. But that very night, hearing that Rangoji had reached Bálásinor, Sher Khán stole off towards Kapaḍwanj. Punáji and Fakhr-ud-daulah followed in pursuit but failed to prevent Rangoji and Sher Khán from joining their forces.

Siege of Kapadwanj by Fakhr-ud-daulah, 1746.

Shortly after, in A.D. 1746, a battle was fought in which Sher Khán was wounded. He was then forced to take shelter with Rangoji in Kapaḍwanj, while Fakhr-ud-daulah, Gangádhar and Krishnáji laid siege to that town. At this time Malhárráv Holkár, on his way back from his yearly raid into Málwá, was asked by the Lunáwárá Chief to join him in attacking Virpur. Holkár agreed, and Virpur was plundered. Rangoji, hearing of the arrival of Holkár, begged him to come to his aid, and on promise of receiving a sum of 20,000*l.* (Rs. 2,00,000) and

At the approach of Holkár the siege is raised.

two elephants, Holkár consented. Gangádhar, Krishnáji, and Fakhr-ud-daulah, hearing of the approach of Holkár, raised the siege of Kapaḍwanj, and marching to Dholká expelled the governor of that district. Shortly afterwards Rangoji went to Baroda on a summons from Dámáji and Khánderáv Gáekwár; while Fakhr-ud-daulah, Krishnáji, and Gangádhar went to Jetalpur, and, taking possession of it, expelled A'mbar Habshi, the deputy of Jawán Mard Khán. Leaving Baroda, Dámáji and Khanderáv Gáekwár advanced to Wasu, where they were met by Krishnáji and Gangádhar, whom Dámáji censured for aiding Fakhr-ud-daulah. On this occasion Dámáji bestowed the districts of Baroda, Naḍiad, and Borsád on his brother Khanderáv. Then proceeding to Goklej, he had an interview with Jawán Mard Khán. From Goklej he sent Kánoji Tákpar with Fakhr-ud-daulah to Sorath, and himself returned to Songarh. As Borsad had been given to Khanderáv, Rangoji fixed on Umreth as his residence.

Safdar Muhammad Khán, Governor of Surat, 1746.

In this year Tegbakht Khán, governor of Surat, died, and was succeeded by his brother Safdar Muhammad Khán, who, in acknowledgment of a present to the emperor of seven horses, received the title of Bahádur. At this time Talib Ali Khán died, and the writer of the Mirat-i-A'hmadi was appointed minister by the emperor. In A.D. 1747, Rangoji returned to A'hmadábád, and Jawán Mard Khán had an interview with him a few miles from the city. Shortly after this the Kolis of Mehmudábád and Mahudhá rebelled, but the revolt was speedily crushed by Sháhbáz Rohillá.

Momin Khán II., governor of Cambay, 1748.

During this year Najam Khán, governor of Cambay, died. Muftákhir Khan, son of Najam-ud-daulah Momin Khán I., who had also received the title of Momin Khán, informed the emperor of Najam Khán's death, and himself assumed the office of governor; he was afterwards, in A.D. 1748, confirmed in this office. On hearing of the death of Najám Khán, Fidá-ud-din Khán marched to Cambay on pretence of condoling with the family of the late governor, but, not being allowed to enter the town, was obliged to retire. He afterwards went to Umreth and lived with Rangoji. Kánoji Tákpar, who had gone with Fakhr-ud-daulah into Sorath, now laid siege to and took the town of Wanthali; but, as it was now time for the Maráthás to return to their own

Chapter III. Moghal Viceroys.

country, Kánoji and Fakhr-ud-daulah, retiring to Dholká, expelled Muhammad Jánbáz, the deputy governor. Rangoji, who had at this time a dispute with Jawán Mard Khán regarding his share of tribute, now came and joined them, and their combined forces marched upon Sánand, where, after plundering the town, they encamped. It was now time for Kánoji to withdraw to the Deccan. Rangoji and Fakhr-ud-daulah remaining behind to collect tribute from the neighbouring districts, marched to Isanpur, where they were opposed by Jawán Mard Khán. On this occasion both Jawán Mard Khán and Fakhr-ud-daulah sought the alliance of rájá Ráisingh of Idar. But, as he offered more favourable terms, rájá Ráisingh determined to join Fakhr-ud-daulah. Sher Khán Bábi also joined Fakhr-ud-daulah, who, thus reinforced, laid siege to A'hmadábád. While these events were passing at A'hmadábád, Haribá, an adopted son of Khanderáv Gáekwár, at that time in possession of the fort of Borsad, began to plunder Rangoji's villages under Pitlád, and, attacking his deputy, defeated and killed him. On hearing this, Rangoji withdrew from A'hmadábád, attacked and captured the fort of Borsad, and forced Haribá to leave the country. Jawán Mard Khán now sent for Janárdan Pandit, Khanderáv's deputy at Nadiád, and, in place of Rangoji's representative, appointed him to the management of the Maráthá share of A'hmadábád.

Increased strength of Fakhr-ud-daulah's party.

Dissensions among the Maráthás.

Surat affairs, 1748.

During this time important changes had taken place in the government of Surat. In the year A.D. 1734, when mullá Muhammad A'li, the chief of the merchants and builder of the Athwá fort, was killed in prison by his brother Tegbakht Khán, the nizám sent Syad Mathan to revenge his death. Syad Mathan was, however, unsuccessful, and was forced to return; but after Tegbakht Khán's death Syad Mathan again came to Surat and lived there with his brother Syad Achan, who held the office of paymaster. He now tried to get the government of the town into his own hands, but, again failing, committed suicide. His brother Syad Achan then attacked, and took the citadel, expelling the commander; and for several days war was waged between him and the governor, Safdar Muhammad Khán, with doubtful success. At last Syad Achan called to his aid Malhárráv,[1] the deputy at Baroda, and their combined forces were successful in taking possession of the whole city. During

---

1 Probably Malhárráv Khuni.

Chapter III.

Moghal Viceroys.

Syad Achan gets possession of Surat, 1747.

the sack of the city Malhárráv was killed and the entire management of affairs fell into the hands of Syad Achan. Safdar Muhammad Khán, the late governor, though obliged to leave the city, was determined not to relinquish Surat without a struggle, and raising some men opened fire on the fort. Syad Achan now begged the Arab, Turk, English, Dutch, and Portuguese merchants to aid him. A deed addressed to the emperor and nizám, begging that Syad Achan should be appointed governor, was signed by all the merchants excepting Mr. Lamb, the English Chief, who at first refused, but at the end was also persuaded by the other merchants to sign it. The merchants then assisted Syad Achan, and Safdar Muhammad Khán retired to Sindh.

Safdar Khán retires to Sindh, Mallá Fakhr-ud-din escapes to Bombay.

Meanwhile, on account of some enmity between mullá Fakhr-ud-din, the son of mullá Muhammad Ali, chief of the merchants, and Syad Achan, the mullá was thrown into prison. On this Mr. Lamb went to Syad Achan, and remonstrating with him for what he had done, suggested that the mullá should be sent for. Syad Achan agreed to this proposal, but on the way Mr. Lamb carried off mullá Fakhr-ud-din to the English Factory, and afterwards sent him to Bombay in disguise. In the meantime Kedárji Gáekwár, a cousin of Dámáji's, who along with Malhárráo had been asked by Syad Achan to come to his help, now arrived at Surat, and though Syad Achan had been successful without his aid, Kedárji demanded the sum of 30,000*l*. (Rs. 3,00,000), which had been promised him. As the syad was not in a position to resist Kedárji's demands, and had no ready money to give him, he made over to him a third of the revenues of Surat until the amount should be paid. And as before this another third of the revenues of Surat had been assigned to Háfiz Masud Khán, the deputy of Yákut Khán of Jhanjhirah, the emoluments of the governor of Surat were very seriously reduced.

Cession of Surat revenue to the Gáekwár, 1747.

Year of famine, 1747.

Dissensions among the Maráthás.

In the same year (A.D. 1747, S.1803) there was a great famine in Gujarát and many persons died. In the following year Jawán Mard Khán endeavoured to recapture Jetalpur, but failed. About the same time Umábái died, and Dámáji procured, through his brother Khanderáv, who was on good terms with Ambiká, wife of Báburáv Senápati, the guardian of Umábái's son, his own appointment as deputy of the Maráthás in Gujarát. Immediately on being

Siege of Borsad, the fort taken and Rangoji imprisoned

raised to this post Dámáji, with his brother Khanderáv, marched against Rangoji to recover Borsad, which, as above mentioned, Rangoji had taken from Haribá. Their forces were joined by two detachments, one from Momin Khán under the command of A'gá Muhammad Husain, and the other from Jawán Mard Khán, commanded by Janárdhan Pandit, and the combined army besieged Borsad. After a five months' siege Borsad was taken, and Rangoji was imprisoned by Khanderáv. Upon this Sher Khán Bábi and rájá Ráisingh of Idar, who were allies of Rangoji, returned to Bálásinor and Idar; Fakhr-ud-daulah was sent to Pitlád, and Fidá-ud-din Khán, leaving Umreth, took shelter with Jetha, the chief of Autarsumbá.

AhmadShah Emperor, 1748-1754.

MA'HA'RA'JA' WAKHA'TSINGH, 60th Viceroy, 1748.

In this year the emperor Muhammad Sháh died and was succeeded by his son Ahmad Sháh (A. D. 1748-1754), and shortly after his accession máhárájá Wakhatsing, brother of the máhárájá Abhyesingh, was appointed sixtieth viceroy of Gujarát. When, however, he learned the state of the province, he considered that his presence would be more necessary in his own dominions, and accordingly never took up his appointment. Khatsingh was the last viceroy of Gujarát nominated by the imperial court, for although Fakhr-ud-daulah, by the aid of the Maráthás under Rangoji and others, was of some little importance in the province, had never been able to establish himself as viceroy. In this year also occurred the death of Khushálchand Sheth, the chief of the merchants of A'hmadábád.

Fakhr-ud-daulah retires to Delhi. Spread of disorder.

Khanderáv Gáckwár appointed Rágbavshankar his deputy at A'hmadábád, and Safdár Khán Bábi issued from A'hmadábád with an army to levy tribute from the chiefs on the banks of the Sábarmati. Fakhr-ud-daulah, the former viceroy, when he heard of the appointment of the máhárájá Wakhatsingh, retired to Delhi, seeing no chance of deriving any benefit from a longer stay in Gujarát. In this year, A.D. 1748, A'sáf Jáh, Nizám-ul-Mulk, died at an advanced age, leaving six sons and a disputed succession.

About the same time Bálájiráv Peshwá, who was jealous of the power of the Gáekwár, sent a body of troops, and freed Rangoji from the hands of Khanderáv Gáekwár. During these years certain adventurers in different parts of the country, taking advantage of the decay of the central power, endeavoured to establish themselves in positions of independence. Of these attempts the most formidable was a revolt of one of the Pátan Kasbátis who took possession of that city, and Jawán Mard Khán found it necessary to proceed in person to reduce him. Shortly afterwards he demeed it advisable to recall his brothers Safdar Khán and Zoráwar Khán, who were then at Unjá under Pátan, and took them with him to A'hmadábád. Janárdan Pandit now marched to Kairá and the Bhil district to levy tribute, and Khanderáv Gáekwár appointed Shewakráv as his deputy. In the meantime at Surat, Syad Achan endeavoured to consolidate his rule, and with this view tried to expel Háfiz Masáud Habshi, and prevent him again entering the city; but his plans failed, and he was obliged to make excuses for his conduct. Syad Achan then oppressed other influential persons, until eventually the Habshi and others joining, attacked him in the citadel. Except Mr. Lamb, who considered himself bound by the deed signed by him in A.D. 1747 in favour of Syad Achan, all the merchants of Surat joined the assailants. Among the chief opponents of Syad Achan were the Dutch, who sending ships brought back Safdar Muhammad Khán from Thattá, and established him as governor of Surat. The English Factory was next besieged, and though a stout resistance was made the guards were bribed, and the factory plundered. In A.D. 1750 Syad Achan, surrendering the citadel to the Habshi, withdrew first to Bombay and then to Poona, to Bálájiráv Peshwá. Shortly afterwards, in consequence of the censure passed upon him by the Bombay Government for his support of Syad Achan, Mr. Lamb committed suicide. Wearied by these continual contests for power, the merchants of Surat asked rájá Ragunáthdás, minister to the viceroy of the Deccan, to choose them a governor. Rájá Ragunáthdás accordingly nominated his own nephew, rájá Harprasád, to be governor, and the writer of the Mirat-i-A'hmadi to be his deputy. Ere however rájá Harprasád could join his appointment at Surat, both he and his father were slain in battle.

Surat affairs, A.D. 1750. Syad Achan unpopular.

Safdar Muhamad brought back by the Dutch.

Syad Achan retires.

In the same year, A.D. 1750, occurred the deaths of rájá Ráisingh of Idar, Safdár Khán Bábi of Bálásinor, and Fidá-ud-din Khán, who for some time before had been settled at Broach. Jáwan Mard Khán, who, seeing that they were inclined to become permanent residents in Gujarát, was always opposed to the Gáekwár's power, now entered into negotiation with Bálájiráv Peshwá. Choosing Patel Sakdev to collect the Maráthá revenue, he asked the Peshwá to help him

Alliance between Jawán Mard Khán and the Peshwá, 1750.

Chapter III.

Moghal Viceroys.

in expelling Dámáji's agents. The Peshwá, however, being now engaged in war in the Deccan with Salábat Jung Bahádur, son of the late nizám, was unable to send Jawán Mard Khán any assistance. Towards the close of the year Jawán Mard Khán started from A'hmadábád on an expedition to collect tribute from the chiefs on the banks of the Sábarmati. Returning early in A.D. 1751, at the request of Jethá Patel, a subordinate of Bhávsingh Desái, he proceeded to Nabud under Viramgám and reduced the village. Ali Muhammad Khán, the author of the Mirat-i-A'hmadi, was about this time raised in rank with the title of Bahádur.

The Peshwá obtains a share of the Gáekwár's interest in Gujarát.

It was in this year, (A.D. 1751,) that the Peshwá, decoying Dámájiráv into his power, imprisoned him and forced him to surrender half of his rights and conquests in Gujarát. Taking advantage of the absence of the Gáekwár and his army in the Deccan, Jawán Mard Khán marched into Sorath. He first visited Gogo, and then levying tribute in Gohelwár advanced into Káthiáwár and marched against Nawánagar, and, after collecting a contribution from the jám, returned to A'hmadábád. In the following year, (A.D. 1752,) as soon as the news reached Gujarát that the Maráthás share in the province had been divided between the Peshwá and Gáekwár, Momin Khán, who was always quarrelling with the Gáekwár's agent, sending Vrajlál his steward to Bálájiráv Peshwá begged him to take Cambay in his share and send his agent in place of the Gáekwár's agent. This was agreed to, and from that time the Peshwá's agent was sent to Cambay. In the same year Raghunáthráv, brother of the Peshwá, entering Gujarát took possession of the Rewá and Mahi Kántá districts and then marched on Surat. Shiáji Dhangár was appointed in Shewakrám's place as Dámáji's deputy, and Krishnáji came to collect the share of the Peshwá.

Governors of Broach become independent, 1752.

Up to this time the city of Broach had remained a part of the nizám's personal estate, managed by Abdulláh Beg, whom A'saf Jáh the late Nizám-ul-Mulk had selected to be his deputy with the title of Nekálam Khán. On the death of Abdullá Beg in A.D. 1752, the emperor appointed his son to succeed him with the same title as his father, while he gave to another son, named Mughal Beg, the title of Khertaláb Khán. During the contests for succession that followed upon the death of the nizám in A.D. 1752, no attempt was made to enforce the claims of that family upon the lands of Broach; and for the future, except for the share

Chapter III.

Moghal Viceroys.

of the revenue paid to the Maráthás, the governors of Broach were practically independent rulers.

Pándurang Pandit marches on A'hmadábád, 1752;

The Peshwá now sent Pándurang Pandit to levy tribute from his share of Gujarát, and that officer crossing the Mahi marched upon Cambay. Momin Khán prepared to oppose him, but the Pandit made friendly overtures, and eventually Momin Khán not only paid the sum of 700*l.* (Rs. 7,000) for grass and grain, for the Pandit's troops, but also lent him four small cannons. Pándurang Pandit then marched upon A'hmadábád, and encamping near the Kánkriyá Tank laid siege to the city which was defended by Jawán Mard Khán. During the course of the siege Pándurang Pandit, sending some troops, ravaged Nikol, part of the lands of Ali Muhammad Khán Bahádur, the author of the Mirat-i-A'hmadi. Meanwhile the operations against A'hmadábád, not succeeding, Pándurang Pandit made offers of peace. These Jawán Mard Khán accepted, and on receiving from him the present of a mare and a small sum of money under the name of 'entertainment,' the Maráthá leader withdrew to Sorath.

But has to retire.

About this time, the Peshwá released Dámáji Gáekwár, on promise of helping the Peshwá's brother Raghunáthráv, who was shortly afterwards despatched with an army to complete the conquest of Gujarát. Meanwhile Jawán Mard Khán's anxiety regarding the Maráthás was for a time removed by the departure of Pándurang Pandit; and as the harvest season had arrived, he with his brother Zoráwár Khán Bábi, leaving Muhammad Mubáriz Sherwáni behind him as his deputy, set out from A'hmadábád to levy tribute from the chiefs of Sábar Kantá. At this time certain well-informed persons who had heard of Raghunáthráv's preparation for invading Gujarát begged Jawán Mard Khán not to leave the city but to depute his brother Zoráwar Khán Bábi to collect the tribute. Jawán Mard Khán, however, not believing their reports, said that he would not go more than from 45 to 60 miles from the city, and promising, should the necessity arise, to entrust his brother with the charge of any more distant excursion, he marched from the city levying tribute as he went, and arrived on the Pálanpur frontier about 75 miles distant from A'hmadábád. Here meeting Muhammad Bahádur Jhálori, the governor of Pálanpur, Jawán Mard Khán was foolishly induced to join with him in plundering the fertile districts of Sirohi, conti-

Unexpected invasion by the Maráthás,

In the absence of Jawán Mard Khán.

Chapter III.

Moghal Viceroys.

nuing to advance till at last he was not less than 150 miles from his head-quarters. While he was thus engaged Raghunáthráv, joining Dámáji Gáekwár, came suddenly by an unaccustomed route into Gujarát, and news reached A'hmadábád that the Maráthás had crossed the Narbadá. On this the townspeople of A'hmadábád sent messenger after messenger to recall Jawán Mard Khán, and building up the gateways prepared for defence, while the inhabitants of the suburbs, leaving their houses, crowded into the city for protection with their families. Raghunáthráv, on hearing that Jawán Mard Khán and his army were absent from the city, pressed on by forced marches, and crossing the river Mahi despatched an advance corps under Vithal Sakdev. Kosáji, landlord [1] of Naḍiád, at Dámáji Gáekwár's invitation also marched towards A'hmadábád, plundering Khokhri, only three miles distant from the city. In the meantime Vithal Sakdev reached Kairá, and taking with him the chief man [2] of that place, Muhammad Daurán, son of Muhammad Bábi, continued his march. He was shortly joined by Raghunáthráv, and the combined forces now proceeded to A'hmadábád and encamped by the Kánkriyá Tank. Next day Raghunáthráv marched thence and camped near the tomb of Hazrat Sháh Bhikan, on the bank of the river Sábarmati to the south of the city. Raghunáthráv now proceeded to invest the city, distributing his army of from thirty to forty thousand horse, into three divisions. Operations against the north of the city were entrusted to Dámáji Gáekwár; those on the east to Gopál Hari; while the troops on the south and west were under the personal command of Raghunáthráv and his officers.

The Maráthás invest Ahmadábád.

Return of Jawán Mard Khán.

Meanwhile Jawán Mard Khán, after leaving Sirohi, had gone westwards to Tharád and Wáv, so that the first messengers who were sent failed to find him; but one of the later messengers, Mándan by name, who had left A'hmadábád immediately after the arrival of Raghunáthráv at the Kánkriyá Tank, made his way to Wáv Tharád, and told Jawán Mard Khán what had happened. Immediately on hearing the news Jawán Mard Khán set out by forced marches for Rádhanpur, and eaving his family and the bulk of his army at Pátan, he himself pushed on with 200 picked horsemen to Kaḍi,

---

[1] The word is *tálukdár*.

[2] " " *watandár*.

Chapter III.

Moghal Viceroys.

He enters A'hmadábád.

and from that to A'hmadábád, contriving at night to enter the city. The presence of Jawán Mard Khán raised the spirits of the besieged, and the defence was conducted with ardour. But, in spite of their watchfulness, a party of about 700 Maráthás succeeded on one occasion, under cover of night, in scaling the walls and entering the city. Ere they could do any mischief, however, they were discovered and driven out of the town with much slaughter. The bulk of the besieging army, which had advanced in hopes that this party would succeed in opening one of the city gates, were forced to retire disappointed. Raghunáthráv now made proposals of peace, but Jawán Mard Khán did not think it consistent with his honour to accept them. On his refusal, the Maráthá general redoubled his efforts and sprung several mines, but owing to the thickness of the city walls no practicable breach was effected. Jawán Mard Khán now expelled the Maráthá deputies, and continuing to defend the city, with much gallantry contrived at night to introduce into the town by detachments a great portion of his army from Pátan. At length, embarrassed by want of provisions and the clamour of troops for their pay, he collected a sum of 5,000*l*. (Rs. 50,000) from the townspeople, and making it over to the soldiery persuaded them to continue the defence.

Gallant defence of the city.

Jawán Mard Khán surrenders.

Raghunáthráv beginning to despair of taking the town had determined, should the siege be protracted a month longer, to depart on condition of receiving the one-fourth share of the revenue, and a safe conduct. Jawán Mard Khán's troops at this time, however, were again becoming clamorous for pay, and the townspeople, who had unwillingly submitted to the former levy, were growing disaffected. Much to Raghunáthráv's relief Jawán Mard Khán was therefore reduced to treat for peace through Vithal Sakdev. Eventually, it was arranged that the Maráthás should give Jawán Mard Khán the sum of 10,000*l*. (Rs. 1,00,000) for the payment of his troops, besides presenting him with an elephant and other articles of value. It was at the same time agreed that the garrison should leave the city with all the honours of war, and that for himself and his brothers Jawán Mard Khán should receive free from any Maráthá claim the districts of Pátan, Waḍnagar, Sami, Munjpur, Visalnagar, Tharád, Kherálu, Rádhanpur with Terwárá, and Bijápur in jágir. It was further agreed that one of Jawán Mard Khán's brothers should

Chapter III.

Moghal Viceroys.

alway serve the Maráthás with 300 horse and 500 foot, the expenses of the force being paid by the Maráthás. And, finally, that the estates of other members of the family, namely, Kairá, Kasbá, Mátar, and Bánsa Mahudhá, which belonged to Muhammad Khán, Khán Daurán and A'bid Khán were not to be meddled with, nor were the lands of Káyam Kulikhán or Zoráwar Khán to be encroached on. This agreement was signed and sealed by Raghunáthráv, with Dámáji Gáekwár (half sharer), Malhárráv Holkár, Jye A'pá Sindhiá, Rámchandar, Patel Viṭhal Sakdev, Sakháram Bhagwant, Mádhavráv, and Gopálráv, as securities. This treaty was then delivered to Jawán Mard Khán, and he and his garrison marching out with all the honours of war, A'hmadábád was taken possession of by the Maráthás April 1753.

The Maráthás take possession, 1753.

On leaving A'hmadábád, Jawán Mard Khán retired to Pátan. At A'hmadábád, Raghunáthráv with Dámáji arranged for the government of the city, appointing Shripatráv as his deputy. He then marched into Jháláwár to exact tribute from the Limbḍi and Wadhwán Chiefs; and was so far successful that Harbhamji of Limbḍi agreed to pay an annual tribute of 4,000*l.* (Rs. 40,000). As, however, the rainy season was drawing near, Raghunáthráv did not go further, but returned to Dholká. In the meantime Patel Viṭhal Sakdev forced Muhammad Bahádur, the governor of Pálanpur, to consent to a yearly payment of 11,500*l.* (Rs. 1,15,000). From Dholká, Raghunáthráv went to Tárápur, about ten miles from Cambay, and compelled Momin Khán to submit to an annual payment of 1,000*l.* (Rs. 10,000). At the same Ali Muhammad Khán Bahádur was appointed collector of customs, and his former grants were confirmed, Dámáji Gáekwár, after levying tribute in the Wátrak Kántá. went to Kapaḍwanj, which he conquered from Sher Khán Bábi. Thence he went to Naḍiád and appointed Shevakrái to collect his half share of the revenue of Gujarát. In the A'hmadábád mint, coin was now no longer struck in the name of the emperor, and the suburbs of the city which had been deserted during the siege were not again inhabited. The Kolis commenced a system of depredation, and their outrages were so daring that women and children were sometimes carried off, and sold as slaves. After the rains were over (A.D. 1457.) Shetuji, commander of the A'hmadábád forces, and Shankarji governor of Viramgám, were sent to collect tribute from Sorath. At the close of the year Shripatráv,

Collect tribute.

Coin no longer struck in the name of the Emperor.

Chapter III.

Moghal Viceroys.

Failure of an attempt on Cambay, 1753.

Koli disturbances.

who was anxious to acquire Cambay, marched thither against Momin Khán, but after two doubtful battles in which the Maráthás gained no advantage, it was agreed that Momin Khán should pay a sum of 700*l.* (Rs. 7,000) and Shripatráv departed for A'hmadábád early in A.D. 1754. When the Kolis heard of the ill-success of the Maráthás at Cambay they revolted, and Rághoshankar was sent to subdue them. He in a battle fought near Luhárá defeated them, but afterwards again collecting, they forced the Maráthás to retire. At this time Shetuji and Shankarji returned from Sorath, where they had performed the pilgrimage to Dwárká. Shetuji was now sent to the Bhil district against the Kolis, but he was unsuccessful, and, ashamed of his failure, returned to the Deccan, and Dandu Dátátri was appointed in his place.

Maráthás attack Cambay, 1754.

In this year died Nek A'lam Khán II., governor of Broach, and was succeeded by his brother Khertalab Khán. At Bálásinor, about the same time, a dispute arose between Sher Khán Bábi and a body of Arab mercenaries who took possession of the fortress on the hill, but eventually peace was made between them. Bhagwantráv, the Peshwá's deputy, now conceived the desire of conquering Cambay, and obtaining the Peshwá's permission marched on that town. But Vrajlál, Momin Khán's steward, then at Poona, sent word to his master, who prepared himself against any emergency. Bhagwantráv arrived at Cambay, and displaying no hostile intentions, was well received by Momin Khán. Subsequently, however, Bhagwantráv wrote to Sálim Jamadár at A'hmadábád to march against Cambay, and this letter falling into Momin Khán's hands, he at once surrounded Bhagwantráv's house and made him prisoner. When the Peshwá heard that Bhagwantráv had been captured, he ordered Ganesh A'pá, governor of Jambusar, as well as the governors of Viramgám, Dhandhuká and other places to march at once upon Cambay; and they went and besieged the town for three months, but without success. Eventually Shripatráv, the Peshwá's deputy, sent the author of the Mirat-i-A'hmadi to negotiate, and it was agreed that Bhagwantráv should be released and that no alteration should be made in the position of Momin Khán. Shortly afterwards Shripatráv was recalled by the Peshwá and his place supplied by an officer of the name of Rágho. About this time Khertalab Khán, governor of Broach, died, and quarrels arose regarding the succession. Ultimately Hamid Beg, nephew of Khertalab Khán, obtained the post, and he afterwards received an imperial order, con-

Chapter III.

Moghal Viceroys.

Alamgir II. Emperor, 1754-1759.

firming him as governor, and bestowing on him the title of Neknám Khán Bahádur.

At Delhi, during the course of this year, A.D. 1754, the emperor A'hmad Sháh was deposed, and Aziz-ud-din, son of Jahándár Sháh, was raised to the throne by the title of A'lamgir II. Bhagwantráv, who after his release had established himself in the Cambay fort of Nápáḍ,[1] not long afterwards commenced a warfare with Momin Khán; several battles were fought with doubtful success, and peace was at last concluded on condition of Momin Khán paying 1,000*l.* (Rs. 10,000), on account of the usual share of the Maráthás which he had withheld. This arrangement was made through the mediation of Tukáji, the steward of Sadáshiv Dámodar, who had come to Gujarát with an army, and been ordered by his master to help Bhagwantráv. As Momin Khán had no ready money, Tukáji offered himself as security for the payment of the amount agreed upon, and this difficulty being removed, Bhagwantráv and Tukáji withdrew to the Deccan. Momin Khán's soldiery were now clamorous for pay, and as he was not in a position to meet their demands, he sent a body of men against some villages to the west belonging to Limbḍi and plundered them, dividing the booty among his troops. In the following year, A.D. 1755, Momin Khán went to Gogo, a port which, at one time subordinate to Cambay, had afterwards fallen into the hands of Sher Khán Bábi, and was now in the possession of the Peshwá's officers. The town easily fell into his hands, and placing a garrison of 100 Arabs there under Ibráhim Kuli Khán, Momin Khán returned to Cambay, levying tribute as he went. He then sent the bulk of his army under the command of Muhammad Zamán Khán, son of Fidá-ud-din Khán, and Vrajlál his own steward, to plunder and collect money in Gohelwár and Káthiáwár. Here they remained until the arrears of the soldiery were paid off, and then returned to Cambay. Momin Khán next marched against Borsad, and was on the point of taking the fort when Siáji, son of Dámáji Gáekwár, who resided at Baroda, hearing of Momin Khán's success, came rapidly with a small body of men to the relief of the fort and surprised the besiegers. The Muhammadan troops however soon recovered from the effects of the surprise, and Siáji fearing to engage them with so small a force retired. On his departure Momin Khán raising the siege returned to Cambay.

Contest with Momin Khán renewed, 1754.

Momin Khán takes Gogo, 1755.

[1] Nápád is now in the British District of Kairá.

Chapter III. Moghal Viceroys.

and recovers A'hmadábád,

In this year, A.D. 1755, the rains were very heavy, and the wall of the city of A'hmadábád fell down in many places. Momin Khán hearing of this as well as of the discontent of the inhabitants, owing to the oppression of the Maráthás, resolved to endeavour to capture the city. He accordingly sent spies to ascertain the strength of the garrison, and also commenced making allies of the chief men in the province and enlisting troops. About this time Rághoji, the Maráthá deputy, was assassinated by a Rohillá. As soon as Momin Khán heard of this he sent his nephew, Muhammad Zamán Khán, with some men in advance, and afterwards himself at the close of the year, A.D. 1755, marched from Cambay and camped on the Wátrak. From this camp they moved on to Kairá, and from Kairá to A'hmadádád, and after one or two fights in the suburbs the Muhammadans, finding their way through the breaches in the walls, opened the gates and entered the town. The Kolis commenced plundering, and a hand-to-hand fight ensued, in which the Maráthás were worsted and eventually were expelled from the city. The Kolis attempting to plunder the English Factory met with a spirited resistance, and when Shambhurám, a Nágar Bráhman, one of Momin Khán's chief supporters, heard of what had taken place, he ordered the Kolis to cease attacking the factory and consoled the English.

Jawán Mard Khán allies himself with the Maráthás

In the meantime Jawán Mard Khán, who had been invited by the Maráthás to their assistance, set out from Pátan, and when he arrived at Pithápur Mánsá he heard of the capture of the city. On reaching Kálol he was joined by Harbharám, governor of Kaḍi. They resolved to send Zoráwar Khán Bábi to recall Sadáshiv Dámodar, and to await his arrival at Viramgám. Momin Khán himself now advanced, and entering A'hmadábád appointed Shambhurám as his deputy. Sadáshiv Dámodar now joined Jawán Mard Khán at Viramgám, and at Jawán Mard Khán's advice it was resolved, before taking further steps, to write to the Peshwá for aid. Jawán Mard Khán and the Maráthás then advanced to Sánand and Jitalpur, and thence marched towards Cambay. On their way they were met and, after several combats, defeated by a detachment of Momin Khán's army. Momin Khán now sent some troops to conquer Kaḍi, but Harbharám, the governor of Kaḍi, defeated this force, and captured their guns. When the emperor heard of the capture of Gogo, he sent a sword as a present to Momin Khán; and when the news of the capture of A'hmadábád reached A'grá,

Chapter III.

Moghal Viceroys.

Momin Khán prepares to defend the city.

Momin Khán received many compliments. Bájiráv Peshwá, on the other hand, much enraged at these reverses, at once sent off Sadáshiv Rámchandra to Gujarát as his deputy, and Dámáji and Khanderáv Gáekwár also accompanied him with their forces. Momin Khán on his part, refusing to give up A'hmadábád, prepared for defence. Upon this Sadáshiv Rámchandra, Dámáji and Khanderáv Gáekwár advanced and, crossing the Mahi, reached Kairá. Here they were met by Jawán Mard Khán and the rest of the Maráthá forces in Gujarát, and the combined army advancing to the capital camped by the Kánkriyá Tank.

The city invested.

The Maráthás now regularly invested the city, but Momin Khán, aided by Shambhurám, made a vigorous defence. After a month's siege, Momin Khán's troops began to clamour for pay, but Shambhurám, by collecting the sum of 10,000*l*. (Rs. 1,00,000) from the inhabitants of the town managed for the time to appease their demands, when they again became urgent for pay. Shambhurám diverted their thoughts by a general sally from all the gates at night. On this occasion many men were slain on both sides, and many of the inhabitants deserted the town. The copper vessels of such of the townspeople as had fled were now melted and coined into money and given to the soldiery. When affairs were in this state an order arrived from the imperial court, bestowing on Momin Khán a dress of honour and the title of Bahádur. It is a singular sign of those times that although the imperial power had for years been merely a name in Gujarát, yet Momin Khán asked and obtained permission from the besiegers to leave the city and meet the bearers of the order. The Maráthás now redoubled their efforts, and were successful in intercepting some supplies of grain for the garrison, who however fought gallantly in defence of the town.

Respect still shown to the imperial power.

Help sent to the garrison by the ráv of Idar, 1757.

At this juncture, in A.D. 1757, rájá Shivsingh of Idar, son of the late A'nandsingh, who was friendly to Momin Khán, sent Sajánsingh Hazári with a force to assist the besieged. On their way to A'hmadábád, Harbharám with a body of Maráthás attacked this detachment, while Momin Khán sent to their aid Muhammadlál Rohillá and others, and a doubtful battle was fought. Shortly afterwards Sadáshiv Rámchandar made an attempt on the fort of Kálikot. It was, however, successfully defended by Jamádár Nur Muhammad, and the Maráthás were repulsed. The Maráthás endeavoured but in the vain to persuade Shambhurám to desert Momin

Khán, and though the garrison were often endangered by the faithlessness of the Kolis and other causes, yet they remained staunch. Momin Khán, though frequently in difficulties owing to want of funds to pay his soldiery, continued to defend the town. The Maráthás next tried to seduce some of Momin Khán's officers, but in this they also failed, and in a sally Shambhurám attacked the camp of Sadáshiv Rámchandar, and burning his tents all but captured the chief himself.

Successful sally under Shambhurám.

When the siege was at this stage, Hasan Kuli Khán Bahádur, viceroy of Oudh, relinquishing worldly affairs and dividing his property among his nephews, set out to perform a pilgrimage to Mecca. Before he started Shuja-ud-daulah, the nawáb of Lucknow, requested him on his way to visit Bálájiráv, and endeavour with him to make some settlement of A'hmadábád affairs. Accordingly adopting the name of Sháh Nur, and assuming the dress of an ascetic, he made his way to Poona, and appearing before the Peshwá offered to make peace at A'hmadábád. The Peshwá assenting, Sháh Nur wrote to Momin Khán to give up the city, and return to his former position as governor of Cambay. On condition that the Peshwá should allow him to enjoy Cambay and Gogo free of all tribute, and give him a sum of 10,000*l*. (Rs. 1,00,000) with which to clear off the arrears due to his troops, Momin Khán consented to surrender A'hmadábád. These proposals were approved, and the Peshwá sent Ranchordás Gujaráti, accompanied by Sháh Nur, with an order to Sadáshiv Rámchandra to accept these terms. Before their arrival, however, Momin Khán had, under the influence of Shambhurám, Sulimán Jamádar and others, changed his mind, and now refused to agree to give up the city. Upon this Sháh Nur left in disgust, and shortly afterwards Momin Khán was himself obliged to make overtures for peace. After discussing the state of affairs with Dámáji Gáekwár, it was agreed that Momin Khán should surrender the city, receive 10,000*l*. (Rs. 1,00,000) to pay his soldiery, and be allowed to retain Cambay as heretofore, that is to say that the Peshwá should as formerly enjoy half the revenues. On the other hand, he had to promise to pay a yearly tribute to the Maráthás of 1,000*l*. (Rs. 10,000) and to give up all claims on the town of Gogo. Accepting these terms Momin Khán finally surrendered the town to the Maráthás. In the beginning of April 1757

Negotiations for peace.

Surrender of the city.

April 1757. Maráthá arrangements in A'hmadábád.

Sadáshiv Rámchandar and Dámáji Gáekwár entering the city undertook the management of it on behalf of the Maráthás. Of the other chiefs who had engaged in prosecuting the siege, Sadáshiv Dámodar returned to the Deccan, and Jawán Mard Khán receiving some presents from Sadáshiv Rámchandar departed for Pátan after having had a meeting with Dámáji Gáekwár, at a village a few miles distant from the capital. Shambhurám, the Nágar Bráhman who had so zealously supported Momin Khán, when he saw that further assistance was useless, in vain tried to escape, and eventually was taken prisoner and sent in chains to Baroda. Sadáshiv Rámchandar, on taking over the charge of the city, had interviews with the principal officials, among whom was the author of the Mirat-i-A'hmadi, and receiving them graciously confirmed most of them in their offices. He then having chosen Náro Pandit, brother of Pándurang Pandit, as his deputy in A'hmadábád, started on an expedition to collect tribute in Sorath. On receiving the government of the city the Maráthá generals ordered new coin bearing the mark of an elephant goad to be struck in the A'hmadábád mint. Siájiráv Gáekwár remained in A'hmadábád on behalf of his father Dámáji, and shortly afterwards went towards Kapadwanj to collect tribute, and thence at his father's request proceeded to Sorath to arrange for the payment of the Gáekwár's share of the revenues of that district. Momin Khán, on his return to Cambay, was at first much harassed by his troops for arrears of pay; but on the timely arrival of his steward Vrajlal with the Peshwá's contribution of 10,000*l.* (Rs. 1,00,000), their demands were satisfied without any actual mutiny.

New coins struck.

Momin Khán at Cambay.

Momin Khán now began to oppress and extort money from his own followers, and it is said that he instigated the murder of his steward Vrajlál, who was assassinated at this time. Meanwhile Sadáshiv Rámchandar went from Porbandar to Junágarh, where he was joined by Siájiráv Gáekwár. Sher Khán Bábi was there presented with some horses and appointed Maráthá deputy. In accordance with orders received from the Peshwá, Shambhurám and his sons, who were still kept in confinement, were now sent to Poona, and Dámáji Gáekwár was also summoned there, but did not go. In this year ráo Lakhpat of Cutch presented some Cutch horses and Gujarát bullocks to the emperor, and in return received the title of Mirzá.

Chapter III.
Moghal Viceroys.

Expedition from Cutch against Sindh, 1758.

About this time the rúv of Cutch, who planned an expedition against Sindh, solicited aid from both Dámáji Gáekwár and Sadáshiv Rámchandar to enable him to conquer Thattá, and as he agreed to pay the army expenses, Sadáshiv sent Ranchordás, and Dámáji sent Shewakrám to help him. In this year also Neknám Khán, governor of Broach, received the title of Bahádur and other honours. In A.D. 1758, Sadáshiv Ramchandar advanced to Kairá, and after settling accounts with Dámáji's agent proceeded against Cambay. Momin Khán, who was about to visit the Peshwá at Poona, remained to defend the town, but was forced to pay arrears of tribute amounting to 2,000*l.* (Rs. 20,000.) In this year Sher Khán Bábi died at Junágarh, and the nobles of his court seated his son Muhammad Mohobat Khán in his place.

Levy of tribute by the Maráthás.

Sadáshiv Rámchandar besieged Cambay until Momin Khán paid 2,000*l.* (Rs. 20,000,) being arrears of tribute for two years. Shortly afterwards Dámáji Gáekwár at the invitation of the Peshwá went to Poona, and sent his son Siájiráv into Sorath. After his success at Cambay, Sadáshiv Rámchandra levied tribute from the chiefs of Umetá, and then passing southwards withdrew to Poona. On his way back, on account of the opposition caused by Sardár Muhammad Khán, son of Sher Khán Bábi, the chief of Bálásinor, Sadáshiv Rámchandar besieged the town, and eventually forced the chief to pay tribute. Next marching against Lunáwárá, he induced the chief Dipsingh to pay him the sum of 5,000*l.* (Rs. 50,000). Sadáshiv then went to Visalnagar and so to Pálanpur, where Muhammad Khán Bahádur Jhálori resisted him; but after a month's siege he agreed to pay a tribute of 3,500*l.* Rs. (35,000). Marching south from Pálanpur, Sadáshiv then went to Unjá-Unáwá, and from that to Katosan, where he levied 1,000*l.* (Rs. 10,000) from the chief Shujá, and then proceeded to Limbḍi.

Affairs of Surat, 1758.

During the course of this year, A.D. 1758, important changes took place in the city of Surat. In the early part of the year Syad Moin-ud-din, otherwise called Syad Achan, visited the Peshwá at Poona, and received from him the appointment of governor of Surat. Syad Achan then set out for his charge, and as he was aided by a body of Maráthá troops under the command of Muzafar Khán Gárdi, and had also secured the support of Neknám Khán, the governor of Broach, he succeeded after some resistance in expelling A'li

Chapter III.

Moghal Viceroys.

Nawáz Khán, son of the late Safdár Muhammad Khán, and establishing himself in the government. During the recent troubles, the English factory had been plundered and two of their clerks murdered by the Habshi, commander of the fort. They therefore determined to drive out the Habshi and themselves assume the government of the castle. With this object men-of-war were despatched from Bombay to the help of Mr. Spencer, the chief of the English factory, and the castle was taken in March A.D. 1759, and Mr. Spencer appointed commander.

The English take command of the Surat port, 1759.

Momin Khán of Cambay visits Poona, 1759.

Shortly afterwards Momin Khán, by the advice of Syad Husain, an agent of the Peshwá, contracted friendship with the English through General Inglis, who commanded the British troops at the capture of Surat. Momin Khán then asked Mr. Erskine, chief of the English factory at Cambay, to obtain permission for him to go to Poona by Bombay. Leave being granted, Momin Khán set out for Surat, and was there received by Mr. Spencer. From Surat he sailed for Bombay, where the governor, Mr. Bourchier, treating him with much courtesy, informed the Peshwá of his arrival. The Peshwá sending permission for his further advance to Poona, Momin Khán took leave of Mr. Bourchier and proceeded to Poona.

The Maráthás in Káthiáwár, 1159.

From Limbḍi, to which point the course of his tour for the collection of tribute has been already traced, Sadáshiv Rámchandra advanced against Dhrángadhrá, when the chief who was at Halwad sent an army against him. The Maráthás, however, informed of his designs, detaching a force, suddenly attacked Halwad at night, and breaching the walls forced open the gates. The chief retired to his palace, which was fortified, and there defended himself, but was at last forced to surrender, and was detained a prisoner until he should pay a sum of 12,000*l*. (Rs. 1,20,000). The neighbouring chiefs, impressed with the fate of Halwad, paid tribute without opposition. Sadáshiv Rámchandra now went on to Junágarh, but ere he could commence operations against the fortress, the rainy season drew near, and returning to A'hmadábád, he prepared to depart for Poona. Siáji Gáekwár, who was also in Sorath collecting tribute, amongst other places besieged Kundlá, and levying from that town a tribute of 7,500*l*. (Rs. 75,000) returned to the capital. Khanderáv Gáekwár had during this time been levying tribute from the Kolis, and after visiting the Bhil district went to Bijápur, Idar,

Kaḍi, Dholká and Naḍiád. The chief of Halwad now paying the sum agreed on, was allowed to depart, and Dipsingh of Lunáwárá, who was also a prisoner, was sent to Lunáwárá and there released after paying his tribute. On the news of the capture of the Surat fort reaching the emperor, he issued an order, in the name of the governor of Bombay, confirming the command of the fort to the English instead of to the Habshis of Janjirá, appointing the Honourable East India Company admirals of the imperial fleet, and at the same time discontinuing the yearly payment of 2,000*l.* (Rs. 20,000) formerly made to the Habshi on this account. When in the course of the following year, A.D. 1760, this imperial order reached Surat, Mr. Spencer and the other chief men of the city, went outside of the walls to meet and escort the bearers of the despatch.

Concluding Remarks.

The tribute-collecting expedition not purely Maráthá.

The above sketch, if its accuracy be allowed, will have shown that the system of collecting tribute by yearly military expeditions, was by no means, as is usually supposed, an invention of the Maráthás, but on the contrary had been the custom of the previous rulers, and may possibly have dated from the time of the A'nhilwáḍá kings. Perhaps the only distinctive Maráthá levy was the claim to the one-fourth share of the revenue. For the rest the *khanḍni*, their general term for tribute, is in effect synonymous with the Persian word *peshkash,* while such minor claims as those for grass and grain were no doubt enforced by the Muhammadan, not less than by the Maráthá governments.

General instability of Maráthá rule in Gujarát.

The sketch may also have shown that the Maráthá rule in Gujarát was at no one period on any stable basis, and had the intervention of the British been delayed for another half century, it seems as likely as not, that so far from the Maráthá yoke being more firmly riveted on the Gujarát chieftains, they might have regained their independence, and the Gáekwár might have been curtailed of his tributary rights, if not of his territorial possessions. In A.D. 1761 the decisive battle of Pánipat was fought, and that battle shook the Maráthá power to its base. Taking advantage of the confusion that followed, the Delhi Court despatched instructions to the chief nobles of Gujarát, directing Momin Khán, Jawán Mard Khán, and the governor of Broach to join together in driving the Maráthás out of the province. In consequence of this despatch, Sardár Muhammad Khán

Chapter III. Moghal Viceroys.

Bábi defeating the Maráthá garrison, regained possession of Bálásinor,[1] while the governor of Broach with the aid of Momin Khán succeeded in winning back Jambusar. Sadáshiv Rámchandra, the Peshwá's viceroy, remonstrated with Momin Khán for this breach of faith. But in reply his envoy was shown the despatch received from Delhi, and was made the bearer of a message, that before it was too late, it would be wisdom for the Maráthás to abandon Gujarát. Things were in this state when Dámáji Gáekwár, wisely forgetting his quarrels with the Peshwá, marched to the aid of Sadáshiv with a large army. Advancing against Cambay he attacked and defeated Momin Khán, plundering one of his villages. But the Maráthás were too weak to follow up this success, or exact severer punishment from the Musalmán confederates. Sadáshiv inviting Muhammad Khán Bábi to Kairá, on condition of his assenting to the payment of tribute, agreed to allow him to keep possession of Bálásinor. Subsequently Dámáji's energy enabled him to enlarge the power and possessions of the Gáekwár's house, recovering the districts of Visalnagar, Kherálu, Waḍnagar, Bijápur and Pátan from Jawán Mard Khán, besides acquisitions from other chiefs. Still, after the death of Dámáji, the real importance of the Gáekwár's power was sensibly diminished; and had it not been for its alliance with the British, it is impossible to say what might not have happened when the sceptre passed to the feeble hands of Siájiráv. If in the zenith of the Gáekwár power Momin Khán could reconquer, and, for so long, successfully defend A'hmadábád, what might not have been possible in its decadence?

Their charater as conquerors.

Defects have, I think, been attributed to the Maráthá rule which are common to all conquering powers, and by no means peculiarly Maráthá. Thus greed, rapacity, and encroachment are terms ordinarily applied to the Maráthá rule by historians; yet in point of fact, they do not appear to have been more rapacious or encroaching than the Muhammadans, while by the side of Nádir Sháh and other invaders of India, they contrast very favourably.

Date of the first capture of A'hmadábád by the Maráthás.

One more remark is necessary, before concluding. The first capture of A'hmadábád by the Maráthás has been here, on the authority of the Mirat-i-A'hmadi, stated

---

[1] Bálásinor had been conquered from Sardár Muhammad Khán Bábi about a year previously by the Maráthás under Bhagwantráv, a Maráthá commander under Sadáshiv Rámchandra.

to have taken place in A.D. 1753. This is at variance with the account commonly accepted on the authority of Grant Duff,[1] who, on the evidence of the Maráthá records, and the statements made by General Walker, has fixed A.D. 1755 as the date of that event. The question therefore is, which are we to prefer as an authority, the Persian or Maráthá account, and which date—A.D. 1753 or A.D. 1755—fits in best with the history of the time. To this I would unhesitatingly reply, the Persian. For the Persian history was compiled not by an ordinary person, but by a minister of the empire, who, and his father before him, were actors in the scenes recorded. The author had access to the imperial archives, and his uniform exactness, the fact that the date he gives of a famine which occurred about this time coincides with the date of the Samvat year by which that famine is ordinarily known, and that only shortly before the fall of A'hmadábád his own private estate of Nikol had been plundered, are circumstances which necessarily give weight to his assignment of the date, which moreover fits in more aptly than A.D. 1755 with the general history of the province. On the other hand, Mr. Grant Duff, though he frequently quotes the Mirat-i-A'hmadi, was not, I venture to think, thoroughly acquainted with that important work; else why should he have omitted—and many subsequent historians also following his lead have done the same—all mention of the reconquest of A'hmadábád by Momin Khán and its second capture by the Maráthás. Able as is Mr. Grant Duff's history of the Maráthá power as a whole, it seems probable that, in this particular, he erred in adopting the loose Maráthá records to the well digested history of an imperial functionary. The confusion of thought which, from adopting A.D. 1755 as the date of the fall of A'hmadábád, his own history displays, is best illustrated by the following quotation[2]:—"The occupation of Gujarát, the siege of A'hmadábád, and the Karnatic expeditions prevented the Peshwá from joining to reduce Surat, or from cooperating in attacking Tulájí Angria, until the beginning of the year A.D. 1755." Now, if A'hmadábád, was not taken till April A.D. 1755, how could its siege be said to delay the Peshwá till the beginning of that year? This passage alone is sufficient to cast a doubt on the accuracy of this date. General Walker's source of information being probably the

1 History of the Maráthás, II., p. 51, (Ed. 1863).

2 History of the Maráthás, II., p. 60, (Ed. 1863).

Chapter III.

Moghal Viceroys.

same as Mr. Grant Duff's, the same remarks would apply to his reports; and valuable and interesting as all his reports are, I venture to think that no one would assert that they are models of historical accuracy. On these grounds I have adopted A.D. 1753, instead of A.D. 1755, as the date of the first conquest of A'hmadábád by the Maráthás.

Since writing the above I have ascertained, through the courtesy of Sir T. Mádhavráv, minister of Baroda, that the official records of that State confirm the account given in the Mirat-i-A'hmadi. And this is the case both as to the date, A.D. 1753, of the original capture of A'hmadábád, as to the fact of its subsequent recapture in A.D. 1755-56 by Momin Khán, and as to its final acquisition by the Maráthás in A.D. 1758. This is, I think, conclusive, and not only shows that the first conquest of A'hmadábád has been post-dated by two years, but that the important facts of its conquest by Momin Khán and reconquest by Sadashivráv, Dámáji, and Khanderáo Gáekwár have hitherto been entirely lost sight of, all subsequent writers following the version given by Grant Duff.

As in A.D. 1760, the Maráthá power was firmly established, and the imperial power subverted, it is unnecessary to prolong further this sketch of Gujarát under the Muhammadan rule.